THREE SUMMERS

A MEMOIR OF SISTERHOOD, SUMMER CRUSHES, AND GROWING UP ON THE EVE OF WAR

AMRA SABIC-EL-RAYESS

with LAURA L. SULLIVAN

FARRAR STRAUS GIROUX
NEW YORK

The names of some persons described in this book have been changed.

Content warning: The reader should be aware that the following content exists in this book before proceeding: genocide, depression, death of a disabled child, disappearance of a disabled person, racism, prejudice, and ableist and racist slurs. The publisher would like to thank the sensitivity readers who considered this manuscript's depiction of people with disabilities, especially that of Marfan syndrome.

Farrar Straus Giroux Books for Young Readers
An imprint of Macmillan Publishing Group, LLC
120 Broadway, New York, NY 10271 • mackids.com

Our books may be purchased in bulk for promotional, educational, or business use. Please contact your local bookseller or the Macmillan Corporate and Premium Sales Department at (800) 221-7945 ext. 5442 or by email at MacmillanSpecialMarkets@macmillan.com.

Library of Congress Cataloging-in-Publication Data

Names: Sabic-El-Rayess, Amra, author. | Sullivan, Laura L., 1974– author.
Title: Three summers / Amra Sabic-El-Rayess with Laura L. Sullivan.
Other titles: 3 summers
Description: First edition. | New York : Farrar Straus Giroux, 2024. | Audience: Ages 8–12 | Audience: Grades 4–6 | Summary: "An epic middle-grade memoir about sisterhood and coming-of-age in the three years leading up to the Bosnian Genocide. Three Summers is the story of five young cousins who grow closer than sisters as ethnic tensions escalate over three summers in 1980s Bosnia. They navigate the joys and pitfalls of adolescence on their family's little island in the middle of the Una River. When finally confronted with the harsh truths of the adult world around them, their bond gives them the resilience to discover and hold fast to their true selves. Written with incredible warmth and tenderness, Amra Sabic-El-Rayess takes readers on a journey that will break their hearts and put them back together again" —Provided by publisher.
Identifiers: LCCN 2023024519 | ISBN 9780374390815 (hardcover)
Subjects: LCSH: Sabic-El-Rayess, Amra—Childhood and youth—Juvenile literature. | Teenage girls—Bosnia and Herzegovina—Bihać—Biography—Juvenile literature. | Muslim teenagers—Bosnia and Herzegovina—Bihać—Biography—Juvenile literature. | Muslims—Bosnia and Herzegovina—Bihać—Biography—Juvenile literature. | Bihać (Bosnia and Herzegovina)—Biography—Juvenile literature. | Bihać (Bosnia and Herzegovina)—Social life and customs—20th century—Juvenile literature. | Bosnia and Herzegovina—Ethnic relations—History—20th century—Juvenile literature.
Classification: LCC DR1748.S34 A3 2024 | DDC 949.742/020922—dc23/eng/20230812
LC record available at https://lccn.loc.gov/2023024519

First edition, 2024
Book design by Samira Iravani
Printed in the United States of America by
Lakeside Book Company, Harrisonburg, Virginia

ISBN 978-0-374-39081-5
1 3 5 7 9 10 8 6 4 2

With boundless and infinite love for my daughters, Jannah and Dinah

—Amra Sabic-El-Rayess

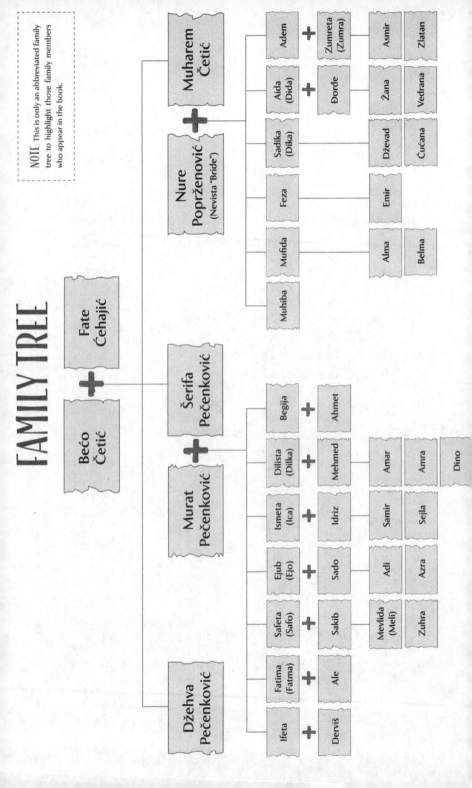

TABLE OF CONTENTS

BEFORE

1

I DON'T REMEMBER a knock. Nobody let her in. Yet there she is like magic, a fortune teller with a face as soft and brown and wrinkled as last year's apple, sitting at our sofra, holding Mama's hand. She's wearing a dimije, the traditional full trousers favored by grandmothers and village women. She is both. Her jacket is embroidered with vines and flowers. I can tell from here that her jacket is a little dusty, a little threadbare, but it is still beautiful. I wonder if she made it herself when she was young.

Mama catches me peeking around the corner and gives me a look that sends me back to the other room. We're at the home of Tetka Fatma and Tetak Ale, my aunt and uncle. I go back to sitting on a cushion between my two brothers, pulled this way and that. Dino wants me to play with his little toy cars. My older brother, Amar, sitting at the table, wants me to help him learn more Chinese characters. No one studies Chinese here in Bosnia and Herzegovina! Russian, yes. English, maybe. But my brilliant brother wants to learn something no one else knows. He's memorized a thousand characters already.

I push the cars, I hold up flash cards ... but my ears are pricked to listen to the fortune teller. How strange that my practical Mama will let her read her palm. I make one of the little cars race across the carpet just so I can chase it and get close enough to hear.

"This is all nonsense," Mama scoffs. "There's no such thing as magic. There's only reality, and we make our own fortunes by hard work." But she doesn't pull her hand away. The old woman with lines in her cheeks like deeply plowed furrows in a field bends over Mama's palm. I'm a little afraid of her. I've never seen anyone so ancient, outside of the tapestry in Tetka Fatma's living room that hangs just above their heads. It shows an old man from centuries past smoking a pipe in front of a shop, wearing traditional Bosniak (Bosnian Muslim) clothing. This woman could have stepped out of that very painting to join us from generations ago. But her voice is gentle, and maybe those lines come from a lifetime of smiles.

"You are worried about someone you love," the fortune teller says.

Mama gives a nervous little laugh. "That's an easy one. Everybody is worried about someone."

"It is a child."

I hear Mama's breath catch.

"I tell you that your worry will end."

Mama gasps, and for an instant her eyes light with hope. "He'll be well again?"

"Soon the one you love will be free of all pain."

Mama snatches her hand away, and just then Tetka Fatma comes bustling in, taking the old woman to the kitchen to give her coffee and hurmašice syrup cakes before sending her on her way. Tetka Fatma feeds everyone: family and neighbors and stray kittens. Mama gets up quickly and rushes into another room, her eyes glistening.

I feel tears in my own eyes, tears of joy. Can it be?

"Amar, did you hear?" I whisper.

He gives me his sweet smile and gathers up his homemade Chinese flash cards. Then he picks up his long, long legs with his long, long arms, one at a time, straightening and settling them until he can haul himself to his feet. He stifles a grunt, a moan of pain. Then, with agonizing slowness, he forces his body to limp and shuffle across the room.

But in my mind's eye I see him healthy at last, free of the disease in his body. I see him running up stairs, riding his bike like he used to do when he was younger. He's starting high school in a couple of weeks, and the world will be opening up for him. Thinking about what awaits him—success in school, his first girlfriend, a fulfilling career—I realize that what I hope for is not necessarily for him to be well and strong, but for the world to see him as he really is. I want others to look beyond the physical and see his brilliance, his uniqueness, his kindness. I want those bullies who plague him to wake up one day and see that he is a person of value. Yes, I want him to be free of pain, but even more than that, I want him to be free from prejudice.

My brother Amar has Marfan syndrome. He told me that the American president Abraham Lincoln had it, too. "So see," he tells me when I fret, "not only will I turn out just fine—I may even be president someday!" But if Lincoln had it, he had a mild version. My brother's bones have grown so fast that his muscles and joints can't keep up. He gets weaker every year. Now, his friends have to carry him up the stairs at school.

But worse than the pain, worse than the legs that won't

cooperate and the arms that aren't strong enough to hold his heavy books, Marfan syndrome affects his heart. Each heartbeat is sluggish and slow. He can't go more than a few steps without losing his breath.

But there's hope. We've been trying a new medicine to help protect his heart. My cousin Meli, a nurse, comes over twice a day with her huge needle to give him shots. I hold his hand while he bends over so she can inject him in the muscle of his buttocks. His backside is covered in bruises, all colors from fresh blue to dark purple to fading sickly yellow. He pretends it doesn't hurt. He's gotten really good at that. But I feel the pain for him.

The medicine must be working. I really believe the old fortune teller. Soon we won't have to worry about Amar anymore. His pain will be gone.

I know he heard the fortune teller, too. Like me, he must be filled with hope now. So why does his smile have a tinge of sadness?

2

OUR APARTMENT BUILDING is ugly, a brutal rectangle with tiny windows. It is gray and yellow concrete, the color of an old bruise, and was made in the days of the Communist leader Tito, all function and no form.

It is also beautiful because, for as long as I can remember, it has been home.

Tomorrow, we are leaving it.

We've scrimped and saved, dreamed and designed. While we could smell our neighbors' roasted chickens and the grilled spiced meat kebabs called *ćevapi*, we've mostly eaten beans and onions to save money. While my friends parade in new Levi's jeans and designer sneakers, we mend holes in our old clothes. I remember when I was little I had pretty dresses, puffy fluffy things in bright yellow and pink. For years now, though, I've had nothing but hand-me-downs from Amar.

But it is all worth it because our new house is ready for us now.

Mama and Tata designed it themselves. Everybody has their own bedroom, and each bedroom has a balcony. *I want windows everywhere,* Mama told the architect, so natural light streams into every room. It is our dream home, and I see it as part of the miracle the old woman foretold. Everything in our life is about to change. The suffering is over. I feel bouncy with hope.

Amar does, too. He wants to be outside, even though I can see thunderclouds in the distance. "It's nicest just before a storm," Amar says. "I love the breeze, the fresh smell that comes with the first raindrops. That smell even has its own name: *petrichor.*" I help him downstairs and outside to the cement Ping-Pong table next to our apartment for a game. It is in a shared space that several apartments can use. Painted bright spring green, the table is the most colorful thing I can see from here.

Amar has to lean against it while he plays. He's really good. He sends me a backhand shot with spin that I catch but slam way too hard, sending it off the table. He laughs while I run after it.

"You shouldn't just hit it as hard as you can, Amra," he tells me. "That's not how you win. You need subtlety."

Then his laughter breaks into a wheezing choke, and I have to pretend I don't notice because he hates it when people worry about him.

Suddenly I hear crowing and shouts from outside a nearby apartment, a building even grayer and uglier than ours. It's the despicable twins, Milorad and Ratko, mirror images of evil.

"What do you think it will be today?" Amar whispers when I run back with the ball. "Will they call me spider, crab, or grasshopper?"

"They better not dare call you anything," I say, glaring at the twins. They're like angry bees, always wanting to sting. Amar is their favorite target. They call him names, mocking his long, skinny limbs, his stretched face. They seem to feed on his pain, getting bigger and stronger and meaner whenever they manage to make him miserable. He learned long ago to deny them the satisfaction. Now he ignores them when he can, shrugs off the insults, the pinches, the punches. He laughs at them, which drives them to worse and worse cruelty.

"Hey, cripple!" one of them shouts.

Amar ignores them but says to me in a conversational voice, "Cripple, huh? I hoped for better. I wish they knew bigger words. I wouldn't mind being called an arthropod or arachnid for a change. At least that would be entertaining." He lifts one long, skinny leg like a grasshopper, gives me a grin that turns into a grimace of pain. "Maybe I could teach them a better vocabulary?"

"Why aren't you dead yet?" the other twin shouts across the street. I see a couple of heads look out of windows, but nobody says anything, nobody does anything. I think even the grown-ups are afraid of Ratko and Milorad. Or they don't think Amar is worth defending.

Amar wants me to ignore them, hoping they'll get bored and go away. But I can't help shouting back, "Just wait until my brother gets better. You won't dare say anything then! He'll beat you up!"

"No I won't!" Amar calls out affably. "I'm a pacifist." In a lower voice he says, "Amra, hush! It doesn't matter what they say or do to me, but you ..."

Before he can finish, the twins start crossing the street. The closer they get, the bigger they loom. Over their heads, the sky begins to darken.

"Just ignore them and keep playing," Amar says calmly, and serves me the ball. My anger and sadness are building inside me like a geyser. I'm going to erupt in tears. Why can't they leave him alone? Hasn't he suffered enough?

The world is blurry. I slam the ball as hard as I can, wishing it was the twins' faces. The ball flies high over Amar, right at Ratko. He snatches it midair.

"Give it back!" I shout at him.

"It's okay," Amar whispers.

"It's our last ball," I mutter, then yell again at Ratko. "That's ours!"

To my surprise, he holds it out. It lolls in his palm. "Here you go," he says. But when I reach for it, at the last second, he lets it fall. It gives one bounce...then he crushes it under his foot.

I breathe hard, telling myself I will not cry. I see a flash, and the darkening sky lets out a dangerous rumble.

Milorad and Ratko walk past me, one on each side, chuckling like they just told the best joke. *Be calm, Amra,* I tell myself. *None of this matters.* The fortune teller's words nestle inside me like a secret treasure. *Soon we'll be in the new house, and Amar will be free of pain. Be like Amar. He lets the hateful words flow over him. You can, too.*

But I'm burning with rage when they start imitating the way Amar walks. His legs don't straighten all the way or bend properly, so sometimes he has to tug on his pants to force his legs to move where he wants them to go. The twins lurch and stagger, cracking each other up. Amar catches my eye, and though I fume, I do nothing.

When they come up right beside him, though, Milorad says, with almost casual cruelty, "You don't deserve to be alive, you stupid cripple." Ratko adds, "I hope you die soon, moron." I want to scream at them that Amar is brilliant, the smartest person in

Bihać. Amar's so smart he could change the world. Amar's so kind he could bring world peace. But these bullies think he's worth nothing just because his body is sickly.

Words can't hurt you, Amar always tells me. I know he's wrong. Words, ideas, hate can kill people. I know that instinctively. But I try my hardest to be like him. To be good and kind and patient. To forgive.

Then the brothers bump into him as they walk past, and that I will not forgive. They jostle him hard, back and forth like a pinball game, and he falls to his knees with a cry while the twins walk on.

I roar like a lion, and when they turn, I see real fear in their eyes. They're older, bigger—but I am an almost-six-foot-tall kid full of fury. I am a wrecking ball that smashes into them, demolishes them.

This feels good, releasing my anger. I don't even know what I'm shouting, curse words I've heard on the street, never in my home. All the words of insult and hate I've heard from the twins themselves. I hope my words burn into their brains forever. They run in different directions to distract me, but I zero in on one—I can't tell them apart now—and slam into him, knocking him against the gray wall of his apartment building. His hair is shaved, and his ears stick out like perfect handles, so I grab them, squeezing like a vice, and slam his head against the cement wall over and over and over. It makes a ringing sound like the school bell.

"Never make fun of my brother again!" I scream as I bang his head. "Say it! Say it now! 'I will never make fun of Amar again!'"
Bang!

He stammers it out: "I—I'll never make fun of him again."

"Swear it!" *Bang!*

"I swear it!"

I let him go, and the twins run back to the safety of their apartment. And I know, as certainly as I've ever known anything in my life, that they will never tease Amar again. That no one will ever tease him again. I won't let them.

I feel powerful, just for a moment. I've defended my brother. I'll always keep him safe.

I think this, even though I know it's not true. This was one moment, not his whole life. I can't protect him from everything that awaits him. I wish I could be his hero, but what I wish even more is that the entire world would change so he could always be recognized as the hero he truly is.

The rain starts to fall in such hard, stinging drops that I can't even feel the tears on my cheeks.

3

"IT'S NOTHING, JUST a cold," Amar says with a sniffle and a shiver.

"Because you were out in the rain," the doctor says. "Of course if you get soaked to the skin at night you'll have a cold the next morning."

Amar flicks a wry look my way before telling the doctor innocently, "That's funny, I always thought rain was just water. But I've taken showers at night and haven't woken up with a cold. There must be more to rain than water. Some kind of . . . cloud chemicals?" He's making fun of our old family doctor, but the doctor nods sagely and tells Mama and Tata that Amar is fine. "Nothing that a good rest won't cure."

So we take him to Fatma and Ale's house, wrap him up in Fatma's warmest, fluffiest pink robe, and set him comfortably on the couch in front of the TV. When Fatma hands him a cup of steaming chamomile tea she winks and says, "I know your clever ways, Amar. You just wanted to get out of helping on moving day."

Amar laughs and flexes the marble-sized muscle in his gangly arm. "I always do all the work. Time for my lazy family to pull their own weight for a change!" I give him a long hug and head back to our apartment to help Mama and Tata move the rest of our things. The furniture is already in the new house, but we still have to make a lot of trips back and forth with the little items. I never thought we had very much … until we had to put it all into boxes and move it!

There's still some work left to do on our house. The walls and roof and windows are complete—the house won't fall down, but some of the details are still missing. The facade of the garage still has to be finished. But my parents ran out of money and decided it was better to move in as soon as the house was livable rather than waiting. We could finish the rest of the house bit by bit. Dino says he wants to help us unload boxes at the new house, but after a while he gets bored and stares longingly out the window at the sand pile left by the construction crew.

The sand pile is a paradise to the neighborhood kids. Dino has already made a lot of friends just because all the neighborhood children flock to our tiny mountain. They could dig holes and bury their feet and play there all day.

"Please, can I go, Mama?" Dino begs. "Just for a little while?"

She lets him so he's not underfoot. I head down to see if one of the mothers will keep an eye on him. Soon he's laughing and shrieking with his friends, utterly happy. To him, the best part of the new house is the sand pile.

Then it's back and forth, back and forth, in our little orange Communist car. The car is nothing like the American cars we see on TV when they show film marathons on New Year's Day. Like so many things under communism, the car is rudimentary, uncomfortable, and barely functioning. I can run faster than this car drives. We shuttle boxes of books and clothes, knickknacks and glasses and bowls. Finally we have just one more trip for the things we'll need until the end: a broom to sweep the empty apartment clean and our telephone.

I didn't think I'd be sad to leave this place, but now that the moment is here, I'm overcome with melancholy. The apartment seems naked without our things inside it. Even without our possessions, there are signs of our years in this home. Here are pencil marks on the wall, charting our heights. A black charred streak on the windowsill reminds me of the fire: One day Mama and Tata had left me alone, watching little Dino while they took Amar to the doctor. Our neighbor had decided to roast a pig in the basement, and, of course, started a fire. I remember the choking smell of smoke, the licking tongues of flames. I ran to this very window, screaming for help, and a passerby, a tall man like a basketball player, ran up and told me to throw Dino down to him. I was terrified, sure he'd miss and my brother would crack his head on the pavement. But Dino went flying through the air, the man caught him, and Dino laughed and shrieked, "Again! Again!" Then I had to jump down myself. The firemen had the flames out within a few minutes, and our building was saved.

"Goodbye," I whisper, as I walk from room to room through all the memories.

Mama and Tata are carefully carrying the TV down the stairs when the phone rings. "Answer that, and then unplug it and bring it along," Tata calls as they head to the car.

It's Tetka Fatma. "You have to hurry here, come at once!" At first, I'm not worried. Fatma talks like this all the time, always rushing us over. She makes it sound like the world is about to end, when really, she just took her burek meat pie out of the oven and wants us to be there for lunch before it gets cold.

"You have to come now, Amra! Tell your parents!"

Now I hear the panic in her voice, and my heart goes cold.

"What is it, Tetka? What's wrong?"

"It's Amar. Something's very wrong. He's not . . ."

I drop the phone before she can say any more and my legs fly downstairs. "Mama! Tata! Something's happened to Amar, we have to go!"

The television falls from their nerveless fingers, and we pile into the car. Tata swerves around traffic, so upset that he mistakes the gas for the brake and we almost crash. Cars honk their horns at us, but we speed on.

Amar is still where I left him, nestled in the corner of the L-shaped sofa, wrapped up in Tetka Fatma's bright pink robe. But his long face is limp, his mouth hangs open.

"Amar, Amar, my beautiful boy. Look at me!" Mama chafes his cold hands, trying to bring life into them. I hear Tata on the phone, calling for an ambulance. "Come now, it's an emergency. Oh, I cannot lose my son!"

I kneel by his side and take over rubbing his arms while Mama gives him mouth-to-mouth resuscitation. "Ako, Ako," I plead, calling him by his pet name. "Come back to us."

I see his eyes open, just a little. He finds me, and as the world grows still and cold around us, l remember the fortune teller's words: *Soon the one you love will be free of all pain.*

Then his eyes slowly close, never to open again.

His pain is over. Our worry is over.

And our sorrow has just begun.

4

EVERYTHING THAT HAPPENS in the next few minutes is like a tragic play, actors playing their parts. I hear the ambulance scream up to the house, and paramedics rush in. I know it is too late. They know it is too late. But they check Amar's pulse, do a few mysterious things, go through the motions of trying to save him, like they are onstage and this is their role. I watch and wait to see if magic is real. But I know it isn't. They aren't magicians, and they can't bring my brother back. If all my love, all my mother's anguished cries, can't bring him back, what can?

Still, they don't say out loud that Amar is dead. They simply take my mother aside and tell her that they are sorry. That word, *sorry*, says it all.

There is no limit to our grief, but we all express it differently. I go very quiet, like a black hole that has sucked all the sorrows of the universe inside it. Mama explodes like a supernova, tearing her sweater apart like she's tearing her heart in two.

They take my brother away on a stretcher, and I wait for someone to stop them. He is ours, brother and son, family. How can strangers be taking him away? Tata follows them slowly, half carrying Mama, who can barely stay on her feet.

They won't let us go in the ambulance with them. As Tata and Mama get into Tetak Ale's car to follow, Mama stops me and says in a voice that's ragged and empty, "Amra, go pick up Dino."

Dino has been completely forgotten in the last hour. For a moment I can't even remember where he is. Yes, the sand pile at our new house, a short walk from Tetka Fatma's home. How joyous everyone was just a little while ago. Now I trudge down the street with tears streaming down my face. Strangers pass by, people who will be my neighbors in this new neighborhood. They don't even notice the depth of my grief. Or is it that they don't want to notice, don't want to be enmeshed in someone else's troubles?

When someone dies, you're supposed to feel sad for *them*. Sad for all the things they will miss, being gone. But as I walk, tear-streaked, I can't help mostly feeling sad for myself. It doesn't seem right but I can't help it. All of my thoughts are about me. Why did I have to lose my brother? We were all supposed to be so happy together, and now I'm crushed. What is our family going to do? What am *I* going to do? Because I have to do something, right? I have to find a way to make this all better.

But I feel so helpless.

The fortune teller's words mock me. Now she looms in my memory like a demon, a wicked witch who cursed us. How dare she tell us everything would be fine when it wouldn't? But then I realize, she did tell us, in her tricky way, exactly what would happen to Amar, and I hate her for that, too. Now that he's gone, Mama will never have to worry about his pain, his illness. We'll never have to worry about him being bullied. He'll never have to worry about people only seeing his body, not his kindness or his humor or his brilliant mind.

I know I'm thinking these things only to try to salve my own pain. There is no bright side. The pain of his loss is so deep that even my bones feel frozen. Amar made me a better person. Without him, I am not me.

Is he at peace now? The old fortune teller didn't look like a wicked witch when she told Mama's fortune. She looked like she was telling Mama something kind. Maybe, in a way, she meant it to be reassuring.

But it's not fair! Amar should have gone to college. He should have been a professor and written books and engaged other clever minds in heated debates. He should have fallen in love, gotten married, had children and grandchildren. He should have led the way for his younger brother and sister so that we could have followed in his great footsteps.

And now I have to tell Dino. How am I ever going to do that? He worships Amar.

Night is falling, and my new neighborhood is dim and shadowy. There are no streetlights, and the trees wave strangely in the early autumn wind. Other houses are lit inside, their windows giving off a welcoming golden glow. I can hear laughter inside one, the clatter of dinner dishes inside another. But our house is dark. Our house is empty and silent, inside and out.

There is the tall sand pile, but where are the children?

Where is Dino?

A sense of danger swells within me, and panic starts to rise. *He's nearby,* some small rational voice inside me tries to say. I can't listen to it. I've lost one brother today, and now I'm completely certain that the worst has happened and I've lost another.

"Dino! Dino!" I call, louder and louder, but no one answers. I run all around the outside of the house, throw open the doors, and search through each room, through the furniture that is ours in the space that doesn't seem to properly belong to us yet. The house is empty.

No, no, no, I scream inside my heart. This can't be happening. This whole day has to be a dream. A nightmare.

Laughter echoes down the street, and my head snaps to attention. I sprint outside to the children kicking a soccer ball back and forth, and I don't know what they must think of me, my face red, my eyes swollen, grabbing them by the shoulders and screaming for my brother. They back away, and only the bravest stammers out that yes, Dino was playing with them earlier, but they have no idea where he can be. I pound on door after door, but no one has any idea where he is.

I'm supposed to protect them—both of my brothers. I thought I could protect Amar... and I could, from simple things like bullies. But there was a force more powerful that I couldn't fight.

Dino's so young... how could I have left him alone? Anything could have happened to him. That mother who was supposed to watch him, where is she? I hadn't even bothered to find out what house she lives in, what her name is.

He could have been hit by a car. He could have wandered off to the banks of the rushing River Una and tumbled in. He's a good swimmer, but he's so small, and the river can be merciless.

I'll never be able to live with myself if I can't find him.

What do I do now? I have to tell Mama and Tata. Where are they, at the hospital? That's too far to walk, and I'm not sure I could find it anyway. I'll go back to Tetka Fatma's and Tetak Ale's house. The need to hurry is at war with my dread of having to tell them Dino is missing. My shoes feel like lead boots, every step dragging me back, but I have to make myself run.

Mama and Tata aren't there, but my Tetka and Tetak are there, doing those small everyday things people do when they don't know what else can be done. Tetak Ale is wiping down the table where, earlier today, we all had our lunch together. He rubs a damp cloth across the same place, over and over, numbly. Tetka Fatma is rearranging the cupboards, moving the honey they harvest from their little bee farm here and there and back again, just to be doing something.

I burst in on them, crying, "Dino's gone!" They look at me with horrified faces, frozen, shattered from another tragedy until they realize that Dino is simply missing. It's not *that* kind of gone. There's hope.

There's something they can do. We pile into their Škoda car and drive back to the new house.

They're more sensible than me—they go door to door, every home, in an organized search, where I had run around like a chicken with its head cut off, banging at this door, missing the next. And they demand that the neighbors help us. Soon everyone is out, calling Dino's name, searching for him or for the mother who said she'd keep an eye on him. The night is deep, and we move through the black streets like ghouls, howling his name.

Finally we come to a house around the corner. The door is answered by a little grandmother with bright black eyes like a sparrow's. "The boy who likes playing in the sand? Yes, he's in here with my grandsons. When it got close to evening I thought he might be hungry."

There is Dino, happy with his friends, snacking on a slice of burek meat pie and clutching a plastic toy in his hand. He's been having the time of his life, and has no idea why his sister, aunt, and uncle squeeze him like they'll never let him go and wash him in a flood of tears.

5

DAYS LATER I'M in the classroom. School is harder now. We don't just study "science" but also its specialties: physics, chemistry, biology. I'm starting to learn Russian. I'd always gotten good grades, but it was never easy. Not like it was for Amar. Everything came so naturally to him. I'd rather run wild in the neighborhood than do homework. Mama always had to call me in from my fun, sit me down in the most uncomfortable chair in the house, and stand over me to make me do my homework.

Now I don't want to do anything at all.

Even though we moved, Mama kept me at the same school this year. I'd almost rather be among people who don't know me. At least they'd have an excuse to not talk about my brother. Here everybody knows, but nobody says anything. Not *we're sorry*. Not *we really liked Amar*. Not *we know you miss him*. Nothing. It's like he never even existed. Like it would be bad luck to speak of him.

I know all these kids around me, but I've never felt so alone. Would they even notice if *I* died? If Amar's life doesn't matter to them, what does? I thought they were my friends. Being in a new school with strangers would have been easier. Strangers can't disappoint you the way friends can.

I haven't studied. I alternate between memories of Amar and numbness.

Today my physics teacher calls on me and two other students.

We have to stand up in front of the classroom while he quizzes us. Each student gets a turn. If they can't answer, he asks the next person. I stare at him without seeing anything. I'm not even there. I'm sitting with Amar at sunrise at Šumatac, watching the morning sky grow pink while Amar explains how energy is heat and light and sound and waves and particles in a way that helps it all make sense.

My teacher barks a question. The first person can't answer it. Neither can the second.

"Amra?" he asks without much hope.

I rattle off the answer almost without thinking. As Amar explained it to me, the concepts are easy. My teacher asks another question, harder this time. I answer, and he nods. At last he gives me a complex scenario, a set of numbers that would have made me panic not long ago. But I feel Amar's voice move through me, and I go to the board and solve the problem.

"I taught Amar, you know," my teacher says. It is the first time anyone in this school has mentioned Amar's name since he died. "I'm so sorry you lost him. But you didn't disappoint me. It is clear that you're Amar's sister. He would be proud of your brilliance."

As I go back to my seat, the connection I felt with Amar fades a bit. The loss aches as much as ever. I want that feeling back, the way I could channel him through me. I can't talk to him anymore, but maybe if I do my best to emulate him, a part of him will survive. I can never be as brilliant as he was. But maybe, if I devote myself heart and soul to my studies, I can have a way to commune with Amar again.

The bell rings for lunch. When Amar was here I'd run to the

line before anyone to pick up his lunch and mine. We don't have a cafeteria, just a kitchen on the ground floor. There's a tiny opening. All we ever see is a hand poke through with our food. Amar used to say that prison cells have the same kind of little door to slide prisoners their meals. Every day it is the same: two thick, uneven slices of bread with a thin piece of chicken salami between them and a box of a sugary drink that is supposed to be orange juice, though it is obvious that beverage has never met an orange. I used to urge Amar to eat, just a bite, just for me. He had a hard time chewing and swallowing, so he'd never take more than a few mouthfuls. I did everything I could to help him gain weight. But in the end, I'd usually finish his lunch for him.

Now I don't even bother getting in line. I just go behind the school and sit by myself. Sometimes I watch kids fight. Once, I would have jumped up to help the underdog. Now I know that no matter how hard you fight, you can't win. I fought for Amar, and look what happened.

"You're getting so skinny," Mama says when I get home. Tetka Fatma is there with a dish of my favorite stuffed peppers. Usually the rich smell of meat, smoked paprika, and rice makes my mouth water. Now it just turns my stomach.

"No, thank you. I'm not hungry." I go up to my room and try to find Amar in my studies. As I climb the stairs I hear Mama say, "I have to do something. What can I do?"

"Give her time," Tetka Fatma says. "The wound is raw, but all wounds heal."

"No, they don't," Mama says with an edge of fear in her voice. "Sometimes people die of their wounds."

Sometimes l try to remember myself the way l was before Amar died, bubbly and adventuresome and bold. Now I'm like a snail in a shell, tucking all my soft raw parts inside. Studies are my hard, protective covering. l can't be wild anymore because l don't want to give my parents anything else to worry about. If l am quiet and perfect, their lives will be easier. If l get top grades and do all my homework, Mama won't notice the way my ribs stick out.

l catch them crying sometimes. Tata makes up some silly reason that he's crying: a favorite sports team lost, a glass broke, he found a new gray hair. He won't talk about it. Mama takes less trouble to hide her tears. I'll see them leak out of her as she grades her students' papers or cooks green beans. l threaten to call Tetka Fatma if she doesn't stop.

ALL THROUGH THE winter l stay at home in the room that was supposed to be Amar's but is now mine. l read, l study, l listen to the youth program on the radio. All those freezing months my parents let me hibernate. But when the warm weather returns, they pester me to go outside and play. After a week of moping around alone in my yard, Mama takes things into her own hands and asks other girls my age to come and play with me.

Anyone who's ever been eleven can imagine how that goes.

First Mama asks Zumreta to come and take a walk with me. She used to be one of my mom's students and is too polite to say no. But she's a year older than me, and we have nothing in common. Anyway, l want a friend who likes me, not one who is just doing a favor for my mother. Bored of the spring flowers and foraging honeybees, she takes me to her house to watch TV. It's bigger than our house, and her room is stuffed with more things than she could possibly need. She dumps a bunch of chocolate-covered almonds into a bowl—something I've never even seen, let alone tasted—and she eats them as freely as if they are peas. I take one and suck on the chocolate slowly, wanting to savor this unheard-of luxury.

While we're watching TV, I hear a commotion from the next room—shouting, then a crash. I think it might be a burglar, but Zumreta is unconcerned. "My dad just got home from a 'business trip' with lipstick on his collar," she says nonchalantly. "So Mom has to make sure he knows that she knows. She buys cheap ashtrays to keep around the house, just to throw. Then he brings her a necklace or fancy perfume and everything goes on like before...until the next 'business trip.'" I want to leave the house, but Zumreta seems perfectly comfortable. When the shouting gets louder, she simply turns up the volume on the TV.

I've never heard my parents raise their voices to each other.

Next Mama tries Valbona, and the sisters Fatima and Anela, whose family runs a corner store down the block. Valbona is nice, Anela is boringly benign, but Fatima has a sharp jealous streak that eventually seems to lash out at any other girl around her. I try hanging out with them to make Mama happy, but I'd rather be alone.

One night when I'm falling asleep over my math homework, Dino knocks on the door.

"I can't stand not talking about him," he whispers like it's a secret. "Why won't anybody talk about him?"

"I don't know," I say, cuddling him close. "I think they think that it will hurt more to talk about Amar."

"But I miss him. I don't want to forget him."

"We'll never forget Amar," I assure him.

"You're wearing his clothes. At least you have that."

It's true, I'm wearing some of Amar's old pants. We're still saving money, still trying to finish the house. No matter how many times I wash and iron them, the pants still bag out above the knee in the place where Amar would tug at them to help his legs move.

"Tell me about Šumatac," Dino says, curling up in my bed.

"You know the story well enough to tell me. You were there. It was only a year ago."

"Tell me," he insists.

So I lie down beside him and recount the story of our last trip as a family. It's not a story you'd read in a book. There's no plot, no twists. Just us, a family, together. The best kind of story, really. I tell it with questions: *Do you remember? Do you remember?*

"Do you remember the ride up to the mountain village in our little orange Stojadin car?"

"I do! The roads were so twisty I thought I was going to be sick. Amar taught me to stare straight out the front window and pretend I'm riding a dragon. That kept me from throwing up."

Amar had a solution to every problem except his own.

"Do you remember the chestnuts?"

"I do! They jumped right out of the fire, didn't they? Amar made me wait to eat them so I wouldn't get burned. And then you fed chestnuts to the ducks, right? The duck that went to sleep?"

I'd wanted to share the delicious chestnuts with the ducks

that walked in orderly rows up and down the hills like schoolchildren in uniforms. I gave one duck a piece that was too big and he choked. Amar said he knew just how to save him, though, and he and my uncle took the duck away. Later, he told us the duck was sleeping, and since all the ducks looked alike to me, I never knew if he was just protecting me. We each wanted to protect the other.

"Do you remember the baby chicks?" I ask Dino.

"I do! They were still wet from inside the egg, and shaking, trying to get near the light to warm up."

Amar and I had bent over those adorable fuzzballs for hours, marveling at how they could run and peck at bugs as soon as they were born. Most were yellow, but a few were covered in soft black down. I asked Amar if those chicks would be treated any differently. I was always expecting anyone who was different to get picked on. Me for my height, Amar for his disability. But he said no, to the flock of hens, chickens are all just chickens no matter what they look like. It made me wonder why humans can't be as good as chickens.

"And I remember the mushrooms!" Dino says sleepily. "Cousin Imo taught Amar which ones were poisonous. I was never sure, but Amar always was. Amra, did he know *everything*?"

"He would have," I say softly, and send Dino back to his own bed. Alone, I let more and more memories of happy times in Šumatac swirl in my head. Nothing ever tasted as good as those wild mushrooms roasted over the outdoor wood-burning stove. There was always that little thrill of defying death, because the cousins and uncles on my father's side were full of tales of people who mistook one mushroom for another and died horribly. Then the campfire stories changed to memories of World War II. My father and his brothers were old enough to remember. Heroic tales, gruesome tales, of multiethnic partisan groups fighting Nazis, Ustashe, or Chetniks. When the stories got too frightening, Amar would distract Dino and me with fables of his own, beautiful stories he made up on the spot about friendly wolves and magic trees.

I fall asleep on a tear-damp pillow, thinking about him.

I wake in the middle of the night drenched in sweat and gasping.

It was a dream, I tell myself, wanting to scream for Mama and Tata but not daring to disturb them. They've hardly slept in the last year. Instead I keep it bottled in, pounding inside me like my terrified heartbeat.

I dreamed about Amar. He was on his hands and knees, crawling across hard ground, jagged rocks, broken glass. His palms were bloody. "Amra, help me!" he cried out. But in the dream, I couldn't move, couldn't ever get any closer to him. I could only watch him drag himself painfully along. It seemed so real.

When I'm awake I'm so sad, I feel half dead. But there's no escape in my dreams either. I feel haunted in this room that was supposed to be his. Still panting, feeling like I might faint, I throw back the covers and creep downstairs.

I only mean to sit on the couch for a little while, to let the sweat dry and the terror of the dream dissipate. But there, on the table, reflecting the faint light of a streetlamp like a dim jewel, is the chocolate.

Few things can shake me out of my depression these days.

Chocolate is one of them. Here in Bosnia chocolate is cheaply made, dusty gray, mostly sugar, and almost no rich chocolate flavor. Still, the three of us always lived for the days Tata would bring home a chocolate bar. Amar would carefully break it into three exactly equal pieces, and we'd enjoy our special treat together. Toward the end, when it was hard for him to chew, chocolate was one of the few things Amar would still eat.

But this box of chocolate! It is a treasure, something you'd present to a queen! A week or two ago it was given to me—not to us, the family, but to me in particular—by some distant relatives who work in Germany. A lot of Bosnian Muslims do that, work in Germany as truck drivers or cleaners, making more than they ever could here even at much better jobs. They scrimp and save so they can visit in their Audis and Mercedes, bringing expensive gifts we can't get here. Our stores have no variety, and the prices just go up and up and up. If I forget something at the store and Mama sends me back, the shopkeeper is already putting out new higher prices.

So this chocolate is something I could only dream about. There is a clear plastic window to see the candy inside. Each glorious piece is wrapped in a different color of bright shiny paper. Fancy antique writing tells me what kinds they are: praline cream, amaretto fondant, double dark chocolate ganache. The words are foreign and thrilling.

But the night I got it, just as I was getting excited about tasting these rare chocolates, Mama had snatched the box away from me. "You know we always save the best gifts to give to other people, Amra," she chides. "These will be perfect for Sado."

Oh, Sado! I'd rather throw the chocolates into the River Una!

Now, having been thinking about these chocolates for days, I stare at the tempting box. It seems to stare back at me.

My life has been nothing but misery for months. I haven't had a single thing to live for. Don't I deserve to taste a little happiness just this once?

I run to the kitchen and take the sharpest knife we own, one that Tetka Fatma brought back from Italy. Then, hunkered in the dark, I perform precise surgery on that fancy box. I've decided I want to be a doctor, to save people. This will be my first operation.

Biting my lip in concentration, I slice through the sticker that holds the box closed so neatly that no one would know it was cut, then ease open the glued seal. When I open the box, a cloud of chocolate smell washes over me. I'll only have one. If Sado finds a single empty wrapper, she'll think it was a manufacturing error.

It's a big decision. My hand flutters over one, then another. Finally, I snatch up a hazelnut chocolate. Nuts are so expensive in Bosnia. At most we have walnuts in the baklava we serve at Eid, a holiday we have twice a year that is as important to Muslims as Christmas is to Christians. (This is a secret sort of Eid, since no one ever talks publicly about being Muslim here.) I only taste precious hazelnuts the rare times we go with Tetak Ale and Tetka Fatma to gather wild ones. To me, a hazelnut chocolate is like gold: priceless. The candy is even wrapped in gold foil like a treasure. Before I eat it, I reshape the wrapper so it looks like there's still a bonbon inside, then place the hollow decoy back in its section. When I sink my teeth into the smooth chocolate and feel the nut crunch between my teeth, it is like heaven. I've never tasted anything so good. It's creamy and heavy, nothing like our pale chalky chocolate.

I want more.

I want it all!

So I take more. I eat with a kind of desperation, a greedy hunger that is more spiritual than physical, trying to fill the emptiness inside me. I want to feel something again. I tear open one after another, savoring it at first but soon hardly tasting the rest. By the end I feel sick, but I choke down the last piece with a kind of defiance. I spend the rest of the night forming the wrappers back into perfect little empty cubes, and seal the box with tape.

Mama calls me as soon as I doze off again at dawn. "Get up, and dress nicely, we're visiting Sado and Uncle Ejo today. And don't let me forget to bring them the chocolates."

6

YOU CAN NEVER give up on family.

In a household of sisters, Uncle Ejo is Mama's only brother. He was coddled and protected by his many sisters, given good advice that he rarely followed. Ejo is so handsome that everyone loves him, no matter what mistakes he makes. When he married the awful Sado (after some mysterious love story with another woman that no one will talk about) it would have been easy to abandon him. Sado seemed to have married Ejo out of spite. She never shows him the slightest affection in front of us. Nor has she ever been welcoming to her new family. His sisters have showered the couple with presents, even signing over the title to a riverside home and another parcel of land, just to help out their marriage. Nothing anyone does seems to soften Sado. They have a son, Adi, who is always in trouble, and a girl, Azra, a few years older than me, who is a lot like her mother.

Now Mama and I present ourselves at their front door. I clutch the chocolates behind my back, trembling at what will happen when my crime is discovered. Sado always has something mean or critical to say. When she found out I was playing volleyball, she said it would make my body hard and sinewy like an old piece of rawhide. "You won't have a nice fluffy feminine body, and no one will want to marry you," she'd told me. What a thing to say!

Who is thinking about marriage? I just want to play my sport and have fun.

Hospitality in Bosnia is taken so seriously it might as well be a law. When people visit, you invite them in. You feed them. You welcome them. It doesn't matter whether you like them or not. If they are family or neighbors, or even strangers, you take them into your home and share whatever you have with them. Whether it is Tetka Fatma's lavish meals or the most humble cup of coffee, you do your best to make people feel appreciated in your home.

If Sado ever invites us in, she hovers with instructions: *Wipe your feet, don't touch that, don't sit there.* She never offers us so much as a cube of sugar or glass of water from the tap.

Most of the time, though, she doesn't even let us cross her threshold. Today, when Mama gives a cheerful rap on the door, Sado opens it just an inch and peeks out like we might be a troupe of vagabonds looking for a handout.

"What do you want?" she snaps at us.

"Good morning, Sado! You look very nice today." Mama is trying to butter her up. Sado is always thinking about her looks. She's short and has thin hair that she spends an hour styling every day. She always wears heavy makeup, even though you can barely see her face past the constant cloud from all the cigarettes she smokes.

Sado doesn't reply to the compliment. "The floors are clean," she says, and we know what that means. She's telling us we're too dirty to enter her nice, clean house. That's ridiculous! Everyone takes off their shoes when they go into someone's house, so how could we get the floors dirty?

Mama's smile never leaves her face, but it gets stiff. "We brought you a present, some lovely chocolates from Germany."

Sado opens the door just enough to receive our offering. She looks it over critically, and I hold my breath. If she opens it and discovers it is empty, there will be a family scandal! She'll hate us even more than she does already.

But she just sniffs and says, "I prefer milk chocolate to dark chocolate. Anyway, Belgians make better chocolate than the Germans." She tosses it on the table behind her, and with a sigh of relief I realize she'd rather starve than eat anything we give her. She'll probably regift it to someone she wants to impress. Knowing the Bosnian way, everyone will think this box of chocolates is too special to eat, and it will be passed from family to family for years to come, never opened, never eaten. My secret may never be discovered.

"I'll get Ejo," she says, and slams the door in our faces. We're left standing on her doorstep for a long time. I wonder if the neighbors are watching, wondering what kind of family would do such a thing. Even if we were traveling salespeople, we should be invited inside.

Finally Uncle Ejo comes out, and Mama's face lights up. He's the family pet. I try to imagine being Mama's age, with Dino a grown man trapped in a bad marriage. How can a life stray so far from what you hope it will be when you're a kid?

Ejo, at least, is glad to see us. He suggests a paddle on the river, and we climb into his wooden lađa boat. "Azra, join us!" he calls to his daughter. She grumbles and starts to say no, but when she sees me she changes her mind.

On the short paddle to the little sand island in the middle of the river, Azra primps and worries about her hair. It is long and huge, elaborately curled and teased at the top. She's short like her mother but uses her hair to make herself inches higher.

One side of the island has a nice little beach of hard-packed sand and clear, calm water. Mama and Ejo sit there and shoo us to the other side so they can talk about serious, grown-up things. I've listened before. It's usually Mama giving him advice about how to endure his unhappy marriage.

Azra and I walk over to the far side of the island. Here there is no firm sand and clear water. The sand is alive, soft, and so hungry that if you step on it, it sucks you down as far as your knees. Off the shore, green weeds dance and wave like a water witch's hair. Azra starts in on me right away.

"Ugh, when are you going to stop growing? You're even taller than before." Apparently in her world it is okay to be tall because of big hair and high heels, but not from long bones. She looks at my height like it is freakish, like I belong in a circus. "Are you going to be like your brother, never stop growing until you get sick and die, too?"

I catch my breath but don't say anything. I don't want to upset Mama by letting her know what Azra is like. Neither she nor her mother ever once said they were sorry about Amar. They did their best to ignore him when he was alive, and now that he's gone it's like he never even existed to them.

"You look like a boy, you know. And not even a proper boy with muscles, like my boyfriend, Davor."

"You have a boyfriend?" I ask, surprised. Maybe she's nicer to boys than she is to me.

"Well, not exactly, but he's going to ask me out soon. He's had a crush on me for ages. But really, you should grow your hair out. If you look like that in a few more years they'll conscript you for army service like a boy." She tosses her extravagant hair, smacking me in the face with the hair-sprayed strands.

I stare at the waving water weeds that look like octopus arms ready to grab me and fight back tears. With all the overwhelming things my mom had going on over the last few years, she never had time to put my hair in pretty curls or braids. My hair is cut in a short, boyish bob. On a special occasion, a school play or a celebration, she might twist a piece of hair in the front round and round into an organic loose swirl, but that was the extent of any feminine hairdo for me. I would have liked long, cascading hair, though.

Why should I care what Azra thinks of me? If I'm ugly or beautiful, what does it matter to her? She's like Milorad and Ratko, someone who would say anything as long as it caused pain. How can she treat a cousin like that? Doesn't family mean anything to her?

She notices me staring into the swirling emerald-green river. "Are you afraid of the Una? I saw someone drown here just last year. Their boat hit a rock and they flipped over and never came up again."

The River Una is beautiful and dangerous. The Romans called it Una—*the One*—and it is everything a river can be. Calm and gentle with quiet lagoons and pretty beaches. Rough and wild and twisting over boulders, through canyons, ready to smash anyone who lets their guard down. It is like Bosnia itself. I love the Una, but I respect it, too. My family are all strong swimmers, but the Una can swallow even the strongest. There's even a saying, that people who can't swim never drown in the Una. It is the swimmers who get into trouble, so entranced by the river's beauty that they underestimate her power.

"Since you don't have to worry about your hair, you should go swimming," Azra suggests.

But I'm not in a bathing suit, just shorts. Anyway, I'd have to go back to the safe side, where Mama and Ejo are still talking.

"Go on, are you afraid?"

Pride makes me take a step closer to the bank. My feet sink into the sand, up to my ankles. I can't risk going any deeper, or I might be sucked under.

Suddenly, Azra shoves me from behind, and I fly forward onto my knees. My head goes underwater, and the slimy weeds wrap around my neck like they want to choke me. I hear Azra laughing, and I come up sputtering, furious, ready to yell at her.

But then the unbelievable happens. It is so unbelievable that at first, I can't even react.

She steps up behind me, grabs the back of my head, and thrusts my face back underwater.

For a second, time is frozen. I see bubbles, seaweed, a tiny snail. Then my unbelieving mind accepts that this is real, and I thrash and struggle, scream underwater. Her fingers grip my short hair, holding me down. She's not big or strong, but she's leaning all her weight on my head, and I can't escape!

I manage to turn a little bit under her grasp. Looking up through the bright prism of the water, I see her face, laughing, distorted, ugly. Sweet air is only an inch away, but she won't let me reach it. I scream and choke and beat at her hands. How can this be happening? People don't do this kind of thing. Not to family, not to anyone.

Suddenly, she lets me up, and I take a great choking gasp of air, then roll to my knees to cough up all the water I swallowed.

"What are you kids up to?" Mama calls from the other side of the island. I hear her footsteps coming closer, crunching softly in the sand.

"Amra's just playing in the water," Azra says with a goody-goody voice.

"Oh, Amra, you're soaked!" she says when she's near enough to see me. "And we need to stop at the market on the way home. I thought you'd be more sensible than that."

I want so much to tell Mama what happened. But it seems unbelievable. *Azra almost killed you, drowned you?* How can I put the impossible into words? I feel like I've entered some alternate universe where nobody is who they seem. Where evil—real evil, not the storybook kind—is truly possible. Where a cousin can turn on you because you're tall or different or for no reason at all.

I can't burden Mama with all of that. So I mutter, "Sorry," and wring the water from the hem of my shirt.

On the way home Mama can tell I'm upset. She thinks it's because she chastised me and tries to make amends with swirly ice cream, but I tell her I'm not hungry. All I want is to be home with my head under my pillow, free to cry where my tears won't upset anyone. Being eleven is horrible. I just want this time of my life to end.

LATER, WHEN I slip out to use the bathroom, I hear my parents talking downstairs in low, worried voices.

"We have to do something, Dilka," Tata says. "She's fading right before our eyes. I want to see the joy back in her face."

"She needs a friend," Mama says.

"I thought you said she has friends. The girls you invited over."

"They came because they had to. They're nice enough girls, but...No, Amra needs someone to talk to, someone who will stand by her through anything."

"She can talk to her parents. We'll stand by her. She knows that."

"Mehmed, have you ever been a preteen girl? She needs someone like her, a girl to share her feelings with. If only..."

"If only what?" Tata wants to know.

"I think I should get in touch with Aida."

"I thought she was calling herself Dida now."

"She's still my cousin, no matter who she married. Look at Ejo. My sisters and I still fight to be close to him even though he married Sado. Just because Aida married Đorđe is no reason we should be estranged."

"She's the one who left. She's the one who pretends to be something she's not."

"Still, it has gone on long enough."

"I don't know."

"Well, I'll think about it," Mama says. "But seeing Amra like this is breaking my heart. If only she could have something like I had at her age. You know how close my sisters all were. We were like a gang, always ready to fight for one another, always supportive no matter what. Amra needs a girl like that in her life."

"But you don't even know what Žana is like."

Žana! That's my cousin who I've never met, a girl who lives with my aunt and her Serb husband in Belgrade. I've heard their names a few times, but no one really talks about them. When I hear Žana's name, it sounds so pretty, so exotic and exciting. Žana sounds like she should be a character in an adventure story, a heroine.

"It might be time to take a chance. But like I said, I'll think about it a while longer. It's summer now. The holidays might help her snap out of her depression."

I go back to my room and put my head under the pillow again.

THE FIRST
SUMMER

7

TO KEEP TATA and Mama from worrying, I make myself go outside at the beginning of summer break. Some of Mama's students, the girls she forced to meet me, are hanging out under a neighborhood basketball hoop. Nobody is playing, but I suspect they think if they wait long enough, a boy will show up. I wander over to them and listen to their conversation. They're only a couple of years older, but their topics are mysterious to me: boys, boys' bodies, and their own bodies. Thanks to Amar, my thoughts range much wider. I want to discuss how the universe began, or whether aliens exist. I don't know how to join in on these girls' discussions. One teases another for having to bleach or pluck the fine hairs on her upper lip. Another starts talking about Saša, and suddenly my ears perk up.

Saša! He is the boy version of German chocolates, beautiful and rare. His parents are Bosnian but work in Germany. He's home for the summer. I've seen him playing basketball, riding his fancy BMX bike, talking with his friends. He is the most interesting person I've ever seen, with his flashing white smile, wavy caramel-colored hair, and alluring German accent. I've always wanted to be his friend, but somehow whenever he comes near I can't seem to get a word out.

I want to take part in the conversation, and Saša is the first thing I think of to talk about. "Saša seems really nice," I say.

Instead of taking me into the conversation, they all just stare at me. Probably thinking, *Who does this baby think she is, talking about teen things like boys?* Like I don't have a right to admire him.

So I drift away, and they don't even notice. Instead I take Amar's old bike and start riding lazy loops around the block. At least I'm getting the fresh air my parents are always talking about, though how it's any fresher than the air in my bedroom next to my open window, I don't know.

What would it be like to have a friend…a *real* friend, like Mama mentioned? Someone who would laugh *with* me, not *at* me. Someone who would like me no matter what. Lost in these thoughts, I make my loop too tightly and crash my bike onto the road. For a moment, I sit stunned, watching red blood well from the long scrape on my knee.

Then Saša is running up out of nowhere like a hero. "Are you okay? No, don't try to get up. Stay there, I'll be right back." He sprints off to his family's fancy German car and takes a bag from the trunk. When he opens it, bandages and gauze spill out. "We always carry a first aid kit for emergencies," he says in his fascinating accent as he cleans bits of gravel from my wound. "This is the first time I've had to use it, though. Does that hurt?"

I shake my head.

"What's your name?"

"Amra."

"I'm Saša."

"I know," I can't help saying, and he laughs. When he dabs Mercurochrome on the scrape I flinch, but I'm so thrilled to actually be talking to him that it barely even hurts.

That's when the other girls come over—Zumreta, Valbona, Anela, and Fatima. Saša puts a bandage on my knee and stands up. The girls look at me with new interest. All except Fatima, whose face is scrunched up in a scowl.

He puts out a hand to help me up, and when I reach to take it my short sleeve slides up. Fatima bursts into laughter like a crow's cawing. "Now that you're old enough to *fall* for boys, you're old enough to shave your armpits, Amra. It looks like a jungle in there. I'm surprised I don't see monkeys swinging around under your arms!" The other girls giggle along with her.

I feel like the earth has opened up beneath me. I wish it would. I wish it would swallow me so Saša can't see my burning face. Everything felt so nice for a moment. Now I feel too young and naive and embarrassed. I knew I had armpit hair. I didn't know I had to do something about it. What about my other hair? Do I need to take it all off to fit in?

I ride my bike home, never looking at Saša's face. Mama and Tata have gone somewhere, maybe the store. I don't want to ask them anyway. I can take care of this myself. How hard could it be? I see Tata shave every day. Here's his silver razor, his shaving cream, his shaving brush with boar's hair bristles. Once I take off all this hair, maybe I'll feel normal again. Maybe Saša won't think I'm weird. Maybe one of the girls will truly want to be my friend.

I lather up my armpit, and slash the jungle with my razor like an intrepid explorer.

When Mama and Tata come home, it must look like a slaughterhouse. I'm curled up on the bathroom floor, blood dripping down my arms, my legs, the razor on the tile beside me.

"My baby! What have you done?" Mama screams, falling to her knees in the blood, and it's only then I realize what she must think I've tried to do. Tata's face is ghostly white.

"I needed to shave," I sob. "The other girls said so. They laughed..."

"You shaved? Is that all? Oh, Amra! Why didn't you talk to me first? You don't have to shave. I never do, you know." She doesn't, I realize now—not her legs or underarms or anywhere—and she is still a beautiful, elegant woman. "You've hurt yourself."

"It doesn't matter." I weep into my hands.

"Look at me, Amra," Mama says, taking my hands in hers, pulling them away from my face. "Never do something because some girl laughs at you. Never! No true friend would do that." She turns to Tata and makes a decision. "Mehmed, tonight I'm calling up Aida. We're reconciling the family. Amra needs her cousins."

8

I DON'T HAVE high hopes for meeting my cousins. After all, Mama has tried to find friends for me before, and look how that went. Those girls either barely tolerated me or were outright mean to me. And the fact that Žana and her little sister, Vedrana, are family doesn't make me any more hopeful. My own cousin, who I've known all my life, tried to drown me. What will a stranger-cousin be capable of?

Still, I'm curious about this part of my family that has been lost for so long. Amar taught me to always be curious. Before they arrive, Mama sits me down to tell me more about the family history.

"I call Žana your cousin, but really her mother Aida is my cousin, the daughter of my uncle." In Bosnia, we tend to give everyone a closer family title than they were born with. Every distant relative is a cousin, and first cousins are often called *brother* or *sister*. "We were close when we were young," Mama tells me. "But then Aida fell in love with a Serb."

The way she says it, it sounds like something is wrong with that, but I'm not really sure what. Bosnia—and when we say Bosnia, we always mean Bosnia and Herzegovina—is part of a bigger country, Yugoslavia, which also includes the other states of Serbia, Croatia, Slovenia, Macedonia, and Montenegro, as well as Kosovo and Vojvodina, the autonomous regions closely controlled by

Serbia. They were originally bound together after the Second World War by a leader named Tito, linked by Communist ideals. Now Tito is gone, and the news reports say we are held together by brotherhood. There are Serbs and Croats here in Bosnia, so I never understood why people sometimes talk about them like they are all separate people. And no one calls us Bosniak, only Muslim. Serbs are Orthodox Christian and Croats are Catholic, but they aren't identified by their religion. I don't ask why. But we are all Bosnians and Herzegovinians. Most of the time I can't look at someone or talk to them or meet their family and figure out if they are Serb or Croat or even Bosniak.

"Aida's father would not accept the marriage. It wasn't that she was marrying a Serb, but a Serb from a Chetnik family. And not only a Chetnik family—people aren't responsible for their ancestors—but from a *proud* Chetnik family."

"What are the Chetniks?" I ask, even though I sort of know. I suddenly feel like there's a lot I "sort of" know but don't really understand.

Mama pauses for a moment, draws a breath, and lets it out in a slow sigh. "Amra, if we talk about this, you have to remember that some things are just said among family inside four walls. They're not to talk about with the rest of the world, do you understand? It could cause problems for our family." She looks at me earnestly until I nod, then goes on.

"They were a Serb nationalist group, a guerrilla force of fighters in the Second World War. The Chetniks have always been for Serbs first, Serbs last, Serbs only and always. Sometimes Chetniks sided with the Nazis, but they also fought everyone else depending on which side was winning, which side could help the Serbs the most...or whoever they hated for simply not being Serb. When the war was already ending, when the partisans were winning against the Nazis, plenty of Chetniks joined the partisans. But before that a lot of Chetniks spent a lot of the war killing Muslims. Aida's husband Đorđe's family are Serbs from the small village of Tovrljane in Kosovo, and they were known in World War II for slaughtering Muslims. And Đorđe himself is a high-ranking military officer. Aida didn't just marry *any* Serb boy. She married into a family of known Muslim-killers."

A shudder passes through me. World War II always felt so far away from me, like it might have happened hundreds of years ago. But for the first time, I see that history is much closer than I ever realized. I've heard—or overheard—war stories around the fire at Šumatac. During that war, Bosnia was occupied by Nazi Germany. In so many conflicts Bosnia was always a prize to be fought over by outside forces, while in my land Bosniaks died for other people's wars. I never met my grandfather, my father's father, because he was killed by Nazis near the end of the war. His wife, Grandmother Nura, faced down Nazi soldiers with her children beside her and swore that she had no weapons in the house when she was actually hiding guns for the partisans. And I've heard my family whisper about whole villages of Muslims being killed, of rivers running red with Bosnian Muslim blood. But it all seemed like something that happened in another world, with no relation to the one I'm living in now.

I try to put Aida's marriage into a perspective I understand. What would Amar have thought if I grew up to marry Milorad or

Ratko? Or if my daughter married one of their sons? It must have felt like that to Aida's father. Aida married the enemy.

But shouldn't all these years make a difference? I'm sure Đorđe never killed anyone and never would. His love for a Muslim woman must prove that times are different now. To me, it sounds like a real love story.

"Aida's father never saw her again," Mama tells me. "Aida would secretly visit her mother and siblings every few years, but her father always refused to so much as speak to her. Now my uncle, her father, is dead, and she wants to be able to see her mother more often. When I called them up to reconcile it turned out that she was bringing her family to Bosnia for a weeklong visit anyway. So now they are coming to lunch, and you finally get to meet your cousins. But remember, don't bring up any of the things I told you about our family history, about Bosnia's history." Mama is a history and geography teacher, and her history lessons feel more real than anything I learn in school.

I wish Amar were here to meet his cousins. He always loved meeting new people, and he could approach anyone without fear. Once at the beach he spied a famous Russian chess player and asked him to play a game with him—and Amar won! No one else would have had the audacity, but Amar never hesitated to welcome more people into his world.

When the knock comes we all run to the door. I feel excited, almost scared. All kinds of stories swirl in my head, war and romance. I'll almost be disappointed if these are just ordinary, nice, boring people.

When we open the door I see a giant. We're a tall family, but

Đorđe is six and a half feet tall and has a stiff, proud military bearing that makes him seem even taller. He has big square glasses on a big square head. His thick black mustache is twisted into curling points at the end. He moves with a strange mix of confidence and awkwardness, like with every step he might destroy something. But he greets us with a smile. "The women are fussing with something in the car. Hello, you must be Amra," he says after officially meeting my parents. "And you, young man—Dino, I bet!" He bends down and gives Dino a toy airplane.

"Oh wow!" Dino says, and zooms it around the house. Đorđe has made a great first impression already. But when I smile up at him, look into his eyes, I see that there's no smile there. The smile is only on his mouth, not the rest of his face. He starts to walk around our house like he owns it, or has just invaded it, while we wait for Aida and her daughters to join us.

When Aida comes in, Mama catches her in a huge tight hug. "Aida, how I've missed you!"

"Call me Dida, please," she says, untangling herself from Mama's arms. "No one has called me Aida for years."

She says it lightly, like it hardly matters, but there's tension in her face. She glances at Đorđe, who looks a little annoyed. And I realize, Aida is a traditionally Muslim name. Dida is a name that I've never even heard before. It has no nationality.

A girl about Dino's age tumbles in and stands shyly behind her mother. "This little one is Vedrana. Say hello, Vedrana."

The tiniest murmur comes from behind Aida's skirts. "She's our little owl, all eyes and no voice. Go over there and meet Dino. Žana, are you coming?" she shouts back toward the car.

"I'm getting the presents!" comes a voice.

"That girl!" She sighs as if her daughters are the great trials of her life.

At last, here comes a girl my own age, carrying a pile of pretty, colorful boxes in her arms so high that her face barely peeks over them. Her eyes are crinkled, smiling.

Žana juggles the boxes a bit and then thrusts them at me. Now I'm the one peeking over. I see an unusually pretty face, gleaming teeth, a glint of mischief in her eyes. But all I can say is, "You're taller than I am!"

"What's all this?" Aida wants to know, waving an arm at the packages. "I thought we just brought them chocolates."

"I saw Amra from the car, and as soon as I saw her I could picture the perfect outfit for her. So I went into my suitcase to get it out. I repacked everything to make it more like a real present." She opens the first box on the top of the pile. Inside is something I've only dreamed about—a puffy miniskirt just like the ones in boutique windows. The kinds of clothes my schoolmates have, but we can never afford.

"But those are *your* clothes," Aida protests.

Žana looks at me, aghast. "You don't mind, do you Amra? I know presents should be new, but we're cousins, and I've hardly worn them, and this would look so much better on you than on me! Now that I know how tall and pretty you are I can pick out things just for you next time. Come on, let's try it on!"

Before I know what's happening, she grabs my hand and pulls me up the stairs. "Which room is yours? You don't have to share a room, do you? Oh, this is lovely. You have a balcony!" She walks out onto it, delighted. "I always wanted a balcony. You can play *Romeo and Juliet*. A boy could serenade you from down there!"

Suddenly my room isn't just Amar's old bedroom, a depressing place I inherited after a tragedy. Now, seen through Žana's eyes, my room has beauty and romance.

"You're staring at me," she says. But she isn't mad about it.

"No I'm not! I'm just ..." But I don't have a quick excuse. I *was* staring, because there's something not quite ordinary about her face. I just can't figure out what it is.

"It's my eyes," she says. "Here, let me get in the light." She opens her eyes very wide and beckons me closer.

"They're two different colors!" I cry, and all at once we're both laughing. I look at her, she looks at me, and I feel happy in a way I haven't for months.

"That's amazing," I say, staring first at the blue eye, then at the green one.

Žana shrugs. "It's just me. Come on, try on this skirt. Wait 'til you see how it poufs. My knees are too knobby to make it look good, but it will be perfect on you."

And just like that, easily, naturally, as if we've known each other our whole lives, we're talking and laughing, finding common ground with tales of terrible teachers, cute boys, rude girls. I find myself telling her about Saša and Fatima and my armpit hair, and when I tell it to someone who really likes me, suddenly it's not a sad story but a funny one. Žana laughs—*with* me, not *at* me—and then tells me about a cream you can spread on your skin that just makes the hair all fall off, easy as anything.

Before I know it, though, Đorđe pops his head in and tells Žana it's time to go. I don't dare protest, but Žana doesn't hesitate. "No! I've waited my whole life to meet my cousin, and she's just perfect and I *won't* leave yet!" She folds her arms and stamps her foot. Đorđe looks like he's used to being obeyed. There are probably whole units of soldiers who tremble and jump at his every command. Not Žana. She stares at him defiantly and argues until he agrees that she and Vedrana can stay.

"Just for the night," he says.

"For a week at least! Until we all go back to Belgrade. I'd rather stay here than at Grandmother's house with everyone whispering about us behind closed doors."

It's like watching another species of girl, someone much stronger and bolder than I am. I'd never dare talk back to my parents like that! I might make requests, I might even argue a little, but I could never make demands.

Žana grins broadly at her victory over her father.

Later, as we're setting up the foam mattresses on the floor, Žana says without looking up, "I always wanted a sister my own age."

"Me too," I say shyly.

We stay up late into the night, piled in front of my little black-and-white bubble TV that has a mile-long antenna and still just barely gets one channel. We laugh and shriek at everything and nothing. Near midnight I creep out and apologize to Mama and Tata for being so loud. "Are we keeping you up? We can go to sleep now."

"No," says Tata with tears in his eyes. "Be as loud as you like. You children can laugh until the sun comes up!"

9

THE NEXT DAY I wake up between my two new sisters, listening to the dawn chorus of birds, smelling coffee brewing. We're lined up like sardines in a can on the floor. I tried to give Žana or Vedrana my bed, but they refused, and so my bed was empty all night. With the door to the balcony open and the warm night breeze blowing in, it had seemed like camping out. The floor didn't feel hard at all with my new sisters beside me. I slept as soundly as a princess in a featherbed.

I hear our neighbor Mujesira call out good morning to my parents. They invite her over to join them for coffee on the first-floor terrace. Gentle morning light filters through the curtains, dancing through the leaves of the apple, plum, and quince trees.

That's when it hits me, suddenly and effectively like a hard slap on the back that saves you when you're choking: *Things can get better.* It is such a simple thought, but a profound one for me. My life has been sad in so many ways for the past year that I'd forgotten about the good things I still have in my life. It took Žana to reawaken my sense of hope.

I wiggle out of my sardine pack without waking up my cousins and go out onto the balcony of my second-story bedroom. When Mujesira notices me, she shouts up from the terrace below in the loud classic Bosnian style, "Good morning, Amra! I'm sorry I woke you." I have to smile because though she might be sorry, she doesn't turn her volume down one bit. I think we're so loud because we all grew up near the roar of the River Una. We have to compete with nature to be heard.

"I'm on my way to visit my sister," she yells up to me, and to the whole neighborhood. There aren't many secrets in Bosnia. "But I think I'll take a later bus, so I can spend some time with these two lovebirds." She nods to my parents. "My Medo works so much I never even see him, so here I am, being a cuckoo in the lovebird nest." Mama and Tata are together whenever they can be and hold hands like a teenage boyfriend and girlfriend. I never see any other parents acting like that, so their love must be something out of the ordinary. Will I ever have someone who wants to hold my hand over morning coffee? Someone who looks at me after eighteen years of marriage like we're on our first date?

Mama fills one of the extra fildžan cups they always have ready for unexpected guests. The sun glints on the big gold-filigreed hoop earrings Mujesira always wears. They are a hallmark of Muslim women of a certain age, passed down from generation to generation and worn with silent pride.

Coffee is the drink that binds all Bosnians together. I don't like coffee, but I must be the only person in Bosnia who doesn't. It isn't about getting a caffeine fix. I'm sure Mujesira already had a quick cup in her own home. Coffee is socializing. Bonding. Therapy. Here in Bosnia, people don't go to doctors or therapists when they have problems. They sit with their friends and neighbors and drink coffee. Tetka Fatma always has her girlfriends over for *teferidž*, an old Bosnian word that means enjoying time together while drinking coffee with gusto, and usually feasting on delicious food, too. They have multihour gossip sessions about life, love, children, changes…everything under the sun. Almost every time I'm at her house I witness these coffee-fueled conversations full of laughter and tears. The outpouring of words and emotions doesn't always fix the problems, but it certainly makes them more bearable.

Žana blinks awake, yawning dramatically and then playing with Vedrana's hair until she wakes up—gently at first, then giving it a teasing little tug when she gets impatient. "Come on, sleepyhead! We have a lot to do today."

"What are we doing?" Vedrana asks.

Žana shrugs. "We'll figure that out later. The important part is that we're doing it together with our new sister. I get the bathroom first!" She jumps up, all traces of sleep gone, and races to the bathroom down the hall.

Dino is in there, brushing his teeth with one hand and flying a toy plane with the other. "Hurry up, it's our turn!" Žana says, snatching away his plane and dangling it high over his head. He jumps to reach it, but she's much too tall. She's not being mean, though, and gives it back a second later, and he laughs. "Girls need more time in the bathroom than boys," she explains to him. "You can hang out in the hall and find out all the secret mysteries of girls, though. It will be useful to you later."

"Ew, no!" he says…but all the same I see him reflected in the mirror later, lurking down the hall and watching us. We all wind up squeezed in the bathroom at the same time to wash our faces and brush our teeth. Žana plops an overstuffed toiletry bag on the counter.

"Where's yours?" she asks me. "That's the best way to test new makeup, right? Trying a friend's. It is so disappointing to buy a lipstick that looks good in the store and then it looks weird when you put it on." She pulls out a handful of lipstick tubes and opens one after another, swiveling out the dramatic colors: scarlet, fuchsia, apricot. "This one would look perfect on you, with your coloring." She shows me a dark red that looks frighteningly mature. It's a lipstick for a glamour queen.

"So where are yours? I'm in the mood for something lighter today. Do you have any peach or gold lipsticks?"

"I...I don't have any lipsticks."

"Oh, you like gloss better? Yeah, that's nice in the summer. Juicy lips!" She puckers hers and makes kisses.

I don't want to say it. I feel like she'll think I'm a boring baby. But Mama hasn't taught me about any of this. I see other girls with makeup, or wearing tighter shirts, or walking with a wiggle in their hips. But none of that ever seemed to apply to me. All I know is how to be a kid. I'm clueless about being a girl.

Things with Žana and Vedrana have been going so perfectly, and I'm afraid I'll ruin it. But finally I have to admit, "I don't have any makeup."

"What, none?" Vedrana asks incredulously "Not even a..." She breaks off when Žana nudges her in the ribs.

"You don't need a drop of makeup," Žana says quickly, understanding. "Look at you, perfect skin, rosy lips. Why spoil that with makeup? Me, I have a lot to cover up." Which isn't true at all.

She doesn't make me say that we can't afford makeup. Mama only uses a Nivea face cream and a fire-orange lipstick Tetka

Fatma brought her from Italy, which complements her red hair. She's beautiful, and I don't know if she skips makeup to save money or because she doesn't need it. Maybe both. People sometimes think we have plenty of money because we have such a nice new house. But they don't know what we gave up to build it. And they don't know that we're still saving every dinar to pay for it, and it isn't even finished or properly furnished yet! Our furniture is from the sixties and seventies. It all squeaks and complains when someone sits on it, making a sound like someone is squeezing a juice box.

I almost want her to offer to teach me how to put on makeup... but I'm relieved when she doesn't. Instead, I watch her put her own on. It's the first time I've seen foundation. Imagine, a product made for you to hide behind—a flesh-colored mask that could conceal all of my pain and sorrow and insecurities. Life is so carefree for Žana that makeup can preoccupy her mind. I wish I had that kind of life, a life where I hadn't lost a brother. I wish there was a makeup that could cover up that kind of pain.

A loud, angry rattle and thump interrupts my thoughts, like an army marching through the bathroom, then a sound like a geyser, a rush of splashing water. It breaks through my thoughts so harshly that I scream and clutch at Žana, so lost in my own world that I don't even recognize a sound I hear every day. For a second, it feels like the world is ending.

"It's just the washing machine emptying," Žana says, laughing at my irrational panic. *It isn't irrational to me*, I think, as I watch the soapy water draining out into the bathtub. I used to be so carefree. Death was something that happened to old people, so distant it didn't even require thinking about. But after seeing my brother die, I feel like the world is full of infinite horrible possibilities. Anything bad could happen, at any time. Though Žana is much more sophisticated than me in most things, I am ancient in the ways of trauma. Žana has never lost someone she loved. She doesn't act like someone who has been teased or ever been made to feel inadequate. Never hated herself for being unable to protect the people important to her. Never been haunted by the fear that everyone she loves might die.

But she shows me another way of being. Maybe in time I won't think every loud noise means disaster. Maybe someday I'll be able to say goodbye to people without thinking it may be the last goodbye.

I don't tell Žana any of this. I don't want to scare her off.

Žana keeps complimenting me as she smooths on her makeup. Every feature she criticizes in herself, she praises in me. To me, she is tall and slender like a supermodel, with those unusual, arresting eyes. But to my amazement that seems to be how she sees me! Or is she just saying all these nice things to make me feel better?

In a way, that's almost better than actually being beautiful—having a friend who loves me so much that she tells me I am, whether it is true or not.

It's late morning by the time we go downstairs, and I can tell by the delicious smells, by the bits of phyllo dough on the table, that Mama has been up and busy for hours. So much food!

"Who's coming over?" I ask.

"No one," Mama says. "I've invited our entire family to meet us at the Četić Mill."

It's as if she'd suggested visiting a place from a fairy story. I've heard so many family tales about the Četić Mill, and though we've passed it on the way to Uncle Ejo's house, I've never gone there. We didn't go there for the same reason I didn't have long, curled hair—Mama was simply too busy to organize our social life. Other things came first, like caring for Amar and building our new home, and Dino and I were left to amuse ourselves in the neighborhood as best we could.

Then the other part of what she said hits me. "What do you mean 'the entire family'?"

She can't really mean it! That would be like planning a wedding! Mama has five sisters and a brother, not to mention her first cousins. And all of them have children. Some even have grandchildren since Mama is the youngest. The whole family could easily be a hundred people, maybe more! The whole neighborhood of Hatinac is full of Mama's relatives, people I've either never met or met when I was so small I've forgotten them. They are Mama's distant relatives, not close enough to lean on when Amar was at his sickest, but the perfect guests for a family picnic to welcome Žana and Vedrana. I associate that neighborhood with Ejo's house, with Sado and Azra, so it makes me worry that some of this barely known family might turn out like those two nasty women.

But I push those worries aside because going to the Četić Mill means the River Una, the water and the beach! It means feasting on the delicious-smelling food which even now is making my mouth water! Žana is completely thrilled. She knows some of the cousins about our age fairly well and rattles off stories about them as we pack up the car.

We have to stuff ourselves into the little orange Stojadin for the fifteen-minute ride. I sit on one side of the back seat, and Žana is on the other, with Vedrana in the middle and Dino on my lap. I think of him as a little boy, but he's growing tall and will catch up to me before I know it. Tata has his seat all the way up to give us extra room, and he drives hunched over the wheel.

We have towels, cushions, dishes, and utensils. My feet rest on a propane tank. For one morbid moment I start to worry that the tank could explode. Then I remember that Tata never drives the car faster than I could blow a puff of breath, so we should be safe. Vedrana is given the very important and grown-up task of holding the most precious thing we carry: a huge, rich cake filled with nuts and raisins, topped with a layer of chocolate so shiny I can almost see my reflection in it. She bites her lower lip as she balances it on her knees, awed and thrilled at the responsibility.

All the way there Žana is chatting about how much fun we'll have. "I'm jumping into the water the second we get there!" she says.

Only then do I realize what I've forgotten: a bathing suit.

Not only have I forgotten to bring one, but worse: I don't even own one!

The last time I went to the beach I was inches shorter and years younger. Since bathing suits were less important than the house or Amar's medicine, I wore a pair of Amar's old swim trunks, with just a T-shirt on top. But I have a feeling that's not what Žana or any of the other girls will be wearing. I go quiet, my face red with embarrassment. Maybe I can pretend I don't feel well and just stay on dry land.

The car sputters to a stop, I throw open the door, and suddenly the magical sound of the rushing waters of the Una washes most of my worries away.

10

THIS LAND ALL belonged to Mama's grandfather Bećo. He began life with nothing, orphaned at a young age. Then he got chicken pox and lost an eye from the disease. I always shiver with delicious dread when Mama tells me how it literally leaked on his sister's shoulder. From that poor start he built a small empire of land, a shoe factory, and this mill that once ground wheat into flour. After the difficulty of his childhood, he did everything he could to take care of the rest of his family. He later witnessed Nazis burn all his properties when Germans bombed Bihać and even take his favorite and firstborn son, Muharem, to a Nazi concentration camp. Though he died after the war, he taught his sons and daughters to follow in his footsteps, and the family rebuilt its strength. He didn't want the generations after him to ever suffer.

Though the shoe factory had to be given up after the Communists took over private property, some of the family land remains, divided among Bećo's descendants. And there are many of them—Bećo had two wives at the same time, back when that was still legal. Mama and her sisters are the only ones who don't own land or a house here. They gave up most of their shares to try to help Uncle Ejo's disastrous marriage.

Though the mill and land belong to the Četić family, the recreational area by the river is open to everyone. It is one of the most popular local hangouts for teenagers.

As we spill out of the car and I look around, I'm stunned by the magical beauty of this place. The sights, the sounds, the very air I'm breathing feels different than anywhere else. How did I not know about this? Why haven't I been coming here all my life?

The island is covered in lush shade of ancient birch and linden trees that create a natural harmony with the sounds of Una's waterfalls. The dark green of the trees blends into the deep emerald green of Una with the occasional white flash of a churning waterfall. The sound of the water is a gentle music, with a countermelody of the ritual ezan, or call to prayer from the nearby mosque. I can't hear the sounds of the city, no car engines or trucks honking their horns. It feels like I've arrived in the afterlife, where only beauty and nature engage the senses.

As we walk across the old bridge that speaks of the millions of footsteps that have touched the smooth wood built by my great-grandfather in 1934, we see gigantic trout jumping between ducks with iridescent feathers that shift from purple and blue to bright yellow and orange depending on how the sun hits them. The cold breeze from Una along with the deep shadows created by the old trees makes me cool and comfortable on this scorching summer day.

There are so many people here! At least a couple of these people must be my cousins, but I have no idea which ones. Mama and Tata look serene as young people run past them in tiny bikinis and even tinier Speedos. People are sprawled on the bridges, on the soft grass and moss of the riverbank, on the sun-warmed stones—wet bodies everywhere enjoying the contrast between the sun and the chilly Una. People are relaxed and kissing right in the open. Everyone is tan and free and teenaged, it seems. I think of all the generations of friends and lovers who met here. People must have come here to weep, too, letting their tears fall into the Una. This river has seen everything my family has lived through for a hundred years.

Now it is time for this stretch of the Una to meet me.

We carry Mama's mountains of food over the narrow wooden footpath that crosses half the river to the island we call Lučica. To the left is Brvice, a big curving wooden deck that connects the riverbank with the small waterfalls and the trees growing mid-river. It serves as a beach and basking spot for dozens of bronzing bodies. This part of the river is open and clear, but just upstream and downstream of here, the river bounces down stair-step waterfalls, five, ten, fifteen feet high.

"Can I go swimming right now?" Dino asks.

"Not until after we eat," Mama tells him. "I want Amra to be near you. You're not a strong swimmer yet."

"Yes I am! Please? I'll be fine. Vedrana can come with me."

Vedrana looks at him with her wide-open eyes, somewhere between surprised and grateful to be included. Žana is some-times an affectionate sister when she remembers Vedrana exists, but she sees her very much as the little sister and doesn't try to include her in our plans.

"Later, I promise. Help me with the food first."

"Where's all of the family?" I ask Mama as we set up the food on a huge wooden table that seats twenty people.

"Don't worry, they'll be here soon. The breeze is carrying the invitation." The delicious scents are wafting across the river to the houses lining the banks. Soon enough the first person comes to investigate.

"It's Zumra, Adem's wife," Žana says, suddenly stiffening. "Asmir and Zlatan are her sons. She won't like to see me here!" She gives a nervous chuckle.

"Why?" I ask her.

"Well, my mom was Granddad's favorite, until she married my dad. He cut her out of the will. Now, even though Granddad is gone, all of the other heirs think we'll try to claim their inheritance."

Family is far more complicated than I ever imagined! Before, family had always been about love and acceptance to me. Now I'm sensing the treacherous currents that lie beneath.

Sure enough, when Zumra comes up she asks Mama caustically, "What are you doing here, Dilka? Do you need something?"

Mama completely ignores her tone and says, "How nice to see you too after all these years! All is well with us. We just want to get some fresh air and let the kids have some fun. Sit down and join us."

I can tell from Zumra's scowl that she doesn't want to, but Žana whispers, "She'll stay, because she's sure we have some hidden agenda." Sure enough, Zumra sits down and tries to interrogate Mama, who answers her with bland cheerfulness.

A teen boy with long hair and a Hollywood smile runs up to us, holding an orange basketball. "Žana, you're here! Who's your friend?"

"Asmir, this is Amra, your cousin." I know Asmir's name, and I think I saw him when I was young, but I might as well be meeting him for the first time since we are so distantly related. Asmir's dad and Žana's mom are brother and sister, so they've visited each other before. But Mama is their parents' first cousin.

"And this is my brother, Dino," I say, seeing that Dino is looking at Asmir with awe.

Asmir notices him looking at the ball. "You like basketball?"

Dino nods. "I want to be a basketball star someday!"

I think Asmir is going to laugh but he just nods very seriously. "I'm too hot to play now, but tell you what, let's all go swimming with my friends. Then once I've cooled off maybe we can play a pickup game." He tosses Dino the ball. "Will you keep this safe while I swim?"

"Sure!" Dino says, looking so proud to be included after we've been keeping him on the edges of all of our girl things.

"We just have to put on our bathing suits," Žana tells him. Dino already has his on, a pair of blue terrycloth shorts I know he's a little embarrassed by because they look like something a toddler would wear. Asmir offers to let us use his house to change, but his mother snaps that we should use the mill like everyone else. So Žana swings her bag over her shoulder and we head there.

As soon as we step into the cool shade of the mill, I pull Žana aside. "I have to tell you something," I whisper.

"What's wrong?" She looks instantly concerned, and I realize I made it sound really serious. Well, it is . . . to me!

"I don't have a bathing suit."

I hang my head, but she's unfazed. "Don't worry, I brought my whole collection. Just borrow one of mine."

So easy—just like that! We find a room to change in, and she

72

pulls out at least half a dozen bathing suits: patterned one-pieces with legs cut high almost to the waist and bright-colored bikinis. They're all so beautiful! I didn't think the army could pay so well, but her father must make a lot more than mine. Žana treats it like just an accident that she has six bathing suits and I have none.

"How about this one? No, this one." She throws me suit after suit to try on, and she finally settles on a green bikini. "You have a little more than I do up top, but you won't fall out of it I don't think. Let's go!"

I want more time to get used to having my whole body on display like this. I've never worn a bikini before, not since I've grown these... I look down at the new hills and valleys of my body that I'm not used to yet, a whole new topography of me. What if people look and don't like it? Or—almost as daunting— what if they look and *do* like it?

I think of my ancestors working in this mill back when it ground flour. What would Great-grandfather Bećo think of me standing half-naked in his mill? He'd be shocked not only by me, but by the posters on the wall—Nena with messy layered hair and heavy makeup singing "99 Luftballons" into a microphone, and a topless blond Samantha Fox. But then, I'd also be shocked by someone who had two wives at the same time. Times change, don't they?

What about Grandmother Šerifa, what would she think? She's always covered head to foot, without even a hair showing, always very strict, proper, and respected. But when she'd come to the beach with us when I was little, all of Mama's sisters wore bikinis, and she never batted an eye. She would even join in the tanning by pulling her dimije up to sun her ankles. I think she'd like this bikini because it is green, supposedly the Prophet Muhammad's favorite color. She told me once that in Paradise we will wear robes of green silk.

But I don't have time for self-doubt because Žana takes my hand and pulls me out into the sunshine, and all at once I'm part of it all: the sun, the laughter, the life.

We go to the wooden deck first and dip our feet in the water. It is freezing! Even in the summer it doesn't get more than about sixty-two degrees. But it cleanses my soul from the toes up and freezes any pain. Amar loved to swim here, too. He told me that cold water is like so many things in life: hard at first, but wonderful once you're used to it.

I love looking at the people here. With Žana my nerves vanish, and I smile at everyone. There's a girl named Edita with a shimmery gold bathing suit and the longest, reddest nails I've ever seen. She's styled her long black hair in the "wet look" using a ton of gel and hair spray. I think she could have saved money on hair products and gotten the same look by just diving in the water. But it's clear from the flirty way she poses that she's not here for swimming. There's a set of twins, too—boy and girl—and it is interesting to see almost the same face in two genders.

Asmir calls us over to the waterfalls to watch him and his friends—who aren't related to us—dive in. "I'm going in!" Dino says boldly.

"No you're not," I tell him. "It's too dangerous here by the waterfalls. Later on, you can swim in the cove with Hadžara." Hadžara is a self-appointed lifeguard who can't swim. She stays in the shallow, sheltered place where the younger children swim, wearing dried hollow gourds tied to her arms to keep her afloat. It is fairly safe there, a rare calm place on the Una, but she watches the children like a hawk and never lets one of them drift into more dangerous waters. A whole generation of kids learned to swim with Hadžara. She can't teach them, but she can give them a secure place to teach themselves.

"Aw, that's for babies," Dino protests.

"You are a baby," Žana says, ruffling his hair. He scowls but he doesn't seem too cross. Any attention from his interesting older cousin is valued, and he doesn't want to do anything that will make us banish him. Vedrana stands by him, silent. She already knows how to play the game of tagging along with the older kids.

We find a comfortable place on the rocks and watch as Asmir and his friends splash one another. "They're putting on a show for us," Žana whispers.

"Why?" I ask.

She gives me a look that is both loving and pitying. "Because they're boys and we're girls, silly. They want to impress us." Do they want to impress me, or my green bikini? "Which one do you like best?"

"Asmir, I guess." Of course I'll like my cousin more than strangers.

"No, silly, not *that* kind of like. Which one do you think is the cutest?"

"I don't know," I say as I watch them, mesmerized. They're all so good-looking! Not just because of their smiling eyes or nice muscles but because they are young and suntanned and happy.

They've picked one of the taller waterfalls, maybe ten feet

high. As they line up at the top, laughing and daring one another, I look at the water churning below and have a flashback to Azra holding my head underwater. I'm not at all sure I want to go swimming today. That fear of drowning is still too close for comfort.

Dino is looking at the boys with obvious envy, and I know he wishes he could join them. I'm even more scared for him than I am for myself. Since Amar died I sometimes have panic attacks about Dino. I'll suddenly realize I don't know where he is and have flashbacks to the day Amar died when I thought I'd lost both brothers. Then I have to shout his name and run to find him. He's always safe—playing with his toy plane or talking with a friend—but the sense that something terrible will happen never entirely leaves me, even here in this paradise with Žana.

Even seeing the older boys take risks at the edge of the rocks worries me. "Be careful!" I can't help shouting to them. The boys just laugh, then whisper something to one another. Are they whispering about us?

"Danger is the whole point," Žana explains to me. "If it wasn't dangerous, we wouldn't be impressed."

"Who's going first?" Asmir shouts.

"Not me!"

"You go!"

"I'll freeze my eggs off!" says the troublemaker of the bunch. Žana and I exchange a look, and when it dawns on me what body part he means, I blush and we both explode into uncontrollable giggles.

"Don't use that kind of language in front of my cousins!" Asmir scolds him, and the boy mutters an apology.

"Fine, all you chickens, worried about your eggs—I'll go first," Asmir says when no one volunteers. "*Kukuriku!*" He crows like a rooster, flaps his arms like a hen, and takes a running leap off the waterfall. He seems suspended in midair for a maddening second before plunging down into the foaming water below.

"Watch, they'll all go in now," Žana says. She must really understand how boys think, because every single one seems to forget about the cold and jumps in after Asmir, whooping on the way down and landing with huge splashes.

We're laughing and clapping as they surface, and they slide out onto the rocks like seals, then start throwing back their wet hair, flexing and posing like models at a photo shoot. How did I go from crying alone in my dark room to this glorious world of sunlight and boys in just a couple of days? I feel like another person. Nothing could mar this perfect moment.

"Wait, where's Asmir?" I ask.

"Don't worry, he's a great swimmer," Žana says. "He's fine."

I scan the water, but I don't see him. "I'm serious. Did he come up? I don't think he came up." I jump to my feet. "Asmir!" I shout to his friends, "Did you see him? Is he still under the water?" They start to look around frantically, and I count the seconds, then the minutes. No one can hold their breath for that long.

"He's not here, we can't find him," his friends say.

I don't even think about drowning. I have to do something to help him, even if it is hopeless. I jump in.

The cold water hits me like a punch, and I realize why the boys were splashing one another before they jumped in. The body isn't made to take this kind of shock all at once. My arms feel like they're dead. My fingers go instantly numb. But I strike out for the falls, duck my head under the water even though I can't see anything in the swirling chaos, call his name every time I come up for a breath. I hear a splash behind me. Žana has jumped in now, too—to save Asmir or to save me? I hear Dino call my name, and I recognize the fear in his voice, the same fear I feel whenever I think I can't find him and shout for him through the house or the neighborhood. I'm so cold I can barely move, and my teeth chatter together when I try to talk.

This can't be happening! I just met this new cousin and now he's going to drown. Is this my fate? Am I cursed? Will Žana die next? My parents?

Suddenly, at least five minutes after he jumped in, Asmir shoots out of the water right beside me.

"Worried about me, cousin?" he asks, laughing.

"B-but you ... what?" I stammer, shivering.

"Don't you know there are caves behind the falls?" His friends are all chuckling with him, and I realize they were in on the joke, too. "You thought I was in trouble? Aww, aren't you brave to come after me? Now I know you're really my cousin if you care enough to try to save me. Come on, let's go dry off and eat," he says, and helps me out onto the rocks. I start to slip, but his hand is strong, and I feel secure.

We climb back up the falls to the island and wrap ourselves in warm towels that have been drying in the sun. Dino and Vedrana look at Asmir with awe, like he's some divine, mythical creature—their new superhero! I can't even be mad. It feels too good to be alive.

11

"I'VE NEVER BEEN so hungry in my life!" Žana says as we head back to the island. I know how she feels. My growling stomach, the sharpness of my hunger, is a good sensation, one I haven't felt in far too long. For a while I'd felt dead inside, and the dead don't need to eat. Now, in the sunshine with all these laughing people around me, I'm truly hungry.

We race the boys back to the table and I slide into my seat on the bench before any of them. Mama has mountains of food piled up: burek, krompiruša with spiced potatoes in crispy buttered phyllo dough, and my favorite cheese pie. Mama buys the cheese from an old farmer lady who comes to Saturday market. It is golden yellow with creamy fat and a sweet milk taste. She brings it in a bucket and prices it by the cup, but she and Mama always negotiate about whose cup they will use to scoop it out. The crunch when Mama cuts into the pies is the most delightful sound. Tata is tossing the sliced tomatoes, onions, cucumbers, and cabbage in a dressing of oil and tangy vinegar. He tears up a handful of dill and sprinkles it in. To me, dill smells like summer, sharp and fresh. Next to the salad there's a pyramid of soft, sweet farmer's cheese, creamy like butter but fluffy like cotton candy. Žana sits beside me and takes a deep breath through her nose. "Ah, paradise," she sighs.

Our paradise is luring the rest of the family in, a carefully baited trap. Plenty of their friends and neighbors and even strangers wander in, too. First, local teenage boys come, tempted by the heavenly smells and encouraged by Asmir and his friends to join our family gathering. Next come the girls, tempted by the boys. Finally, the adults use their children as an excuse to follow. Any early suspicions of our motives evaporate with the first bite of Mama's delicious food, and soon dozens of people are crowded around the huge table, chatting and laughing and reaching for seconds. Latecomers stand nearby, nibbling. With a few bites of burek, feuds are reconciled, at least on the surface. And just like that, I have an army of family and friends around me.

"It's so wonderful," I say under my breath, but Žana hears me and knows what I mean.

She gives me a sly look and whispers, "Don't forget about the arguments you can't see. See those two over there? They've been at each other's throats for years over who owns the apple tree that grows on the border between their two houses. I heard Zumra tell someone that one of them crept out in the middle of the night and tried to chop it down with an ax. He'd rather no one have it than let his neighbor enjoy any apples. And I heard the woman over there hates that man sitting at the corner because he told a lie about her when they were both ten years old. Neither of them remembers what the lie was, they just remember the hate. Families are great, but they're complicated and difficult, too."

"Not us, though," I tell her.

"Not us. Nothing can ever separate us. I knew that the moment we met." She hugs me with one arm while she reaches for more food with the other.

One of my aunts says that the world is divided into two kinds of people: those who buy their jufka dough, and those who make it. You can get jufka, or phyllo, ready-made in farmer's markets ... and it is good. But it isn't paradise.

While Žana and Vedrana and I were dreaming on my bedroom floor, Mama was up before the birds to knead and twist and roll out a dough made of flour and water and salt. The ingredients are simple, but the process is a labor of love—and of muscle. Sometimes you'll see tiny old grandmothers with bones like a sparrow's but strong, wiry arms from a lifetime of making phyllo. Mama learned from her sister, my Tetka Begija, who learned from their mother. Tetka Begija is a professional chef who always lovingly teases Mama's jufka for being filled with holes, while her own is rolled out in neat layers. But even if it isn't perfect, Mama's jufka is delicious.

This morning on her impeccably clean kitchen table, Mama rolled out layer after layer of dough to the perfect unbroken thinness, nearly see-through, painting each sheet with butter straight from the farmer's market, butter so fresh it was still inside a cow just three days ago. The layers are stacked and rolled around a filling of ground meat, Hungarian paprika, onions, garlic, and a couple of eggs to bind it together. She twisted the stuffed tube into a spiral shape and baked it to crispy perfection. The whole time she was making them, Dino and Vedrana would come in every few minutes asking if the pies were ready.

"I wish my mom could cook like this," Žana says as she takes a big bite. Watching her eat it is almost as good as eating it myself, hearing the crunch of the jufka, seeing her eyes close in bliss as she chews. I take my first bite, and it tastes like everything I value about my family: nurturing and love. Mama sits at the center of the table, beaming, handing out food to her relatives, and l think l will never forget this moment.

"l will never be hungry again!" l tell Žana later as l lick the last jufka crumbs from my lips.

"Like Scarlett O'Hara in *Gone with the Wind*." Žana laughs. "You should read that book. lt's about a girl who starts out spoiled and pampered, but then it turns into a story about survival and resilience. There's a war, her house is looted, her city destroyed, she's starving, and when she finds the last carrot in the field she gobbles it down and swears she'll do whatever it takes to never let herself or anyone she cares about go hungry again. Plus there's romance, of course! You'll love it."

l make a note to read it someday and breathe a happy, contented sigh. l feel like l won't eat again for a week. But then Žana hands me the biggest slice of cake.

l forgot about the cake!

"l think eventually scientists will discover that people have an extra stomach," Žana says. "A separate dessert stomach. Even when you think you're completely full, somehow there's always just a little more room left for something sweet."

Mama's cakes are always delicious, but she's outdone herself this time. The inside is light and fluffy with chunks of chocolate, crunchy nuts, and sweet, fat raisins. The rich layer of chocolate on the outside is even better than fancy German chocolate—with none of the guilt. Mama puts it on in a thick layer that starts out gooey but hardens when it cools. We're usually so eager to taste it that we don't even let it cool, instead cutting it right away, eating it hot with chocolate dripping down our faces.

The uncles and aunts and grandmothers catch up with Mama and Tata over the feast. Some of them are actual aunts and uncles and grandmothers, others still related by blood but more distant, given honorary titles. Žana helps her grandmother Nura to a slice of cake. "Smaller, smaller," Nura urges, as Žana tries to give her a big helping. "Leave more for the children." Nura is like my own grandmother, Šerifa, Mama's mother, a smiling, beautiful, traditional covered lady. It is so hot today that Nura takes off the outermost of her two head coverings.

Everyone else is enjoying the food as much as I am, especially the boys. I was so focused on Amar's eating habits that it's a revelation to me to see how much other boys can eat. I had to coax Amar to swallow each tiny bite, but these boys inhale their food. "I'll bring more next time," Mama whispers to me as they mop up the last crumbs.

"Asmir, you must still be starving," his mother, Zumra, suddenly says. "This isn't nearly enough for you." She slides her narrowed eyes over at Mama, as if it is her fault a dozen extra people showed up. Why, an army chef could hardly feed all these people. "Let me make you some eggs. This boy loves eggs."

A few minutes later she comes back with her own private feast for Asmir. It is an omelet made to feed an army, with ten eggs in it at least, folded over cheese and herbs. Just as if he's her little prince, she lays out steaming loaves of lepinja and slices mild little onions fresh from the garden. Then she sits smugly and watches him eat, as if she were the only one who could nourish her son properly.

It's all gone in minutes. Where does it all go? Asmir is lean and strong, even though he's just vacuumed up more food than Amar ate in a month. Everything about teenage boys is fascinating to me.

Even though she seems to know more about boys than I do, Žana is just as fascinated by them. After we eat, we find a secluded nook where we can watch the boys swimming and wrestling and talk about them. None of *these* boys are relatives, as far as either of us know.

She talks in a way that seems so much older to me, even though we're the same age. I might say that a boy is cute, or I like his hair, but Žana is on a whole other level. She talks about their lips, their abs, their hands in the kind of detail that never even occurred to me. "See those lines of muscle there, one on each side of his stomach, like a V? That's my favorite part of a man. I could look at his belly all day. Oh, Amra, I love this place! Bihać is a magical city. I want to fall in love on the banks of the Una. I want to kiss a boy with the sound of its waters rushing by."

"Which boy?" I ask her.

"Any boy!" she says with a wild laugh, throwing her arms out like she wants to hug the whole world.

Later we move to a sunnier spot where there are more people. We've spent enough time digesting, so we want to get nice and hot before we jump into the river again. Žana chats with everyone, cousins and strangers alike, and as I watch her I think I might be ready to come out of my shell. What if there's a talkative girl inside me, and she's been asleep all this time?

But I can't quite find the courage to go up to a boy and start talking to him. Who do I pick, and what do I say? I'm standing to the side, watching Žana in action, smiling, but still not actively participating. Suddenly I feel a presence, see something out of the corner of my eye. How long has Vedrana been standing beside me, so quiet like my shadow?

"How are you doing, Vedrana?"

"Dino is sad" is all she will say. I follow the gaze of her large brown eyes and see my little brother looking awkward and alone, near tears on the periphery of all the laughter and fun. No one is paying any attention to him.

Amar always noticed when someone felt excluded, and he'd talk to them, engage them, make them feel welcome. I feel shy and awkward myself, but I know that I have to be more like Amar now.

What I can never do for myself, I can easily do for someone I love. All at once I'm going up to every boy, asking if they have a soccer ball or basketball—Dino gave Asmir's back to him at lunch, and it is still back at the long table. Someone has a basketball, so I get the boys excited about playing a pickup game, and before I know it Dino is playing with all of the bigger boys, and Žana, Vedrana, and I are cheering him on as loudly as we can. He's the youngest, clumsy, and most ungainly in his lanky body, but the older boys are kind and give him plenty of chances to shine. The look of pride on his face when he scores makes my heart soar. I realize how alone he sometimes feels without Amar, still trying to make friends in his new neighborhood, and now his older sister is distracted with her glamorous cousin. I've been so focused on myself that I've forgotten he needs help, too. *I promise I'll always be there for you, Dino.*

The boys flock around us, praising Dino and flirting with us. (I think they're flirting? Maybe they are just talking? How do I tell the difference?) Now that I've broken the ice, I'm comfortable talking with all of them, easy and happy. Then, I hear a voice that shuts me down, makes my smile falter. "There you are," Azra says with scorn, and suddenly I feel like I'm underwater again, panicking, gasping for air. I clutch at Žana's hand, and she looks around but doesn't see anything to be alarmed by, just a short, scowling girl with big, teased-out hair. I know I should do the polite thing and introduce my cousins to each other, but I can't find my voice.

Azra, as rude as ever, doesn't even look at Žana. Instead she looks me up and down and finally says, "I never would have guessed that someone as scrawny as you could have cellulite, but I see that you do." She points to the back of my thighs, shakes her head, and turns away.

I'm numb with confusion and hurt. Not because she's right or wrong. Until today I've scarcely been aware of my body. I know less about the back of my legs than the man on the moon. I have no idea if I have cellulite—I'm not really sure what cellulite even is. But I know she means to be cruel, and it seems so wrong today, like lightning striking me out of a clear sunny sky. At first it makes me want to curl up, take shelter.

But then anger rolls in a few seconds later. I should have a quick, snappy comeback, but I have nothing.

Then, from next to me, laughter. I can't believe it. Žana is laughing at me, too? Then I realize. She's laughing so hard that everyone turns around to look—a big, free, unselfconscious laugh. As soon as she has everyone's attention, she says loudly, "I don't know who you are, but I'm really sorry for you. Apparently you can't stand to see Amra here looking like a gorgeous supermodel in her little bikini. Are you really so insecure that you make up insults about this beautiful girl? I think you need some therapy. You should learn to be happy for someone who is so special that I call her my sister."

There are chuckles from the other teens, and Azra huffs and stammers. Finally she chokes out, "Who do you think you are, anyway? Amra is *my* sister, and I can say whatever I want to her." Azra has certainly never called me *sister* before. She hates me, but she wants to claim me as her own in this weird power play.

"You may be related to her, but there's more to being a true sister than just blood. A real sister, or a cousin, or even a decent human being wouldn't be as mean as you." Žana links arms with me and whirls me away. "Come on, Amra, let's go swimming. Something smells too stinky over here."

The people listening are too polite to laugh out loud, but I hear more than a few low giggles as Žana and I stroll away to the rocky riverbank. Several of the boys follow us, lured by Žana's spirited speech. No one goes up to Azra. She is left alone. I almost feel sorry for her.

Almost.

THE REST OF the day is a delightful dream, the happiest of my life. We freeze in the water and toast in the sun. I know I'm getting burned, but I don't care. It won't hurt until later, and right now I can't let anything interrupt this glorious day. I talk to everyone. Žana flirts with every boy. I study the way she pouts her lips and tosses her hair and lays a hand, as if by accident, on a boy's sun-warmed arm. I take mental notes, because I want to be ready for when the day comes that I want to flirt, too. The boys talk to me, but I don't know if they look at me the way they look at Žana.

She thinks they do. "Amra, did you see the way the blond boy was checking you out?"

I feel like being in Žana's pretty bathing suit tricks people into thinking I'm glamorous like she is. "He was looking at my bikini, maybe, not me."

"So? That's still you. What, you want a boy to love you for your brains and call you ugly when he kisses you? Of course not! You want him to love everything about you, and your body is part of who you are. Whatever you look like, short or tall, skinny or plump, he should love looking at you. So let him love looking at you in a bikini! Why not? Anyway, boys aren't as mature as girls. It will be a while before boys our age realize there are more important things than what a girl looks like in a bikini. That's why I like to kiss older boys."

"You've kissed a boy? Boys? *Older* boys?"

"Well ... not exactly. Not yet. But I will. Soon." She laughs, her big full ringing laugh. "Maybe even today!" She settles back on the smooth slab of rock, arms braced behind her, eyes half-closed like a lizard, watching the leaping, splashing boys from under her long lashes.

I don't want to kiss anyone. Not today. I have enough, just as I am.

12

THE DAYS THAT follow are beautiful in their sameness, and in their variety.

We fall into a routine. Every day Mama gets up early to cook more and more sumptuous meals. I know how much these meals are costing us, and I worry that Mama is sacrificing too much to make this a magical summer for us and bring the family together. For dinner every night we eat kljukuša or "poor people's food"—a simple mix of flour and water and one or two eggs, baked like a big pancake, served with maybe a bit of cheese or butter or garlic, all so we can put everything we've got into our festive communal lunches. Tetka Fatma helps out, bringing over ingredients because she doesn't want Dida to talk about us being poor. And Tetka Begija, who is the head chef for a huge factory that makes plastic packaging, helps us out in a way that may not be entirely ethical but doesn't really harm anyone. When she has supplies like old eggs or oil that is about to expire, she sometimes sneaks it home to give to us.

For Bosnians, feeding people well is a matter of pride. We would rather share one lavish meal with friends and family and then skip the other meals.

We pack them up and head out to the Četić Mill for another glorious day of swimming and sunning and stuffing our faces, a day of laughter and secrets and daydreams, of fun and the most mild flirting. I have so many friends now, but Žana and I are insep-arable. Vedrana is like a girl on a spring, stretched between us and my little brother. She and Dino are the same age and have a good time hanging around, running and screaming and doing cannon-balls into the shallow areas of the Una under the protective gaze of their gourd-wearing guardian. But she's also irresistibly drawn to us and we're happy to have her tag along, watching us with her big owl eyes, dreaming of what it's like to almost be a teenager. I feel like even at her age she knows more than me, living in Belgrade with a big sister like Žana. But I really like her, and it is fun to have a little sister who admires and copies everything I do.

Within this happy pattern, every day is different. Each moment brings a fresh delight, a new discovery about the world or about myself. In chemistry class, we'd learned about catalysts, substances whose job is to start or speed up other reactions. I think Žana is my catalyst. Simply by being with her, I feel like I'm growing, changing, day by day.

All too soon, though, this happy time comes to an end. Žana's father has been working at the military airport near Bihać all this time. What he's doing there, I have no idea. It was one of Tito's biggest projects. The country spent millions building this airport into the side of a mountain. I know military planes fly in and out of there, but I've never been there. And no one I know has ever been there ... except for Žana's father. I don't know why the airport itself has always been a bit of a mystery to me. I guess it is just strange having something that important so near to me and knowing so little about it. When Communists build something so big and expensive, they're usually proud of it. Schoolchildren take tours of it, write essays about it. Not so with the airport. When I ask Žana's dad about it, he's evasive. "It's just an airport, what else is there to know?" he says sometimes. Other times he'll snap a curt, "It's military business."

Žana's mother has been spending time with her widowed mother and the rest of her family—even coming to the Una once or twice—but there are always two lines between her eyebrows. I don't know why, but she doesn't feel comfortable here. It is like she's two different people and is always dizzy from switching back and forth. Sometimes she talks with the distinctively Serbian dialect called *ekavica*. It's a way of talking some people learn to mimic, and they think of it as a more cultured, sophisticated way to speak. She talks like that when she wants to lord it over us, when she talks about her big house or the restaurants she goes to. Or when her husband is there. Other times, though, she talks like we do at home with the Bosnian ijekavica dialect.

Both dialects incorporate a lot of old Ottoman and German words. Our language is like Bosnia itself, a melting pot. Everything about us comes from many sources: Our prominent cheekbones are evidence of Ottoman ancestry, while our fair skin comes from western Europe. Aida talks like us when she's feeling needy, when she wants sympathy. It's funny, though—neither voice sounds real. Whether she's talking like a Bosniak or a Serb, both accents sound faked. Now that I know more about Žana's family, I can see how her mother tries hard to be Serbian, though she must have missed her Bosniak family very much and is trying hard to fit back in. It must take so much effort, struggling to fit in all the time.

When I ask Žana about why her mom is unhappy, she shrugs and says her mom doesn't like anything some days, it's just a mood of hers. But for a second, as Žana answers me, I see two lines between her own eyebrows, just like her mom's, right before she turns away. The next time she faces me they're gone, and she distracts me with a funny story about a male schoolmate who was late to an after-school track meet. He had to change from jeans to shorts in a deserted alleyway, not realizing that some girls preparing for the Tito's Path to Revolution competition were at a late meeting in a room just overhead and saw *everything*.

"I CAN'T BELIEVE you have to leave already!" I moan when the day comes for Žana and Vedrana to leave. "I wish you didn't have to go."

"This was the best summer ever!" Dino chimes in. "Thanks to you I met people who are really good at basketball, and now I'm going to be an NBA star!" It makes me happy to hear him make that big leap from meeting boys who play basketball to being a superstar. I'm glad he can have that kind of optimism. "The only bad part about the summer is that I didn't eat any ice cream." Ice cream is his favorite thing, and a rare treat for our family. We usually have to make it instead of buy it, and churning it until it gets thick and frozen takes forever. Amar was really good at mixing flavors and sticking to the recipe as if it were a scientific formula.... Dino and I, not so much!

"Next summer I'll buy you a big cone of hazelnut gelato," Žana promises him.

"What am I going to do for the rest of the summer without my two new sisters?" I ask them.

"We'll be back next summer, I promise!" Žana says. "The whole summer this time."

"Do you think your parents will let you?"

"I don't care if they do or don't. I'm coming for the whole summer and that's that. If they say no, I'll...I'll run away!" There's a fervor in her eyes, and it strikes me that she looks like someone in love. Yes, I realize—she's in love with Bihać, with the people in it. Sometimes your home isn't the place you're born or the place you live. Sometimes you have to search for your true home. Our new house never really felt like home before because of the tragedy and turmoil we had when moving there. But now it feels like home for me, I think because I have Žana, because I have a friend, and acceptance. I think Žana has found her home here in Bihać. She's more of a Bosnian than her own mom, who was born here.

"And I'll come, too!" little Vedrana adds staunchly, stomping her foot so hard that Žana and I burst into laughter.

"Right," Žana says. "We'll pack our bags and take a train."

"No, a plane!" Vedrana squeals. "The next time Dad flies in we'll just sneak on the plane. When he took me to the airport in Belgrade once he showed me all the huge crates they are flying to Bihać. Stacks and stacks of them, this long." She stretches out her arms. "Surely we can hide in one of those. Then out we'll pop in Bihać!"

Žana smiles at her sister's idea. "I'll walk if I have to. I love my sister, I love the Una … and I love Bihać! Oh Amra, you are so, so lucky to live in a magical city of music and dreams and food and love!"

"Belgrade must have all those things," I remind her. I love my hometown, but Belgrade is the big city. I think of it like I would think of London or New York or Paris, a land of sophisticated people and elegant food and the finest fashions, things that I can only dream of in my little city. Žana told me they opened a McDonald's in Belgrade recently. When she described the addictive quality of the food, held her hands a foot apart to describe a milkshake as big as my head, I thought that nothing here could ever compare to that kind of extravagance.

"No, it doesn't," Žana says, and another quick look of worry or pain crosses her face. "It's hard to explain. It's so gray there, with lots of loud traffic. And it's so bustling, everyone hurrying, no one stops to say hello. Yeah, it's big, everything is bigger—bigger stores, bigger buildings, bigger cars—but a city can be too big. I feel like an ant there sometimes. Like a meaningless speck where nothing I think or want really matters. Here in Bihać, it is different. The air is fresh, the people are friendly. I know where I am here. I know *who* I am."

"And who are you, then?" I ask, not knowing how seriously to take her.

"Here I am Amra's sister!" she says with a little laugh, and shoos Vedrana out of my bedroom to pack up her things in the bathroom.

When we're alone, she goes on in a more serious tone. "Here I am not my father's daughter, not my mother's daughter. I'm not half-Serb, half-Muslim. I'm not too tall or too loud or too bold." She sighs. "I'm just Žana."

"And Žana is my favorite person in the world," I say, throwing my arms around her.

"I'll call you every single day," she whispers into my hair as she hugs me.

"That would be too expensive!"

"Well, I'll write to you every day!"

"You'll be too busy with school to do that," I say.

"And with boys!" She laughs as she releases me. She holds on to my shoulders and looks at me with her strange and lovely two-colored eyes. "Every other day, then. And I mean it, I'll be back next summer no matter who tries to stop me."

"Oh, I have an idea!" I say. "Maybe we can't write absolutely every day, but we should think about each other every day. We can pick a time, and then every day, whatever else happens, we can close our eyes and talk this summer, say a prayer for each other."

"I love that! It will be almost like being with you. We can reach across the miles with our minds. What time should we do it?"

I think for a moment. "How about 5:55 P.M.? I've always tended to notice those kinds of times, 2:22, 4:44. They feel lucky, don't they? And it's near the evening, when things are winding down, so we can relax and visit each other, talk about our day. What do you think?"

"I think I might just barely manage to get through the next year if I get to talk to my sister once a day, even if it's just in my head."

She hugs me again, and though there's a smile on her face, my cheek is wet with her tears. Mine soon join them, and we're crying and laughing until Dida calls us down in a sharp and testy voice.

We've said our personal, emotional goodbye already. The

goodbye at the car is more formal and stilted. The second Žana goes to stand beside her parents, she looks like another person, more closed off, like she's hiding the real Žana under a shell. It's a subtle change. I doubt anyone but me could see it. But for just a second it hurts, seeing how quickly she becomes that Belgrade girl, too sophisticated and jaded to care about a small-town cousin like me.

Then, just as she turns to get into the car, she winks at me, and behind her two-colored eyes I see the memory and magic of the days we spent together. It's there, under the mask she's donned for her parents. I don't fully understand why she has to put on an act for them, but I know suddenly that she is her true self with me.

I felt like Žana was the one saving me from my sadness and loneliness. As she drives away I realize that somehow, I was saving her from something, too. I hope I've helped her as much as she's helped me.

Dear Sister,

I'm back in Belgrade and things feel sad and lonely here without you. I love Vedrana, but she is my baby sister. I just can't talk with her the same way I can with you. I miss laughing and talking with you until 3:00 A.M. every night! Who do I tell my secrets to now? While in Bihać, I lived and felt every day like it was my last one. Oh, how I miss you and Bihać and everyone in it! Remember when we got home from walking all day and I realized I had blisters I didn't even feel because I was so happy? I wish

96

you could come to Belgrade one day and spend some time with me. I think this city would be bearable to live in if I knew I could see you later this fall. Do you think there's a chance? I know I'm still adjusting to being back, but I don't know how I will last until next summer.

Remember my best friend, Ana? The one whose mother is a flight attendant and brings her all the fanciest things from America? Well, that traitor stole Rade even though she knew I had a crush on him. He was mine! Oh, how I loved that boy! He was like a young movie star. I'll send you a photo of him—long, blond hair like a California surfer, perfect teeth, darling dimples . . . Every girl wanted him. But Ana knew that I had claimed him for myself, and she didn't care. I don't even want to think about what she must have done to get him. But as soon as I got home, I found out that she'd spent the whole summer cozying up to him, and now they're dating. Unbelievable! First the pain of leaving my sister, and now I find out that my best friend betrayed me. How will I ever study with all this going on? My parents are already nagging me about my grades. I wish you were here. I'm sure if I had your help I'd get better grades. I'm so sad, Amra. No, not just sad—I'm actually devastated! Your letter will be the only thing that heals my wounds. Please write. I cannot wait to hear how you are!

Love you, sister,
Žana

Dear Sister,

I miss you so much already! I'm so glad to hear that you are home, safe and sound. I can't believe Rade did that to you! He should have known how you felt about him and waited for you to come home. And I can't believe that Ana, your best friend, betrayed you. You told me how many times she came to your house for sleepovers when her mother traveled. You were always there for her, and now she turns on you, trapping the boy who is clearly interested in you? I have never heard of anything like it! Neither Rade nor Ana fully appreciate who you are.

As for our time together this summer, I never imagined it was possible to have a good summer. After Amar's passing, my life was filled with anger—why did he have to be sick? Why did he have to die? But you saved me, Žana. You taught me that fearing things in life prevents us from living. This summer has been the best summer I ever had. I cannot imagine what our next summer will be like!

I cannot wait to see you!

I love you,
Your sister, Amra

13

ALL THROUGH THE freezing Bosnian winter the memory of my time by the Una keeps me warm. As I sit in my classroom figuring out long math calculations, I feel like I'm hiking through a snowy wood toward a roaring golden bonfire. This is cold, this is hard, but if I can get through it, I'll have a joyous sunny reward.

Mama and Tata have promised that Žana can come for the whole entire summer this time!

I'm looking forward to meeting Žana again, but in a strange way I'm also looking forward to meeting myself. The last summer made me think about who I am for the first time. Before, I had always been thinking about protecting Amar, protecting Dino, but no one ever protected me. It made me resilient, but I think it also stifled me a little bit. I've been like a tree that grows on a windy cliff, stunted but strong. In the shelter of Žana's sisterhood, I felt like I had a chance to grow and blossom. It still feels almost selfish to think of myself, but as I reflect on the past summer I realize that I have to figure out who I am. Amar would have wanted for me to work on becoming the version of myself that I want to be. I don't have the answers, but I'm starting to ask the questions.

I still feel the need to be the protector, though. I don't think that will ever go away. In the middle of the winter, Dino starts having trouble with a bully named Radovan who is teasing him about not being as good as him at basketball, even though Dino is a few years younger. Dino doesn't want me to do anything about it, and for a while I don't, but then one night a lot of the neighborhood kids build a big bonfire. Radovan throws a big stone into the flames right near Dino, deliberately sending sparks up into his face and burning him.

"Are you disabled now?" Radovan hoots. "That's not going to help your basketball game. You're as weak and clumsy as your brother was."

I can see the tears in Dino's eyes, see him wishing he could fight but knowing that he's not strong enough, see him wanting to run away but knowing that will just make him get teased more later.

Burning with rage, I snatch up a burning brand from the edge of the bonfire and run at Radovan. "Say that again!" I challenge. He stares at me with his mouth open, but he can't back away. The bonfire is right behind him. "Go on, do you dare to say it now? I didn't think so." I wave the burning stick toward his face. "How do you like it? You better not ever bother Dino again, do you hear me?"

By this point his father has come over to ask what's going on. I drop the stick, but I don't back down. "I'm letting your son know that he shouldn't pick on kids who are younger than him," I say.

"Time to go home, Radovan," his father says. He won't punish his son, but he's not defending him either, so that's something. Radovan never bothers Dino again.

The year drags on, cold and dreary through the winter. Outside the classroom window, white snowdrop flowers poke their heads up through melting snow, like tiny pearls. The folk name for them is "hanging grandma," maybe for the way their white heads nod. A bit later, purple crocuses will sprout in soggy yards and fields. They hardly have any smell, but I will stick my nose in them anyway to breathe in the slightest scent of spring. I'll come away with bright golden pollen on my nose. Soon after the hyacinths will bloom, and they have a smell so sweet it makes me dizzy. They make me think of the sevdalinka song about Emina, the lovely girl whose hair, when it comes unbraided, smells like hyacinths.

The days are getting longer, and I get restless in class, in my room, yearning for summer. With every new bright green leaf that unfurls from bare branches, I think of Žana.

I'm not lonely now, though. Last summer ignited something in me. Maybe I'm bolder now. Maybe I feel worthy of being liked. Maybe after seeing me happy with Žana, people no longer think of me just as that girl whose brother died or the nerdy girl with glasses but as Amra, my own unique person.

I have friends: boys I can joke with, girls I can dream with. None of them hold a candle to Žana, but they are all nice in their own ways. And they are all troubled in their own ways. For a while I was so consumed with my own problems that I forgot everyone suffers about something. Nobody has a perfect life.

I have a complicated friendship with Mersiha, the only other girl in school who is as good at math as I am. While some girls bond over makeup or fashion or boys, we bonded over an argument about proving a theorem.

I had noticed her watching me from the corner of the room for a few weeks once school started. It made me uncomfortable.

Did I spill something on my shirt? Is my zipper undone? *Why is she staring at me so hard?* I'd wondered.

Finally, she walked up to me at the end of class one day. "I don't even want to stand next to you, Amra, but I don't have any choice. You're the only one here I can talk to. Look, I can't make this equation come out right." She shoved a paper under my nose. It was a math problem, but not anything we were doing in school. It was something much more advanced. "I wanted extra work, so I found this in a book, but I can't figure it out."

"I've never seen this kind of math," I said.

"Oh, don't be stupid. See here, you just factor this out and then..." As she explained I started to see it, as she knew I would.

"This is interesting," I said, taking out my own pencil and trying a few things.

She snatched it out of my hand. "I did that already. Think of something else."

So we stayed there for half an hour after school, scribbling out numbers until at last, at almost exactly the same moment, we saw what we were missing and solved the problem.

"Aha! See, I knew it would be worthwhile to talk to the ugly duckling who turned into a swan."

She packed up her books and papers and left without saying goodbye.

I'm still not sure if we're friends. When I'm called on to answer a hard math problem, she'll give me a grudging smile when I get it right. Sometimes she brings me other equations to figure out and then runs away, or she'll walk up to me outside school and make some interesting observation and then stalk off again. It's a long time before she tells me what's wrong.

She's jealous.

When I hear this, I have to laugh. Jealous... of me? Jealous of the girl who is so tall she has to wear boys' clothes, this skinny, nerdy goody-goody? One with big glasses, no less. Even if I try not to wear them more than I have to, I need them to see in class. One lens is falling out, and Mama makes me wear them on a chain around my neck like a grandmother. I dream of one day having contact lenses like a girl in my class, Tatiana. Tatiana's dad works for the military, and she's one of the few people to have a coveted mont jakna, the popular and impossible-to-get, bright-red, down-filled jacket. Of course she has contacts, while my family can barely afford regular glasses. If I got contacts, I'd have to eat nothing but kljukuša for years. The point is, how am I the girl who Mersiha is jealous of?

"I don't like people seeing me next to you," she tells me one day after school when I ask if I can walk home with her. "Maybe if I'm alone they won't notice. But next to you?" She blows a little raspberry with her lips and packs up to leave again.

"Wait!" I call, and run after her as she heads out. "I don't understand."

She gives me the evil eye for a second and then looks confused. "Huh, you really don't, do you? You really have no idea what it's like to be me. Look at me, Amra. Take a good, long look. Tell me what you see."

So I do. I see a short, chubby girl with a face marred by red blotches and angry pimples. "I see Mersiha," I tell her honestly. "I see a math genius. I see you. That's all."

Her lips press together before she says, "Then you're nicer than most people. Or a better liar. It's not fair that you're good at math *and* pretty. Maybe no one wants to look at me, but at least I have my brain. I could feel like I'm better than you and all the pretty, clear-faced girls because I have something they don't. But you have everything, Amra. And I hate you for it."

"Well, I don't hate you for hating me," I tell her. "I'd like us to be friends." I'm baffled by her feelings, because I've never felt pretty. It makes me wonder if the people I think are so beautiful are insecure inside, too. Maybe everyone is like that, with secret fears the world will never understand. Mersiha just snorts and turns away, but she stops at the door and calls over her shoulder, "I don't want to be your friend, Amra, but I guess I have to be. People like you always get their way." I'm left staring at the door she slams behind her.

I guess we do become good friends in a strange sort of way. I respect and value her honesty. She might not always say the nicest things, but she always says exactly what she means. I'd much rather have that than teasing or criticism or cruelty from someone like Azra. Mersiha might envy some things about me, but she never tears me down. I admire her brilliant mind and forthright ways.

Another friend, Hana, lives on my street a few houses down. I first meet her in the spring when she literally runs into me. As I'm walking down the road I hear yelling from one of the houses. The windows are closed so the sound is muffled, and I can't tell what they're saying. I think someone must be hurt, or a wild dog has broken into the house, or maybe a grandmother who is hard of hearing lives there. I literally cannot think of any other reason why a family might shout. Loudness is different than shouting. Everyone who has grown up near the roaring waters of the Una is loud. But it is a happy, boisterous loudness. Shouting is rude at best. If Tata is in a different room from Mama, he won't shout out something to her. He'll walk to wherever she is and talk in a normal voice. Shouting is for grief or pain, or to warn someone of danger.

Or for anger.

Suddenly the door flies open and a girl runs out, slamming the door behind her. I hear a man's voice shout, "How dare you—" and a woman screech, before the door latches and the harsh sounds are suppressed again.

The girl's long, silky black hair almost covers her face, and her eyes are swollen with tears, so she doesn't see me. She crashes right into me and I have to hold her up to keep her from falling. When I look closer I think she has a birth mark or eczema, a big red blotch across her cheek. It looks like the print of a big man's hand.

"Let me go," she snaps. "What do you think you're doing?" But she seems too weak and distraught to pull away.

I don't ask her what's wrong. Some instinct tells me that she won't talk about it. Instead I resort to the time-honored Bosnian method of comfort—food. "Come to my house and have some tea and something to eat. I think there's a slice of cake left." She looks at me resentfully but then hangs her head and accepts my offer. I lead her back to my house. She comes along like she has no will of her own. I've never seen anyone so lost in their own neighborhood.

At home, Tata guides her to the bathroom so she can splash her face with cold water, while Mama toasts thick slices of bread, spreading them with butter and honey. I brew linden flower tea that we get every year from my aunt Ica, who has a big linden tree in her yard.

When the girl comes back she has more control over herself, and says her name is Hana.

"What happened?" I ask her gently.

"Nothing," she says, pouting her lower lip. Behind her, Mama and Tata exchange a worried look.

In the safety of our home, Hana relaxes and opens up, even if it is a long time before she talks about her parents. I take her upstairs and feel some of the fun I had with Žana, talking about makeup and clothes. With Žana, of course, we talked about so much more—about life and dreams and music and politics and love—but it's a start. Žana did this for me, taking me under her wing in my time of sadness, lifting me up. Now I can do it for Hana. My pain makes me understand hers a little better, even if the things we've gone through are different. I wonder if Žana's life had its own hardships that taught her to read my pain?

"My mom has so much makeup," Hana gushes. "You should see it. Ten different kinds of mascara."

"I didn't know there were ten different kinds," I say, thinking about Mama's one lipstick, her Nivea cream.

"Oh, sure," Hana says with the confidence of an expert. "There's a big difference between black and dark brown. And then some make your lashes thicker, some make them longer. She even has a gold mascara, and one with sparkles!"

From her descriptions I'm in awe of her mother, who must be the most beautiful, glamorous woman. After a while I forget the yelling I heard. It must have been some anomaly. Maybe her father dropped a jar on his toe. That would make anyone shout.

"My mom lets me use all her makeup. Or the stuff she doesn't like, anyway. You have to buy a lot of makeup before you find just the right one. I wear makeup all the time. How you look is really important. I could teach you."

Right now, she looks like she ran out of the house without thinking anything at all about how she looks. Her clothes are wrinkled and mussed, her hair uncombed. Like she had to get out that very second.

"Sure," I say, because even though I don't own any, I have to admit I'm a little fascinated by the magic of makeup after my time with Žana. "Maybe we could go to your house now and . . ."

"No!" she shouts. The word echoes in my bedroom. "No," she says again, more quietly, pushing her hair behind her ears. "My parents are really busy right now. Maybe some other time."

Just then Dino comes in and tells me he's heading out to play basketball.

"Who is that?" Hana asks, and something about her tone makes me pause. There's an interest behind the question, and when I see her eyes linger on him as he leaves, I realize that Dino has grown since the summer. To me he is and always will be a little boy I have to take care of, but to someone else he is getting taller and stronger and more attractive.

"That's my brother. My much, much younger brother," I say, and she shrugs. My little baby brother as a boy someone might think is cute? I can barely believe it!

I get to know Hana better, but she only ever comes to my house. She brings half-used lipsticks and crumbling eyeshadows for me to try. I sit patiently while she paints my face. Somehow I never look good in the makeup. Maybe she just doesn't know how to put it on right. After she goes home, I always wash it off right away, happy to see my own face again.

One Monday in late spring, Hana's not in school. Not on Tuesday, either. That afternoon, I knock on her door.

After a long time, it opens. I think the woman who answers must be a sick aunt. This can't be the glamorous woman I imagined Hana's mother to be. Yes, she's wearing a lot of makeup, but the foundation only makes her skin look flat and sallow, and the sparkles in her eye shadow do nothing to hide the fact that there's no sparkle in her eyes. Her lashes are heavily coated with clumped mascara. I can't tell if the dark circles under her eyes are from running eyeliner or lack of sleep or something else. It is the middle of the afternoon, but she's wearing a robe like she just got out of bed. Her hair looks like it was electrified and then slept on for a week without being combed.

"Yes, what do you want?"

"Is Hana at home? I've missed her at school."

From the depths of the house, a man's voice shouts, "Who is it? Tell them never to come at this hour again." Which is strange, because it's not late. It's not even the average Bosnian's dinnertime yet, and in most households, company is welcome at any hour.

"No, she's not here," the woman tells me. I hear a small sound from somewhere in the house, like the whimper of a puppy.

"Is she okay? Is she sick?"

The woman looks me up and down. "Who are you, then?"

Hasn't Hana mentioned me? "I'm Amra, I live down the street. Is her mom here? Maybe if Hana is sick I can just see her for a minute, give her the homework she's missed."

"I'm Hana's mother, and I told you she's not here."

This woman is Hana's mother? "Okay, thank you," I say as politely as I can, and go home.

The next day Hana is in school again. I see her from behind at first. When she turns, I can't keep the shock from my expression. Her face is puffy, like a hundred bees from Tetak Ale's bee farm stung her. There are dark marks on her cheeks, around her eyes. She's tried to cover them up with makeup, but I can see them, purple fading to sickly green, beneath the flesh-colored layers of concealer.

"Oh, Hana, what happened? Who did this to you?" I want to take her in my arms, but she flinches away at my first touch. I want to save her, but I don't know how. If Amar were here, I know he'd have good advice for me, but I feel lost. All I can do is be her friend.

"No one did this to me," she snaps. "I...I fell down the stairs. The doctor told me I was lucky I didn't break my neck. Now, stop staring at me and let's get to class."

As she walks away I stare after her thinking that although my family has had its sorrows, I would never trade my family for another. Better to have one terrible wound in a house full of love than to live with people who hurt you every day, either with their fists like Hana's father, or with more subtle conflicts like Žana's parents.

But most days are good ones. Most days, Hana doesn't have a bruised face. Most days Mersiha just talks about math, about the job she'll have someday as a professor, and not about her jealousy. And I have other friends, too, kids from school and the neighborhood who have much simpler lives than these two, with whom I have less complicated friendships, like Aladin.

He's another friend from school, and he sits next to me in class. Aladin is a true bundle of joy, looking like a cherub, with a full face and the most amazing long eyelashes. Girls are jealous of those lashes, saying it's not fair a boy has them. Once, when I doubt they are real, he invites me to pull them to see. "Ow!" he squeals, then laughs. I'm left with one of his eyelashes in my fingers, dark and thick as mink fur. "Make a wish and blow it away," he tells me.

Thanks to Žana, I've learned to joke and relax with people. Žana saw me differently than anyone else did, differently than I saw myself. Even without her near me, I'm starting to reimagine myself, to see my possibilities and potential as if through her eyes.

I also made friends with Armela. Her grandfather owned many of the bakeries around the city. Most private businesses aren't allowed under communism, but bakeries are one of the exceptions, so he was a rich man by our humble standards. Armela is pretty and fashionable but also very kind and sweet, simple and trusting. I think if she was haughty and mean she would have ruled the school with her looks and money. But she never tries to dominate anyone, and that makes her a perfect target. Jealousy prompts other kids to tease her without mercy.

There's a peculiar menace to the teasing of teen girls. Sometimes they pick out a flaw—acne or uncool clothes—but just as often they criticize an enemy for what should be a good thing.

"Oh, you think you're so pretty," they hiss at her in the halls. "What does that matter when you're so foolish? Look at you, with your fancy clothes. You think you're better than us? You can buy clothes, but you can't buy taste."

Armela tries to smile, let it wash over her—she's been through this many times before—but I see tears glistening in her eyes.

What do these girls want? One of our classmates, Bekira, has a peculiar look. She's not sick, but she's as skinny as Amar was and has huge eyes. The bullies tease her as much for her odd looks as they tease Armela for her beauty. Anything that is different is a fair target for them. I've seen them do it so often before, and it always upset me, but I never knew what to do. It was easy to defend Amar, but how do you defend a girl from being called pretty? I can't fly in with fists and threats like I did if anyone teased my brother.

It wasn't until I knew Žana that I realized how much girls focus on looks. And girls don't fight with strength and muscle, but with words and insults to degrade a girl's power. It is a competition I've never been a part of in the past, and one you don't win with muscle or a bloody nose but with words. Words matter. Words hurt. But words can also empower, and I need to learn how to use them. I remember when Azra made me feel ashamed, and Žana stepped in to save me.

"Leave her alone, you jealous girls," I say, stepping between them and Armela. "What's wrong with you? Armela is pretty and fashionable, and you wish you were, too. Is that any reason to give her a hard time? You should be ashamed of yourselves."

Then just like Žana did for me, I link arms with Armela—who looks almost as shocked as her tormentors—and walk away with my head held high. I realize that reaching out a hand to her, being a friend, helps her even more than my words can.

Hana, Aladin, Mersiha, Armela...I hang out with them all and have some good friends through the school year.

Žana and I write to each other almost every day. I make envelopes out of pictures of movie stars and singers I cut from magazines. I decorate her address with drawings of flowers. Writing to her is like writing in a diary, a free-flowing, intimate expression. We talk about our families, our crushes, our dreams, our fears. Instead of growing apart, the year only seems to make us closer than before.

The year trudges onward with more joys than sorrows, the seasons change and the year warms, and after an eternity, it is summer again.

THE SECOND
SUMMER

14

ŽANA WILL BE here tomorrow!

Her train from Belgrade is coming late at night, at the impossible hour of 1:00 A.M. The day takes forever, moving more slowly than the entire year. Dino is bouncing around all day, excited to see Žana and Vedrana. I didn't realize he felt as close to them as I do, until I listen closely to what he's saying. He wants to show them his free throw and how he can almost dunk the ball. He wonders if Vedrana will notice how much taller he is this year. He says that with Žana here, the cool older boys will play basketball with him, and Žana can cheer when he beats them.

He loves them as family, but more than that he admires them as people whose opinions matter to him. The more he talks, the more I see he has a kind of hero-worship for Žana, and by extension for Vedrana, too. "Something fun always happens when Žana is around," he muses.

At last, after the sun has set, after dinner, after hours of restless pacing, we drive to the station to meet her. My heart is pounding with excitement. I get to see my sister again! Visions of summer joys dance in my head.

I've worked hard to make everything perfect for her visit. The brown-and-white-striped foam mats, like huge sponges, are rolled out on the floor to make comfortable beds. I've picked out the nicest sheets for them, too, washed, crisp, and fresh-smelling.

One set was a gift from my stylish Tetka Fatma, another was a wedding gift from my grandmother Šerifa to my parents. That set is embroidered with tiny beautiful flowers, just like her traditional dimije. I make sure every detail is perfect, as if a foreign dignitary were visiting, even though I know Žana doesn't really care about all those things. She just wants to be with me.

But I feel anxious for Žana, too. She's told me so much about this wonderful boyfriend of hers, Rade the blue-eyed blond dreamboat, the model-looking hunk who loves her with all his heart . . . now that he's broken up with her former friend, Ana. He is the man she wants to marry someday.

This is what she declares about him at the start of every one of her long letters, but as I read more there are always other stories about Rade, too. His parents are divorced, his mother is a flight attendant for the Yugoslav airline, so she travels a lot, and Rade is often out and about on his own. He sounds like a troublemaker to me, a boy who is very free and easy with girls. Žana says that everyone wants to be with him. He has the best clothes that his mom brings from Western countries. All I know about the West comes from movies, so in my head Rade looks like a dream. But for all those charms he sounds scary to me. Žana tries to joke about catching him kissing other girls, then taking him back when he tells her that it isn't his fault—the girls throw themselves at him. She's kidding herself though, and I realize that in such a situation I wouldn't trust him after the first time it happened. I know pain too well and I don't want to get hurt, but Žana is carefree and willing to feel anything, everything, as long as she's feeling something big.

Whether because she honestly loves and misses him, or because she's sure he's having escapades with other girls, I know that being apart from him will be hard for her. I'll do everything I can to soothe her pain, the way she did for me last summer.

The train station is old and rundown. The painted letters on the pistachio-green facade are peeling off. I always feel unnerved by the train station. I know for some it is so exciting, symbolizing the start of some big adventure. But for me, it reminds me of sad departures and separations from the WWII movies we had watched growing up. Once upon a time, on this very spot where I'm standing, someone was being sent off to a war, maybe never to return. Train stations feel like goodbyes.

I don't have a strong desire to go anywhere. Where would I go? Maybe to the beach with my family. Maybe to Belgrade someday to visit Žana. But everything I want and need is right here in Bihać. I know I'll go to college one day. Tata says I should go to Sarajevo, and Mama went to Zagreb, but that feels so far away. I don't want to think about that tonight, though.

There's the train! It has always looked like a big metal monster with red eyes, but tonight it's a more benevolent beast, because my friend is inside. Mama and Tata wait on the platform away from the tracks, but Dino and I can't resist. I run up so fast I barely stop before the edge and Dino catches my arm to pull me back. When the train slows to a stop, I pat it. *Thank you for bringing my friend.*

People pour out, bustling with their suitcases. What if she's not here? What if something happened? Maybe her father forbade her to come. Maybe...So many fears pop into my head at the last minute. I still can't quite stop doing that. I'm almost surprised every morning when the sun rises, because something inside of me always expects the worst.

Then I see her, tall above the crowd, and my heart relaxes.

"Amra! Seka!" she calls out, calling me the nickname for sister. "Oh, I've missed you so much!" She's squeezing me, the big tight hugs my family uses, the kind she says she never gets at home. "I almost couldn't bear it, the year away from my sister." She lets me go only to throw her arms wide. With her head back and a huge grin on her face she shouts out, "Here I am, Bihać! I'm home!" People turn to stare at this silly girl, but she looks so happy they have to smile, too. I notice then that Žana's eyes fill with tears when she's happy, just like Tata's do. They both fill with so much joy that it has to overflow.

Vedrana has come for the summer, too. She's rubbing sleep from her eyes as she grabs her sister's hand, suddenly shy even though we were all so close last year. I scoop her up and give her a whirling hug, and before I know it she's giggling and squealing. "I missed my little sister, too," I tell her as I set her down. Not so little by now, though! Vedrana is almost my height, while Žana is even taller than me. Once I felt freakishly tall, but now I'm the little one!

But Žana makes Dino's day when she takes him solemnly by the shoulders, looks him up and down, and says, "Look how tall you've gotten! I think we girls are done growing, but you will keep growing for years and years and wind up the tallest of us all. How's your game going?"

Dino excitedly tells her about what a good basketball player he's become, talking about his new best friend Muhamed, nicknamed Maše, who plays with him, along with some other not-quite-best friends like a boy named Halid.

"Basketball is my favorite thing! That's all I ever do now."

"Oh, that's a shame. I guess I have to give this skateboard to some other young man, then. Someone who occasionally does something besides basketball."

His eyes get huge in awe when he sees the skateboard, a rarity in Bosnia. It is black with a big neon green skull on it, and it looks like something straight out of an American teen movie. Words fail him, and for the rest of the night Dino alternates between spinning the wheels of his new prized possession and staring at Žana with admiration and gratitude.

We fall asleep on each other's shoulders on the drive home. Just before my eyes close I whisper, "I know how much you must miss him already, but try to be happy this summer."

"Miss who?" she asks sleepily, and settles cozily against me. The "love of her life" is forgotten at the first breath of air in my hometown.

"THIS SUMMER IS going to last forever!" Žana says, throwing open the curtains and stepping out onto the porch in her pajamas for all the neighbors to see. We have slept like babies. "Good morning, Bihać! Did you miss me?"

A neighbor boy named Alen happens to be out and looks up through the branches of our apple tree covered in tiny nubbins of green apples, shocked to think she might be addressing him.

He has glasses as thick as the bottom of a pickle jar and is very shy, and I'd be surprised if he ever talked to a girl besides his sister Alma. When Žana sees his baffled look, she gives him a broad wink, which makes him run home in confusion, tripping over his own feet, blushing red as a beet.

Delicious smells rise from downstairs. We find Mama stirring flour into a mix of milk, butter, sugar, and eggs. I catch a whiff of yeast, too.

"I know what that means," I tell Žana.

"Krofne?" she guesses.

"Krofne!"

Mama puts aside this batch so the dough can rise. We help her with a batch she made earlier that's all ready. She shows Žana how to cut out perfect rounds of dough with a glass. Žana squeals with delight when Mama throws them, three at a time, into the simmering oil. They sputter and squeak and puff up into delightful fluffy doughnuts. She plucks them out with tongs and rolls them in sugar and vanilla, leaving them to cool on a sideboard.

Of course we both burn our fingers trying to get a taste too soon. But it's worth it for the heavenly taste of sugar and oil. One local bakery had experimented with what the Americans call doughnuts. Dino and I tried one once, and we were disappointed. "What a rip-off," Dino had said, winking at me through the hole in the center. "Where's the rest of my doughnut?"

"I'm going to make a mountain of krofne," Mama tells us. She is almost incapable of making a small amount of food. Growing up in a family of seven children, her mother taught her to cook for a minimum of fifteen people. In Bosnia, there are always more people at a meal than you expect. We might get a phone call and someone will say, "I'm coming over for dinner tonight!" and hang up before we even know who it is. More likely, though, they don't even call, just knock or walk in at any time of the day. Unexpected guests are the norm. It's not in our culture to wait for an invitation.

"Do you girls want to go on ahead to Brvice?" Mama asks. "Tata and your sleepy-headed siblings can join you later with lunch."

Žana loves the idea of walking through Bihać, so we run back upstairs and are ready in five minutes. Of course we grab a few more krofne each for the road. I'm wearing the puffy skirt Žana gave me last summer, which still fits. That's one of the benefits of shooting up to six feet tall so early. I got my growing out of the way, and if it is hard to find things that fit, at least I know I won't outgrow them.

We've all grown in our year apart, but I feel like I've grown in more than height. I don't know who I am yet, but thanks to Žana's visit last summer I know enough to at least ask the question.

Even though I've only slept a few hours, I'm skipping down the road. We're laughing, playing a game with our own shadows, and everything is perfect . . .

Until I hear a scream from my friend Hana's house.

"No, Dad, no more. You'll kill me!"

I feel sorry for Hana but also for myself, as horrible as that seems. My perfect first day with Žana is going to be spoiled by sorrow.

Žana, though, looks heroic. With a determined gleam in her eye she says, "We have to save her!" Žana doesn't know Hana, doesn't know that we are friends. But before I can stop her, she charges for their front door. What can I do except follow her? But I'm scared. I've heard these screams too often, and I know there's nothing I can do. That's the way I was raised, not in so many words but by example. Stay quiet, don't draw attention to yourself. It's a feeling more than a lesson, that something bad will happen if a person speaks out too boldly. But Žana never feels this. Why? Is it something about living in Belgrade, having more money, more privilege?

Having a Serb father?

"Žana, no," I try to tell her. "Her parents aren't like my parents. The dad drinks all the time, and he's really mean. If you bother them now, I don't know what he'll do!"

"What's the girl's name?" she asks me.

"Hana."

Žana knocks loudly at the door, loud as the police, a knock than cannot be ignored. After a long wait, Hana's mother answers. She looks like she always does, disheveled hair, a stained robe, smudges of yesterday's mascara under her eyes.

I think even if a dragon answered the door Žana would have greeted her with the same huge smile. "Good morning! Is Hana there? Can she come out to the beach with us?"

"Who are you? Oh, I see you there, Amra. Who is this, another giraffe, then?" She looks up at our height. "No, Hana's got better things to do. Amra, how can your parents let you go out looking like that? You should be ashamed."

She points at my long legs sticking out below my puffy little miniskirt with white and blue sailor stripes, the most beautiful and fashionable thing I own.

"Don't come here so early anymore, I was sleeping."

She slams the door in our faces, and I hear her screech, "Mahmut, you better have breakfast ready soon, or you'll be in serious trouble!" Mahmut is Hana's older brother.

"Wow," Žana says to the closed door an inch from her nose. "And I thought my family was bad."

As we walk away, I tell her the story that Hana didn't tell me for months. The story of how she came to school with two black eyes.

"Her father sent her to buy wine at a shop across town. Apparently it was some special kind, so she had to write it down. But instead she stopped in a local store and bought the same kind. Or she thought it was the same kind. When she got home he could tell the difference, and he slapped her so hard she flew across the room. She said she thought he'd kill her." I have tears in my eyes. "I can't even imagine a family like that, can you?" What parent could harm a child? My parents would sacrifice anything to have Amar with us again. They would take any pain upon themselves to spare us from feeling it.

To my surprise, Žana just shrugs. "Your friend Hana should just learn how to handle her father better."

"How can you say that? He beats her. It's not for her to change—it's for him!"

"But he won't change, will he? She's stuck with him, as long as she's young. My dad is super strict. He's never hit me, but he looks like he wants to sometimes. He'll ground me or yell at me for anything, though. So I learned how to hide things from him. I learned how to flatter him and tell him what he wants to hear.

Bullies like that are simple. You just have to learn to fool them. For instance, if he wants that faraway wine all the time, your friend should get it once and then save the bag from the other store. Next time, she just puts the local wine in the other bag and he has no idea."

This is new territory for me. I have never hidden anything from my parents. I don't want to … but I wonder if there may be times when I'll need to hide things from them, to save them from worry or pain. The thought of that makes me uncomfortable. But it seems like a lot of growing up feels uncomfortable.

"My mom's really strict too, but her, I just tune out," Žana goes on. "I have to live my own life, right? What they don't know won't hurt them. For example, my parents have no idea I smoke."

"You smoke?" I gasp, amazed.

"Well, sometimes, if they're both out. So I made up a friend, Malina, and if they ever find cigarette butts when they get home I just say oh, Malina dropped by to visit."

"You're terrible!" I laugh, shocked and intrigued. I always thought that people who disobeyed their parents were bad, but here is Žana, such a loving and kind person … who still defies her parents. I don't have any desire to do the same, but I'm learning so much about human nature from knowing her.

"You know, I don't even really like to smoke," Žana confesses. "I just do it because it isn't allowed. They're so strict with me, it feels good to get away with something. We should figure out how to help Hana, though," she adds as we walk off.

"Let's tell my parents and see if they have any ideas," I suggest.

The day isn't spoiled, but it has a new edge of seriousness. Part of me feels like a little girl who shouldn't have to deal with things like this, violence and lies. But part of me feels like I need to know more about the real world, beyond my happy family, beyond Bihać. I've started to see that everyone walks on their own unique path, shaped by their family and environment. People are pushed to be one way, pulled to be another, and I can't judge everyone by the same standards. How can you judge a person's decisions until you know the options they had to choose from?

15

WE'RE THERE EARLY, and I guess most people are sleeping in or having leisurely breakfasts because there are only a few people here before us—young parents with young children, an old man with a cane taking a morning stroll.

"This is going to be the best summer ever," Žana says, breathing in the air that is somehow different here by the riverbank than anywhere else. "I'm going to meet the most gorgeous boys and eat every last crumb of your mother's wonderful food and..."

"Wait, what about your boyfriend in Belgrade?"

"Oh, well... he's there and I'm here."

I'm instinctively shocked by her attitude. Shouldn't people always be faithful? But the longer I know Žana, the better I get at seeing the world through other people's eyes. I'd only ever looked through my own eyes before and mostly saw the world in right and wrong, black and white. Now through Žana's gaze I'm beginning to see the world in a kaleidoscope of colors, always swirling and changing through emotions and experiences.

We're sitting on a big flat rock, and she slips off her shoes to dip her toes in the chilly water. Under the water it looks like another world, a crystal palace carpeted in lush waving green plants. "I want to swim, but maybe not yet. We should wait until the sun is higher and all of the cousins are here. The smell of krofne will bring them out for sure. Oh! I just remembered there's someone you should meet." She jumps up and heads barefoot toward the path along the edge of the Una, leaving wet footprints on the stone and deep impressions in the thick moss.

I follow her, still reeling from the comment about her boyfriend in Belgrade.

All of the houses on the riverbank in this area either belong to relatives—some closer, some more distantly connected—or to friends who have known my family for decades. Some are nice, big family homes, others are smaller and crowded onto the same lot. All have splendid views of the Una. At the end of this row of houses, though, is the smallest house I've ever seen. It is a little jewel box, a tiny square house with jumbled, wild-looking flowers around it and an ancient pear tree out front. Most fruit trees don't get very big, but this one is twice as tall as any I've seen before.

"It looks like something out of a fairy tale," I say. "Who lives here?"

"A fairy-tale princess, of course. The nicest, sweetest, prettiest person you'll ever meet. She's my aunt Dika, my mother's sister."

She raps at the door, and a gentle voice calls out, "Come in!"

We push open the unlocked door—the doorway is low, and we both have to stoop to enter—and see a woman sitting on a low couch. She doesn't get up when we come in, which is strange, because this woman has to be family. Only family lives in this part of the riverbank. More than that, she has the high cheekbones that are typical of my lineage. She looks a bit like Mama, and even more like Žana's mother. Žana's mom is pretty, but this woman's face is beautiful.

"Žana! You made it," the woman says as Žana leans over to hug her.

"Amra, this is my Aunt Dika. Dika, this is Amra, Dilka's daughter."

Now I realize why she didn't get up to greet us, to hug us. I know about Dika, though I haven't met her since I was a little girl. Now I can see beyond the lovely face to her weak limbs. It is fortunate her house is small because she can barely move from room to room without a walker.

"Come here, darling girl. I was so sorry to hear about Amar. He was always such a charming, funny, clever boy. I hadn't seen him for years, not since I've had so much trouble getting around. But I can only imagine the pain you must be feeling. He lives in our hearts."

With no more than those few words, I understand that Dika is a woman built completely out of emotion and empathy.

"Žana, pretty girl, come sit beside me. You too, Amra." She pats the couch. "Are you hungry? Thirsty? You can have anything you like in this house ... as long as you get it yourself." She laughs. "Meho is away at work, and Dževad and Ćućana are out at the store."

She gazes beyond us at the big pear tree outside her window. "Amra, did you know that your mother and I were very close friends when we were little girls? Dilka and I were the girls who drank from the Adriatic Sea the first time we went, to check if it was really salty. We used to climb this pear tree. We'd see who could go the highest. Your mother always won. Dilka was the bravest girl I ever met. We'd go so high your grandmother Šerifa made my father Muharem, her brother, chop off the lowest branches so we couldn't climb any more. Do you think that stopped us?"

Žana and I laugh and shake our heads.

"Of course not! We didn't care how dangerous it was—it was fun! Dilka asked my father if we could borrow a chair. He probably thought we were going to make a fort with it, or pretend it was a horse. 'Just return it in the same shape you got it' was all he said. We tended to break things in our escapades."

For almost the first time, I picture Mama as a young girl, suntanned and tomboyish, scraping her knees and stealing pears and having adventures. I've only ever thought of my mother as Mama, the teacher, the caretaker, the wife. The most vivid image of her in my head is bending over Amar, her face furrowed in concern. But she was a child once, innocent, with her whole life before her. Her struggles in life made her who she is, but who was she? The older I get, the more Mama becomes a person as well as a mother.

"We climbed up, Dilka and me. Oh, she was like a squirrel! Up in the highest branches before you could blink. But wouldn't you know it—a branch snapped and down she slithered! Luckily half of her—the head half—landed on soft flowers and herbs. But the other half? Her legs slammed into that chair and smashed it to bits!"

"Was she hurt?" Žana asks.

"Just some bruises. The chair was another story."

"Did you get in trouble?"

"We got some glue and some string and made it look like a chair again, but it was held together with hope. If someone ever tried to sit in it, it would splinter to bits. A breath might even break it. Muharem could see what we'd done and started to get mad, but Dilka piped up, so bold, and said, 'Uncle, you told us to return it in the same shape. What shape is it now? Still chair-shaped! You can't punish us for that.' And he had to give in."

Žana and I brew some rose hip tea while she tells us small stories about the things she sees out of her window—the lives of birds, the changing season, the laugh of lovers passing by. And of course her pear tree, from its bare-limbed days of winter to its blossomy spring sweetness to its golden fruiting glory.

As we sit with tea and buttery cookies in the shape of bear paws, Dika's eyes grow misty, telling us about the past. But though the tale is a sad one, she doesn't sound melancholy. It's like singing a sad song—there is beauty in the feeling.

"You girls are going to have so many new and wonderful experiences on the River Una this summer," she says. "Maybe even fall in love. I met the love of my life on the Una."

Just in the last year, Tetka Fatma has told me bits and pieces, a tale of passion and heartbreak. She's trusted me with the more difficult stories since Amar died. I think they know that having shared the tragedy with them, having gone through the most difficult thing a family can endure, I'm able to handle some of the bitter truths of life.

Dika and her fiancé were so right for each other, everyone said. So much in love. Strangers would smile to see the two of them walking hand in hand. They planned a life together. Dika picked out her wedding dress, her family was planning a huge party . . . and then came her diagnosis.

Muscular dystrophy.

I feel a wrenching pain when I hear the diagnosis, the same as when I heard Amar's, though I understand so much better now what it means. Will I lose Dika one day, too? Will I lose everyone? Death is like a shadow always lurking behind me, clouding even the sunniest days.

It's a disease that weakens the muscles, slowly over time. Or, sometimes, not so slowly. It can run in families. Dika's brother had been diagnosed before her, but his was mild so far, with only minor weakness. But at that time, Dika had no idea how her disease would progress.

Still full of love and hope, she went to her fiancé. When she told him the news she expected comfort, support. They'd still be planning for the future—it would just be a different future. Weren't they about to swear to love each other for better and for worse, through sickness and through health?

Instead of comfort, she got questions: Is there a cure? No, only some treatments that help a little, but can't stop it. How bad will it be? She couldn't answer that one. She might need just a little help and lead a long life. Or she might lose the ability to walk within a year. Her husband might become her caregiver.

The love of her life, the man of her dreams nodded . . .

And walked out of her life the day before their wedding.

Just weeks later, heartbroken, she met Meho on a city bus. He fell in love at first sight, in love with her beauty and her quiet voice and melancholy eyes. He told her he would love her forever.

She married him a few days later, in the wedding dress originally meant for another man.

And Meho did love her. But he had troubles, too, cognitive challenges she never knew about until she was married to him. He can never hold a steady job but just does hourly work. One of his jobs is digging graves. He dug Amar's grave.

"And that's why I'm so glad you've started coming to the Una, Amra. I would have asked Žana anyway." She gives my cousin a squeeze. "But you understand, Amra. You know how someone with a disability can be picked on, shunned. Your mother told me how you always fought when someone was cruel to him."

I didn't even know Mama knew that. Amar must have told her. Amar didn't need my protection, though. He fought back with humor and intelligence, with comebacks the bullies were too dense to even understand. He didn't need a protector, he needed a world with understanding and empathy.

"I want to ask you, you two loving generous girls, to help Ćućana. Look out for her, make sure she's not getting herself into trouble. Make sure she's taking care of herself."

I'm a little puzzled by this because the one other thing I know about Ćućana is that she does everything she can to help take care of her mother—shopping for her, helping her around the house, keeping track of her medicines. Why would a girl who can care for someone else need help taking care of herself?

She doesn't really have any friends. She'll say something strange and people laugh at her. Then she'll just wander away, get lost, hide somewhere. She doesn't understand people, really. So much goes over her head. But she understands sincerity and love. She just doesn't understand how to be in society.

I haven't seen Ćućana in years, but I remember her—quiet

and shy, she seemed then. But once she laughed so loudly about something no one else got. Another time, someone told a silly kid's joke, a play on words, and she didn't understand it.

"Dževad tries to look out for her, but he has his own life now. I see Ćućana slipping away from me, going into some world inside her own head, and I'm scared for her. She spends too much time at home because I'm afraid of what might happen to her out there. But she is still a teen." Ćućana is a couple of years older than we are. "She needs friends and fun and sunshine. I thought maybe with her cousins…"

Dika doesn't have to say any more. Žana and I exchange a look of perfect understanding. Without saying a word to each other, we both know that we will take Ćućana under our wings, look out for her, be her friend.

"She's our cousin," I tell Dika staunchly. "Of course we will include her."

Dika is the most amazingly open and accepting woman, a born confidante. We find ourselves telling her all our secrets as we drink tea and listen to Azra, the most melancholy band in Yugoslavia. (I always think it is ironic that one Azra is so beautiful, while the other, my cousin Azra, is so unpleasant.)

"Nothing is forbidden here in my home," Dika tells us at one point. "A person should have utter freedom in one place, don't you think? You can tell me all your feelings. I'll lock them in my heart and keep them safe. Never be afraid to tell me anything, my beautiful girls. Amra, I know your mother is easy to talk to, but my sister Dida is another story. It must be hard to confide in her, Žana. She is always expecting perfection."

Later in the morning Ćućana comes home, and we have a reunion. "Sisters, you're here!" she screams, and crashes into us like a big teddy bear, trying to hug both of us at once. "I'm so glad! I'm here to do anything for you, to help if you need anything." It seems like a strange thing to say at first, but then I realize Dika has probably spent a lot of time teaching her how to interact with people. Ćućana doesn't always know what to do, but her heart is genuine and loving. "Come on," Žana says, "let's go eat krofne and go swimming. We're going to have the best summer—and now you are, too!"

Dika holds me back for a moment after my cousins leave and looks deeply into my face, seeming to read something there. "I want to tell you, Amra. People aren't necessarily sad because they have a disability. More often they are sad because of the sorrow others feel for them. Amar was a happy person, a complete person. He was not his illness. You can be sad that your brother is gone, but don't be sad for him. He wouldn't have wanted that."

She's talking about Amar, but also about herself with her physical disabilities and Ćućana with her mental and emotional problems. But she's talking about me, too. How do we define ourselves, and how do we let others define us? It is something I have to think about more.

16

"WHERE'S TATA?" I ask Mama as soon as we're sitting down to eat at the big table in the island.

"Oh...he had to work."

"Today? It's a weekend. He works so hard, shouldn't he have a little time off to spend with us?"

"Well, money never stops being earned and spent. As long as money is flowing, your father will have to work."

"Your dad must be really rich if he works with money all day," Ćućana says, too loudly, as we load up our plates.

Žana and some of the others around us look a little shocked. I'm starting to see some of the differences about Ćućana. She blurts her thoughts out where another person would keep them inside. I feel like the world would be a better place if everyone did this, so we didn't have to spend so much time decoding what people actually think and feel.

Before I can answer her, another girl sits down across from us and says in a low, tight voice so the adults can't hear, "Sure, Amra and her family are super rich. Just look at their nice, big house. Look at her fashionable clothes. They're swimming in money. Her father just plucks some bills off the cash assembly line whenever he needs more. Amra can buy whatever she wants, like that boutique miniskirt." The girl herself is dressed in a hot pink Lacoste shirt and Levi's jeans—the height of expensive teen fashion right now.

"Good morning, Sejla," Žana says with chilly pleasantness, narrowing her eyes as she decides how much to jump to my defense.

"That's not true, Sejla," I tell her softly before Žana can say anything else. "You know my parents don't have a ton of money. The house isn't even finished yet. And they didn't buy me these clothes. Žana gave me the skirt, and our aunt Fatma gave me the top." I turn to Ćućana. "My dad is the head of the Service of Public Accounting. He doesn't actually handle any money. He just helps the government keep track of how much companies make."

Sejla goes on as if she didn't hear me. "And your mom's a teacher. What a smarty-pants family. Teachers make good money, too."

"When they pay her. Her paycheck is always weeks late. Sometimes months."

Žana can't control herself anymore. "Cousin Sejla, why are you being like this? What do you care if Amra is rich or poor? What do you care if her parents are economists or teachers or . . . or pirates? Here, take this to sweeten your tongue." Žana thrusts over a plate of krofne.

Sejla bites savagely into a piece of krofne and then seems to deflate. No one can be angry with a mouthful of Mama's krofne.

"I'm sorry," she mumbles. "It's just . . ." She breaks off, sighing.

It's always the same story with my cousin Sejla. She's a few years older than I am, so we haven't spent a lot of time together. Now, I guess, I've caught up enough in age that she can almost see me as a peer—just old enough that I'm not a little kid, but still young enough to tease. Being with Sejla is like eating a handful of wild blackberries. One bite will be sweet, the next sour. And you always have to watch out for the thorns.

She's not jealous like Mersiha, or mean like Azra. I think Sejla's main problem is that she yearns, passionately, to have the good things in life. She sees other people in Converse jackets, Doc Martens shoes, Levi's jeans, Ray-Ban sunglasses, or Swatch watches, and she wants those things the way someone else might long for love or happiness. To her, expensive clothes and fancy accessories *are* happiness.

Her mom is one of Mama's sisters, my Aunt Ismeta. We call her Ica. She's a nice woman, a blonde like my grandmother in a family of redheads, with a cloud-soft touch and the sweetest voice. She always wears white and light colors and reminds me of sunshine. But she works in a textile factory. Sejla's dad does maintenance at a bank. Neither of them are as educated as my parents.

Mama is the baby of the family by almost a generation. Her older sisters are of the generation when their parents didn't think it was appropriate for the well-brought-up girls to go to schools organized by communists. My grandmother was educated in a school for Muslim girls and learned Arabic and the Quran, too, but when communists came to power, they took my family's land from them. My grandparents did not trust this new system to educate their daughters. By the time Mama was growing up, though, there was no other choice, and Mama went to college.

The lack of education made it harder through each generation, I think. We struggle to make ends meet, but for their family, money is even tighter. Though Sejla never takes no for an answer. When she used to ask for red jeans or a sequin shirt, and her mom said they couldn't afford it, she would beg, and shout, and throw tantrums. Now she's too old for that, but I can see the envy in her eyes whenever she spots someone in designer clothes.

When I was little I never noticed how much money someone had or whether they had expensive clothes. I learned Sejla's family was poor when I overheard Mama tell Tata a story. Sejla wanted the lead role in the elementary school play. I remember how much she practiced her lines. She was really good, the only kid in class taking the play seriously. But when it was time for the teacher to cast the leads, she skipped right over the talented Sejla and picked a quiet, clumsy mouse of a girl whose father happened to be a rich, influential doctor. The play was horrible, but the teacher suddenly had new school supplies. That's when Sejla understood how she would always be denied the best opportunities as long as she came from a poor, blue-collar family.

And so Sejla always has some snip to send my way, a little envious, a little malicious, a little sad. I think the sense of inadequacy she has will push her to succeed in life. But for now, I wish she could be a little happier with what she has.

"Well, I'm glad you came to the beach today," I say, forgiving her. It's so much easier to pardon bad behavior when you understand what lies behind it. I know Sejla is genuinely sorry.

"Yes, what *are* you doing here?" Žana wants to know. "Didn't you once say the beach is for babies, that you only go to coffee houses and discotheques?"

Sejla shrugs. "I just wanted to see my cousins, that's all. Is there any harm in that?"

It's only later, once she's lulled us with gossip and compliments, after we're in our sleepy food coma, that her real reason for being here comes out: She's grounded.

"I only stayed out until midnight. Well, twelve thirty, once. And that was on a Friday, not even a school night!"

"What time were you supposed to be home?"

"Eleven. But that's ridiculous! All of my friends can stay out as late as they want. And it's not like I'm getting into trouble or skipping school the next day." She huffs and crosses her arms over her chest, glaring down the long table at her parents. Mama and Ica are chatting happily, drinking their after-lunch coffee. When she sees that her mom is distracted, she leans across the table to whisper to us.

"I'm fed up, staying home with my parents or going to kid places like this. I need your help!"

"What can we do?" Žana asks. "Just serve your punishment, and next time get home by curfew."

"I have to break free—a jailbreak! Come on, Žana, you're supposed to be so adventurous. Help your cousin out. Please? Pleeeeease?" She laces her fingers and bats her eyelashes.

Žana and I exchange a look. It's amazing how well we can read each other's minds. We want to help, but we both think there must be something she's not telling us.

Suddenly Ćućana bursts out loudly, "Who is in jail? If they're bad, we better leave them there!" Adults come over to see what is going on, and Sejla can't say anything else. But later, as we sun-bathe on the rocks, Sejla renews her pleas.

"Amra, you're my mom's favorite, the little goody-goody."

"Sejla," Žana begins in warning.

"I don't mean that as an insult. A goody-goody can get any-thing she wants—from mothers and grandmothers and grandfa-thers. Remember how Babo Murat would always give you an extra piece of Bazooka gum?" Babo is the more uniquely Bosniak word for father, more old-fashioned than Tata, and in our family used as a title for our grandfather. "Bad girls like Žana and me get what we want from everyone else!" She and Žana giggle together. "My mom will listen to you, Amra. Just tell her how much you want to go downtown with all your cousins. We...I don't know, we want to try the new pizza place or something. Oh, and Belma is here in Bihać, too. Have you seen her yet?" Belma is another cousin, a tall, blue-eyed blonde with a fun-loving spirit. "Mom wouldn't let me go out on my own, but she will if I'm with you. She'll think I'm safe with you. Come on, Amra. Please? I have to go out tonight. I just have to!"

She looks really desperate, her eyes wide and shining, almost as if she's about to cry.

Once, I would have said no automatically. Now, although I don't necessarily agree, I can see things from her perspective.

"Of course, I'll do my best," I promise her. But I know there's something she's not telling me.

We swim and sunbathe and flirt—well, Žana flirts while I watch and take mental notes—and later in the afternoon head back to the mill to see if there's any food left.

"Go on, do it now," Sejla hisses, and shoves me toward her mother, who is still talking to mine.

"Um, Mama, do you think we can go downtown tonight? There's a new pizza place we'd like to try." Mama looks skeptical. "Please Mama? Sejla said that Belma is in town, too, and maybe Ćućana can go, too."

"I suppose there wouldn't be any real harm in it," Mama says.

"Sejla can't go," Ica says. "She's grounded."

"I want to get to know Sejla better," I say truthfully. "For all my life I didn't have close cousins, and now I'm trying to make up for lost time."

Ica thinks about it, but still shakes her head.

What can I do? Sejla is going to be so disappointed if I let her down. What would Žana do? She'd come up with some kind of clever story to convince her parents. But I can't lie to Mama and Aunt Ica! The only thing I can do is bend the truth a little bit, and even that gives me an uncomfortable, queasy feeling in my belly.

"Oh no! I really wanted Sejla to go, too. I've never been downtown at night, and she's older so she knows all the places to stay away from. I'd feel safer if Sejla was with us. She'd make sure we didn't get into trouble." I really do want to get to know Sejla better though, even if she can be difficult. She is one of my cousins—my sisters—for life.

Aunt Ica laughs. "My girl is more likely to find trouble than avoid it. I don't know..."

Then I have a brilliant idea. "That's okay, she probably doesn't want to hang out with a bunch of kids like us. She probably likes more exciting people, not a goody-goody like me. A teen like her probably wants to meet older boys, not spend the evening with younger girl cousins. We'd probably bore her."

Aunt Ica thinks a moment. "You know, it would be much better for Sejla to spend time with a nice, studious girl like you than whatever else she usually gets up to downtown. You'll be a good influence on her. Yes, I suppose Sejla can go with you. Just make sure she's home by eleven. I know I can trust you, Amra."

What have I done? I've manipulated an adult to get what I want! This is terrible ... isn't it? But Žana does it all the time. Well, I'm not doing it for anything bad, so I think it is okay.

"We'll be careful," I say. Why does Sejla want to go out so much tonight? A worry creeps over me, that feeling that something bad is about to happen that has never quite left me since Amar died.

"And you'll stay with Sejla all the time, right?" Ica asks. "I don't want her getting up to anything."

"What would she get up to?" I ask innocently, but underneath I worry what that *anything* could be! Luckily Aunt Ica doesn't answer, so I run back to where my cousins are waiting.

"She said yes!" I squeal. Žana and Ćućana cheer.

Sejla pulls me into a hug. "I knew I could count on you, Amra. We'll meet by the clock at seven, okay? Oh, thank you, thank you, thank you!" She runs off, saying she's going home to wash her hair and change.

"I never thought anyone would be so grateful to go out for a few hours and eat pizza," Žana muses. "I wonder what she's up to?"

Before I can speculate, I hear Mama call out, "Mehmed, there you are! Oh, you've spilled the oil." I run up to help.

He's brought one of his favorite dishes, chicken with tomatoes swimming in sunflower oil. Half the juice is running across the table now. I find a rag to clean it up, and Tata sits down heavily. His hands are shaking.

"Tata, what happened? Are you okay?" He looks like he might have a fever, his face flushed, his breath shallow. He even has dark circles under his eyes, though I know he went to bed early.

"I'm fine. Just a little...never mind, it's nothing." He gives Mama a look that I know means *not in front of Amra*. This only makes me more worried.

"Tata, tell me, please." I sit next to him and drape an arm across his shoulders, nestling my cheek against his. Prickles brush my face. He didn't shave this morning, which is strange.

"I was called into work," he says at last.

"But you had the day off. It must have been a real emergency. Was everyone called in?"

"No, just me. I...they wanted to ask me some questions."

They? Who are *they?* The way he says it makes it sound like *they* are opponents: them versus us.

"Is it going to be okay, Mehmed?" Mama whispers.

"I hope so, Dilka." He runs his fingers through his brown silky hair, now with more streaks of gray in it than I remember. He rests his chin on his hand and stares into the distance, his teeth clenched tight as if something might escape if he opened his mouth again.

Nearby, Tetak Ale is playing a mix tape on his boom box. The song switches from a melancholy sevdalinka love ballad to a nasheed, a chant sung by a chorus from a mosque in Sarajevo. I

catch a few words of the song, something innocuous about opening your eyes to a beautiful morning. Suddenly Tata is running
to Tetak Ale. He stumbles to his knees in front of the boom box,
mashing buttons frantically until the music shuts off.

"Ale, are you trying to kill me? Do you want to send me to
prison? You know all they need is something, and this song is
more than something."

"Mehmed," Tetak Ale says in a low urgent voice, "we are
Bosniaks. We've always been here, as long as there was such a
thing as Bosnia. We are Bosnian Muslims who built this country
and have raised generations here."

His words stir something in me. Ever since I was little I've felt a
vague discomfort being Bosniak. It was something we didn't talk
about, and therefore felt almost shameful. There are no Bosniak
girls in the stories I read in school, no Muslim names in the word
problems in math. But with Tetak Ale's words I know that we are
not invisible, not aliens in our own home. I listen more carefully,
so full of questions.

"Why are Serbs not called Orthodox Christians or Croats called
Catholics?" Uncle Ale goes on. "Why can they have their ethnicity,
culture, language, identity recognized, and not us?"

"You know why," Tata whispers.

"Hush, Mehmed," Tetak Ale says. "Let's talk about this away
from young ears. Is it as bad as that?"

They walk away, and I don't hear any more.

"Mama, what just happened? What was wrong with that song?"

"It's a religious song," she says.

"So?"

"A Muslim song. And now is not a good time to be Muslim. Especially for your father."

"But... we *are* Muslim."

She nods. "But it is important that we don't seem *too* Muslim right now."

"How can a song make someone more or less Muslim?"

But she won't answer me, and she won't tell me anything else about what's troubling Tata no matter how much I ask. If Amar were here, I could get the answers I need. He was always my bridge between childhood and adulthood, guiding me through these complex conversations.

Instead of getting annoyed at my persistent questions, her face becomes strangely calm. I've seen her look that way in front of an unruly classroom. When her face is like that, peaceful and pleasant, it spreads to the kids and they miraculously stop misbehaving. If she looks like that, everything must be okay, right? "Don't worry, sweet girl. Your father is exaggerating. It's just a little trouble at work. Nothing at all to worry about."

Any day before today I would have believed her, completely. But today I lied to my family, and this makes me wonder, can my family lie to me?

17

IT'S EASY TO put worry aside when the worry is vague and all of your family is encouraging you to have a good time. Mama gives me one of her necklaces to wear for my big night out. Ćućana has to help her mom before she can go out, so we'll pick her up later, but Belma comes over to get ready with us. She and Žana dress me up until I feel like a supermodel. Then Žana takes out her miraculous bag of makeup and sits me down to paint my face.

"I don't think I want any," I say, remembering Hana's garish attempts at making me up.

"Nonsense," Žana chides as she takes out sponges and puffs and brushes. Belma and little Vedrana watch in approval as Žana smooths foundation over my face. "Blend, blend, blend, that's the secret," she says as she rubs it around my hairline and jaw until it looks exactly like my own summer-tanned skin . . . only better! When Hana did it, it looked like a mask.

I squint and flinch when she applies eyeliner. "Is it supposed to be that close to my eye?" I ask, afraid she'll stab my eyeball. I hate anything too close to my eye, especially something as pointy as this eye pencil. When I was little, two cousins on my father's side, Nafka and Aida, came to live with us for a time while they finished up nursing school. One day, wanting to play nurse, I put on Nafka's white lab coat and her chunky-heeled shoes. But I put them on the wrong feet, and when I tried to walk in them I stumbled and fell face-first into the corner of a table. A long shard of wood broke off and stabbed me almost in the eye. Tata came in to find me screaming and drove me to the hospital with a wooden dagger three inches long sticking out of my face, my blood everywhere. At the hospital they took it out and sewed me up without anesthesia.

Now, it is a mark of supreme trust that I let Žana poke at my eyes. She holds me by the chin and applies a long, sure sweep of chocolate brown eyeliner with her steady hand. "Blue shadow?" Vedrana is all for it, but Belma thinks a smoky eye will be better. I agree.

"Just don't make me look like a clown!" I plead, and close my eyes, hoping for the best.

When I open them, I'm astonished. Instead of looking like a clown, I look like a gazelle peeking out of the forest. My eyes look huge and . . . beautiful.

I've never felt really beautiful before. I never felt ugly either. I guess how I looked just wasn't a priority in my life. Now I think of what Mersiha said about the ugly duckling and the swan. I feel like I'm looking at another person, at a portrait in a gallery instead of a mirror reflecting my own face. Will people look at me with jealousy or appreciation? I can't worry about that. I just need to be happy in my own skin . . . and clothes and makeup.

"Is this me?" I ask them. "Am I allowed to feel beautiful if it is just because of makeup?" And then I blush so much I don't need rouge on my cheeks. Did I just say that? Feeling beautiful is strange enough, but saying it out loud seems forbidden.

Belma starts to tell me that I *am* beautiful even without

makeup, but Žana cuts her off. "Sister, don't even think about being beautiful or not. You are *you*, and that's what matters. Makeup is like clothes. It can make you feel even more special, but it can't cover up what's inside. Would you be *you* naked?"

"Well, not with anyone else around!" I laugh.

"Silly. Would you be *you* in the dark? Of course. Maybe makeup helps you be brave. Maybe nice clothes help you dance and not care who is watching. But it is like using a megaphone to shout. More strangers will hear you, but the only thing that matters is that the people close to you can hear you whisper. I like to dress up as much as anybody, but you can't think that the eye sparkles and scarlet lips are you. They're just…"

"Wrapping paper!" Vedrana bursts in.

"Yes, exactly!" Žana says.

"And Amra is the present underneath!" Vedrana goes on, oblivious to the looks her older relatives exchange. She didn't mean to sound so risqué, but the rest of us are thinking about being unwrapped like a present.

"Who is going to unwrap you, Žana?" Belma asks slyly.

"Oh, I don't know. A mystery boy. He's out there somewhere."

"What about your boyfriend back in Belgrade?" Belma asks.

Before she can answer I jump in with the advice I've been mulling over. "Žana, I think you should officially put the relationship on hold while you're away. Write him a letter, tell him you should both enjoy the summer apart and then see where you are when you get back together. Isn't that more honest?"

"You know, you're right," she says after thinking a moment. "And the fact that I'm the one who says it will annoy him to no end. The whole summer he'll be thinking about me, wondering what I'm up to. Yes, that's perfect." That wasn't exactly what I was going for, but it works out the same in the end. "Now, let me do your lips and we'll go out on the town!"

I've never gone "out" at night before. Sure, I've played in the neighborhood until after dark, after dinner in the summer when the sunset comes late, or bundled up in layers of wool when winter night falls early. But I've never dressed up specifically to go someplace at night with friends.

The clock stands in the heart of the city, tall and iconic, its bright octagonal face illuminated day and night. Every person who has ever lived and loved and had fun in Bihać has made a rendezvous by saying, "I'll meet you at the clock." I've gone with Mama to meet Tetka Fatma there for some shopping and lunch. When a boy dreams of meeting his girlfriend for a first date, he pictures it starting beneath the clock's benevolent glow. How many couples has that clock seen, how many happy families?

We pick up Ćućana but have to wait for her to finish taking care of her mom. Ćućana lays out Dika's dinner, placing everything within easy reach, with her medicines near her plate. "Don't forget to take this pill before you eat, and that pill after. And drink a full glass of water. Do you need me to help you to the bathroom before I go? Are you sure you will be fine without me tonight?"

"Your brother will be home soon, don't worry. You go and enjoy yourself. But remember to come home in time to take your medicine. You're supposed to take it at the same time every night."

They take care of each other, each giving the other what they can, like I fed Amar food and he fed me knowledge. Ćućana can't always take care of herself, but she has a gift for caring for her mom. She never forgets a single thing about her mom's medicines, even if she neglects to take her own. Her care is her gift.

We promise Dika that we'll have Ćućana home by ten for her medicine. The rest of us are going to have a sleepover at my house, but Ćućana refuses to leave her mom overnight even with her brother and dad there to help out.

The sun is setting, pink and gold, and the light gives my cousins a magical glow. Žana's golden-brown hair, already sun-streaked, takes on a fiery hue. Ćućana's big brown Bambi eyes are emphasized with dark eyeliner, and with her high cheekbones and stylish short hair she looks like a rock star. I wish I had a camera so I could capture the splendor of my cousins in the moments before night falls. I know this image will live in my head forever.

"There she is," Belma says, and runs up to greet Sejla, who is dressed in a tiny red leather skirt with a lacy black top that looks like it might have been meant as lingerie, and makeup straight out of a Madonna video. She's wearing an acid-washed denim jacket loosely over her shoulders, but I bet when she left the house it was buttoned up.

"You look amazing!" I tell her.

"I know," she deadpans back. "You girls look … acceptable. For kids." But I can tell from the dancing light in her eyes that she loves us and is happy we came.

The clock smiles down on us as we compliment one another and gossip and decide what to do tonight. "I've only ever been here in the daytime," I tell them. "I'd sit on the terrace with Mama and eat ćevapi. And if we got pistachio and mint ice cream afterward, I'd be in paradise!"

"Well, your mom isn't here tonight, so we may find a different kind of paradise," Sejla scoffs.

"Although I wouldn't mind a gelato," Žana says, and there's still enough kid in all of us that we agree to start the night this way. We walk slowly as we lick our frozen treats.

The clock is near a lovely park that leads to the river. Nearby is the Hotel Park with its public terrace. A band is playing there, one of the best local bands. "What is it called?" Žana asks.

"Okus Meda," I tell her. A Taste of Honey.

She closes her eyes dreamily. "Is that what a kiss would be like, do you think? A taste of honey on my lips?" She makes a happy little humming sound.

"You haven't kissed your Belgrade boyfriend?" I ask her.

"Not yet. Not a real kiss, anyway. I don't get to go out on my own much at home, and it would be no fun sneaking a kiss behind the school or in an alleyway. When I have my first kiss I want it to be supremely romantic. The kind of kiss poets will write about."

Okus Meda plays a mix of Bosnian music and the latest American songs. Now they strike up the urgent, compelling opening notes of U2's "Where the Streets Have No Name." It's not Bono singing, but this musician is almost as good as he belts out the lyrics that speak to my generation all around the world.

"Where the streets have no name!" we shout out together during the chorus.

I'm overwhelmed at how alive my city is at night. There are

hundreds of young people overflowing from the spacious terrace that connects to an adjacent park of ancient trees. The park has remnants of the old city walls and the Captain Tower where the Hungarian king once sought the protection of the brave people of Bihać. There is so much history here…and so much *now*. The faces around me shine as if lit from within, and laughter adds to the music in a glorious chorus. Suddenly, everyone around me is beautiful.

"Now where should we go?" Žana asks.

"Down to the river?" Ćućana suggests.

"No, we're going to be there every day this summer. What about the new pizza place?"

"Mmm, yeah." Ćućana changes her mind. "Let's get pizza."

"But there's a discotheque nearby, right?" Belma reminds us. "I want to go dancing tonight!"

I'm a little nervous about the idea of dancing, and I want to vote for the pizza, but I also don't want to seem like I'm a scared baby. I have a feeling I'm going to be out-voted, though. Žana likes the idea, but to my surprise, Sejla doesn't seem that interested in the discotheque. She's looking all around, detached from our conversation.

"Let's just walk around and enjoy the city," she says at last. "Amra, you and Vedrana can finish your gelato while we walk." I'm a little sad that Dino isn't here to share in the frozen treat, but I make a mental vow to make sure he gets his favorite dessert sometime this summer. It is fully dark now and the world seems to be made entirely of teenagers. It is warm, and the breeze off the Una carries a heady mix of smells: Drakkar Noir cologne, Obsession perfume, the coconut of leftover sunscreen. Vedrana takes my hand and licks melting hazelnut gelato from the edge of her sugar cone.

I know, from the American movies that make their way here on bootleg VHS tapes, that in other places, people our age don't go out on the town at night. To an American it would probably seem strange that girls our age might go to a discotheque—with a kid as young as Vedrana in tow! But here in Bihać the thought of danger never occurs to us. We are together—what could happen?

Still, I feel like I'm on high alert. For what, I don't know. But Dika and Sejla's parents are trusting me to make sure nothing bad happens. I don't know if this is the same kind of responsibility I used to feel for Amar, or if this is just part of my nature.

Romance is in the air. Everywhere we look, people are kissing. Couples retreat to the shadows of ancient trees that were planted during Ottoman rule. I see an extraordinarily tall young man pick up his small girlfriend and stand her on a bench so they can kiss without him having to bend down. I don't care that I don't have a boyfriend—I don't want one. It is life that I'm in love with!

We still can't decide what to do next, and Sejla stalls us whenever we seem close to making a decision. But it doesn't matter. We're laughing and singing and dancing, just happy to be out and together. Belma buys a big bag of popcorn and we all reach our hands in and lick our buttery, salty fingertips afterward.

We find ourselves by the World War II museum. When the Nazis occupied nearly all of Yugoslavia, Bihać was the one area that managed to resist them for a while. We're proud of that fact.

There's an old cannon with big rusty wheels parked in front under a spotlight, a strange metal monster that seems so out of place in this peaceful city. It is hard to imagine that cannons and tanks ever rolled through here. At least l know they never will again. Now, this cannon is just a forbidden playground during the daytime—despite signs warning people not to touch it, what kid can resist climbing on a cannon? Even l did, once. Amar and l used to take guitar lessons near here, and when he wished he could climb on the cannon like other kids l helped him up, and we played there for a while. Amar was a born actor, and he recited lines from war movies we'd watched together, sounding exactly like a general. It was so much fun, but one of my very few acts of disobedience, and l felt guilty for weeks afterward.

Suddenly Sejla gives a little squeal. l turn, and think she's being attacked by an octopus! Arms are snaking around her waist, touching her everywhere!

"Let her go!" l shout, and grab for Sejla's hand to pull her away from her shadowy attacker. But she only laughs and turns into his embrace, kissing him passionately. His lips are on her throat, her cheeks, her mouth...

Oh no! What am l going to tell her parents?

Nothing, l decide at once. Not one word. How unlike the old Amra.

Finally, breathlessly, Sejla pulls away from him and l see a tall, dark-haired, preppy-looking boy, a little older than Sejla, wearing a bright blue Lacoste shirt, Levi's, and new-looking Converse sneakers.

He holds out his hand, the hand that was just touching the black lace below Sejla's collarbones. "Hi, I'm Slobodan, Sejla's boyfriend. I've heard so much about you girls. Let me treat you all to pizza."

So this is why Sejla had to slip free of her punishment and come out tonight, to see this handsome boy! Despite the offer of pizza, we don't move from the spot. Sejla and Slobodan haven't seen each other in a while, and apparently they have some catching up to do.

We're treated to a show I've never seen outside of movies. It is a reunion but they're kissing like it's their final goodbye, the last time they'll ever touch each other. Standing in front of the old cannon, you'd think Slobodan was about to head off to war. Žana is grinning, entranced by their happiness. "Isn't it beautiful?" she whispers to me, squeezing my hand.

I'm happy for them, too. But I can't help being worried. Sejla's parents obviously don't want her to be doing this. And they're counting on me to prevent it.

But I'm scared now as I glance around me. I see some people staring. She shouldn't be doing this out in public! Bihać isn't that big—anyone who passes could be a relative or friend, someone who would report this back to Sejla's parents. She'd be in big trouble . . . and I'd be a big disappointment to all of the adults who trusted me.

But what did Aunt Ica really say? Have her home by eleven, and stay with her the whole time. I'm with her, aren't I? Nothing too bad could happen with her cousins standing right here, could it?

But just as I think it, the very worst thing happens! Luckily I'm so watchful—I spot them half a block away, heading right toward us.

"Danger!" I hiss. "Separate!"

Sejla and Slobodan jump so guiltily I know what they're doing must be wrong. But then, is love ever wrong? He scurries behind the cannon while Sejla smooths down her hair and wipes the skin around her lips to get rid of any smeared lipstick. Only then does she look up to see the danger. Her face blanches.

It is her older brother Samir.

What am I going to do? I feel like I'm going to pass out.

Samir has a friend with him, a boy I know named Haris. Samir is in college, but Haris is a little younger, in high school, a few years older than us.

"Hi, Seka. And look, all my cousins!" He's grinning, as happy to be out in this beautiful night as I was just a minute ago. But now everything feels sinister and dangerous. He introduces Haris to Belma, Vedrana, Ćućana, and Žana, who don't know him.

I hardly remember how to be polite. I'm shaking, sweating like a Bosnian farmer working his fields under a summer sun. Because I see something no one else has noticed yet: Slobodan's long shadow stretching from behind the cannon. I feel like a double agent, working for both sides at the same time.

Any second now, Samir will ask who is lurking back there. And then we'll be caught. Mama will find out, and I'll be yet another disappointment in her life. And Aunt Ica will never trust me or love me again.

Sejla looks cool as a cucumber, talking with her brother as if she didn't just have her secret boyfriend's lips all over her. Belma knows how to handle this, too, and even little Vedrana just watches, learning the teen world through sharp observation.

To my surprise it is Žana who grabs my hand and looks nervous. I squeeze it back and notice how shallow and fast her breathing is. She doesn't say a word. Žana *never* doesn't talk.

Suddenly Ćućana, who has been looking from person to person with a confused frown, says loudly, "Why did that boy just run away?"

There's dead silence.

Finally Sejla gives an awkward laugh and says, "Oh, that must have been some bored tourist. Who else would run at this time of night? Samir, where are you headed? Going to drink coffee and talk politics all night?" She turns to us. "My brother is like you, Amra—always studying, never wants to have any fun." She's retreating into barbed attacks, but I understand her fear and forgive her.

"It looks like Amra is having fun tonight," Samir says. "And actually we're going to the discotheque. Mom wanted me to check on you, but I see you're fine. See you girls later!" To my absolute relief they head off, and we all exhale a collective sigh.

"Amra, who is he?" Žana asks with desperate intensity.

"That's Samir, you know him," I say in confusion, believing she's as upset as I am and not thinking clearly.

"No, not him. The other one!"

"Haris. He's not related, but he's like a cousin. I've known him since I was little. Why?"

Žana takes a deep, steadying breath. "He is the most gorgeous, most perfect boy I have ever seen in my entire life," she declares.

"Is that what you were thinking about all this time?" I ask, laughing with amazement. "Not that we were about to get caught?"

"Oh, what does that matter? Sejla should sing about her love from the rooftops. I should know, because as of this moment I'm officially, totally in love with Haris."

"But you haven't even talked to him! You didn't say a word, and he barely spoke. You know nothing about him."

"Haven't you heard of love at first sight? He's beautiful, an angel."

"I thought you're always telling me looks don't matter," I remind her.

"Well," she says, "they sure don't hurt!" She gazes down the road where Haris disappeared.

Slobodan sneaks around from the back of the cannon. "That was a close one," he says, and resumes kissing Sejla like nothing ever happened.

"Hey, don't eat my sister!" Ćućana says, making me snort with laughter. It really does look like he's trying to eat her. Slobodan tags along with us like a puppy for the rest of the night, and they can't keep their hands off each other.

I'm a little shocked at my own reaction to their passion. I feel a sense of excitement for them, a surge of adrenaline, almost as if it were happening to me and not to Sejla, as if I'm the one feeling those powerful emotions. I feel some guilt at being part of the secret, and I know that I would never behave like Sejla... but just because I can't do something myself doesn't mean they shouldn't.

Luckily we don't get caught by any other relatives. We never make it to the pizza place or the discotheque, but it is good enough just to enjoy the night with my friends. We dance to the music of Okus Meda, and at one point Ćućana grabs Slobodan and dances with him. He has become a part of this magical night for her. Later we lie on the grass, enjoying the breeze off the river and counting the stars. "This has been the happiest night of my life," Ćućana says, and I think I agree. I still feel shaken from our near-miss, but I've read somewhere that a brush with danger makes you feel more alive.

We drop Ćućana off at exactly ten.

"Did you have a good time?" Dika asks her as she welcomes her with a hug.

"I had the best time ever. And my sister didn't get eaten." Dika raises her eyebrows but she's used to Ćućana's odd way of saying things and doesn't question it.

"Was she okay?" Dika asks me anxiously in a low whisper.

"She had fun," I tell her. "In fact, I think she made the night even more fun for all of us just by being there."

"She didn't try to wander off?"

"No, we were together the whole time."

"That's good. I worry so much about her."

The rest of us head to my house, stopping at a late-night bakery that caters to teens and college students who need just a few more carbs to get through the night. At home, to our delight, we find that Tata has brought home a big bucket of chocolate hazelnut spread for us. We smear it on the warm bread and gorge ourselves, talking and laughing so hard that we start to choke. The danger seems like a joke now. Sejla is ecstatic that she got to spend time with her boyfriend. Žana is lost in her own world of her intense crush and keeps bringing him into the conversation.

"Do you think Haris likes hazelnut spread? Do you think Haris likes tall girls?" She frowns. "Do you think Haris is dancing with someone else right now?" Then she brightens. "Maybe Haris is thinking of me as much as I'm thinking of him!"

Later that night I find a moment to talk with Sejla alone.

"Slobodan seems so nice, and he's not much older than you. Why are your parents so against him?"

"Use your head, Amra. What is his name?"

"I don't understand."

"Have you ever heard of a Muslim boy named Slobodan? No. It is a Serb name. Maybe a Croat name. But never a Bosniak name. His mother is Muslim, but his father is Serb. When my father found out, he pitched a fit and said no daughter of his will ever date a Serb. But we love each other. I'm not going to give him up, no matter what my parents say."

She pulls me into a tight hug. "Thank you, Amra. Thank you so much for helping me. You are like a true sister."

I hate keeping secrets, but how can I stand in the way of a love that fights prejudice? Maybe their love can make the world a better place.

18

THE NEXT MORNING, Sejla and Belma leave early. They need to stop home and get ready for the day's adventure on the banks of the Una. The rest of us are sitting around the table nibbling the last crumbs of breakfast. Tata gives Mama a kiss on the top of her red hair as he pours her another cup of coffee. Mama is wearing big earrings and a nice summer dress and looks so happy to have us all around her. I see a dreamy look come over Žana's face, and I'm so proud of my family for its peace and happiness. No couple loves the way Mama and Tata love each other.

"Tetka Begija came by before you sleepyheads were awake," Mama says. "She dropped off this homemade bread and plum jam for us." Tetka Begija gets up before dawn every weekday to make meals for the thousands of workers at the Politilenka factory. Even on the weekends, she can't slow down. If she can't feed thousands, she'll feed us.

Our culture is about family and community. It is about lots of people having little but having more when they bring their resources together. Tetka Begija knows we don't have much—neither does she. But she is the sort of person who makes five dinars out of one, as we say in Bosnia. She makes jams, juices, and pickles herself, because it is cheaper and better. Her mother put her in charge of the family cooking after World War II when she was a girl, and she has taken pride in her knowledge ever since.

Getting up early to cook is her ritual, almost her religion, her way of showing love for her family and for the world.

Tata looks refreshed this morning, I think as I watch him spread plum jam on a steaming heel of fresh bread. Whatever happened yesterday when he was called into work must have been blown out of proportion. I know when I'm troubled, he tells me to sleep on it, and sometimes things will look brighter in the morning. Maybe that advice worked for him.

I remember a problem I needed to talk to him about.

"Tata, remember what I told you about Hana? And her father?"

He presses his lips together and nods grimly.

"He was beating her again yesterday."

"It was terrible," Žana adds. "She was screaming for mercy, begging him not to kill her."

"We went to the door, but her mom wouldn't let us see her. Tata, I'm really worried about her. Can you think of anything to do? Can we call the police?"

He sighs and shakes his head. "The police don't like to get involved in family things like this. They should, but they don't. And even if the police came, would Hana tell them the truth? You said she told you she fell down the stairs the last time. She only told you what really happened a long time after, once she knew you and trusted you. She'd probably be too afraid of her father to tell the police the truth. And then he might be even more cruel to her afterward."

"There has to be something we can do!"

"I can try to talk to him. Maybe I can reason with him, man to man. I know him, a little bit, from work."

"Everyone knows him, or knows of him," Mama says, frowning. "He's one of the corrupt Communist Party officials, siphoning off money and squirreling it away in some secret account in Germany. Mehmed, maybe you shouldn't go over there. What if he hits you? I could try talking to Hana's mother."

They debate for a while but in the end decide that Hana's mother is too depressed and downtrodden to do anything about it. If she hasn't stepped up to protect her own children by now, she never will. Tata thinks maybe if he is gentle and persuasive he can make Hana's father see reason.

"You go enjoy your day, girls," Tata says as he hugs us goodbye. "I'll let you know what happens with your friend when we get there at lunchtime."

Žana is eager to leave. We quickly clean up after breakfast and pack our beach bags. "Will he be there? Do you think he'll be there?" The words bounce out of her mouth. There's no need to ask who "he" is. Only one boy in the world exists for Žana now.

"Probably," I tell her. "I know he goes most days in the summer. He was there last summer some of the times we were, you just didn't notice."

"Impossible!" she says. "I would have noticed him right away. He's the most handsome boy in the universe." She settles her beach bag over her shoulder. "What do you think he'll be wearing? He'd look good in light blue, wouldn't he?"

I roll my eyes. I like seeing her excited and happy, of course, but it is worrying that she seems so obsessed. She usually talks about a thousand different things whenever we're together—from music and books and gossip about friends to her thoughts about life and philosophy and human nature. Talking to her has always been thrilling, her lively mind dancing all around me. Right now—though I'd never tell her this—she's a little boring. Haris this and Haris that, every time she opens her mouth. I don't think I could ever take that leap of faith and love someone that fast. Is love supposed to be like this, an inescapable avalanche that buries you? If I can't do that, doesn't that mean I'll never fall in love?

I can only think of one cure for Žana—getting to know Haris better. Either she will decide he's not worth all this effort, or he'll fall in love with her. I can't imagine any boy not falling in love with Žana if she were interested in him. I decide to do whatever I can to bring them together, and then let nature take its course.

For that, I'll even put up with Žana talking about him nonstop.

It's a brilliant, sunny day, and we're sweating after our walk to Brvice. I'm happy to change into my borrowed bikini. I remember just last year it felt so strange to have so much of myself exposed. Now it feels natural. I'm more comfortable in my skin.

As we're walking along the boardwalk I ask, "Do you want to swim, or—" I break off when Žana grabs my arm and wheels me around like soldiers doing an about-face in perfect military style.

"What? What is it?"

"He's there!" she whispers dramatically.

"Then why aren't we..."

"Shush! He'll hear!"

I look over my shoulder and see him standing by the water with some other boys, mostly his own age, but to my surprise I see Dino there with his friend Maše. Why are they hanging out with Haris? Then I see Haris's younger brother Halid there and remember that Dino started hanging out with him, too. They all love basketball and skateboarding, which also helps them fit in with the older boys sometimes.

Haris's golden hair is shining like a second sun. He is quite attractive, I decide, but to me he is just Haris, a boy a little bit older than me who once caught me a ladybug when I was five. To Žana he is like Apollo, bright and awesome and terrifying.

This is baffling. Here is Žana, the boldest girl I know, who can talk and laugh with anybody, suddenly too shy to face Haris.

"Let's go talk to him," I suggest.

"No, I can't!" To my amazement her cheeks are bright scarlet, and not just from the heat. Even her earlobes are pink.

"Well, then, I can talk to him first. I've known him forever. You can listen for a while until you feel brave and then jump in. I'll even introduce you again, though I'm sure he hasn't forgotten you."

"I don't know..."

"Come on, it's just Haris. And Dino is there. How scary can it be? I'll introduce you to Halid, Haris's brother, too, and then it won't look like you're just going over there to talk to Haris."

Finally we settle on lurking under the trees where we can watch him. She's like a field biologist, taking notes on his behavior, trying to figure him out. "Look, he's with three boys. No girls around. So he probably doesn't have a girlfriend. And see, he's nice to Dino and his friends, so he doesn't mind being friends with younger people. That means he could be my boyfriend even though I'm a little younger."

"He'll never be your boyfriend unless you talk to him."

"Oh, he'll be my boyfriend no matter what. Just you wait and see!" For a moment she sounds supremely confident. But I still can't get her to actually go near him. Where is my courageous sister?

Then before we know it, here he comes, walking along the boardwalk directly toward us. "Here's your chance," I whisper. I smile at him as he approaches, ready to say hello and fade into the background so Žana can flirt to her heart's content. But when I turn to glance at Žana ... she's gone!

"Good morning, Amra," Haris says pleasantly. "Here all alone?"

"I ... well, no, my cousin Žana is here. Somewhere."

"Oh yeah, the blonde one?" he asks.

Oh no! That's Belma. Is he interested in her? Žana will be crushed. "No, the tall beautiful girl with one green eye and one blue eye." I try my best to advertise well for Žana.

He frowns a bit. I don't think he was paying much attention that night. We must have seemed like a generic gaggle of girls to him, and other than me, who he already knew, he didn't bother to tell us apart.

"That's interesting, two different-colored eyes," he says.

"Well, once I find her, come over and take a nice long look at them. We'll be at the island at lunchtime."

He smiles. "I might just do that," he says, then saunters off.

I feel like I've just hooked a prize-winning fish for Žana's lunch.

After he's gone, Žana pops up. "Well, what did he say?"

"He just wanted to say hello," I say evasively. "Why did you run away?"

"I don't know. When I saw him, my heart started beating fast and my mouth went dry, and I knew I'd make a fool of myself."

"Well, you have to talk to him some time," I say.

"Soon," she agrees. "In the meantime, I have an idea."

We track down Dino and his friends, who have broken off from Haris's group to dribble around one another and show off their fancy moves. Suddenly Žana is really cheering every time Dino has the ball in his hands. "You've gotten really good," she says. "I think you're almost ready for the NBA." Dino blushes, pleased to have a pretty older girl compliment him, even if the girl is a cousin. His friends look at Žana with open admiration.

She pulls Dino a little aside from his friends. "That boy you were with before, Haris. You know him well?"

Dino shrugs, not as interested if she's talking about Haris and not him.

"Do you know if he has a girlfriend? What can you tell me about him?"

"I don't know him all that well. But Halid is his brother. I can ask him..."

"No! Haris can't know that I'm curious. Do you think you can find out for me?"

"If he has a girlfriend?"

"Find out anything—everything! If you do I'll...I'll buy you an ice cream for every new thing you find out." Ice cream is a luxury. We have it maybe once a year for a very special treat. Dino's eyes light up.

"But my friend Maše will need ice cream, too," he says. "I won't be able to do it all on my own."

"Fine, just find out something good! And don't let Haris—or his brother—know what you're doing."

"Žana, do you think that's a good idea?" I ask her when the boys have gone. "Wouldn't it be better just to talk to him?"

"I will...as soon as I have some more information." After that we spend the morning basking on the rocks but not swimming. Žana has the idea that her hair won't look good enough if she gets it wet. "Maybe after lunch. I want him to see me looking my best." I want to give her the same kind of advice she would give me—don't lose yourself for a boy—but I don't feel like I have enough experience with boys or life to offer any guidance. So I just agree to her suggestions. I don't tell her about my plan to have Haris gaze deeply into her eyes, though. I think that would make her so anxious she'd run all the way home. Better to let her relax. Then when he comes over she might be able to talk to him naturally.

"He'll come to the island at lunchtime," Žana says. "Amra, what am I going to say to him?"

I decide to drop another hint to help her relax. "You know, now that I think about it, when I saw him he was heading back to the street, so he's probably gone home by now. We can come back tomorrow and look for him. For now, let's just enjoy the day."

Just after noon, Mama and Tata arrive with baskets of food. My mouth starts to water when they unload savory ćevapi, the traditional Bosnian sausage kebabs made of spiced meat. Next to it are fragrant rounds of flat lepinja bread, a big bowl of sliced onions, and jars of Tetka Begija's ajvar, the red bell pepper relish.

Before I make a plate, I ask Tata what happened with Hana's father. Tata looks grim.

"That man! How can he even call himself a man? He wouldn't listen to me. I tried to be reasonable. Someone else would have punched him in the face for the way he treats his children, but you know I'm not that kind of person." My father wouldn't raise his hand to a mosquito. "And that wouldn't do any good with a man like that, one who lashes out and doesn't think or feel. So I was gentle and diplomatic. I talked about his reputation, what people think if his daughter has a bruised face. That's the sort of thing I thought might make a difference to such an arrogant man."

"And what did he say?" I ask.

"He just sneered at me and told me the way he disciplines his daughter is no business of mine. Then he slammed the door in my face. As soon as the door was shut I heard him bellowing for Hana. I'm afraid I might have made things worse."

"Oh, Tata! What can we do?"

He shakes his head. "I don't know. Let me try to figure something out."

I'm talking this over with Žana when Dino comes up, ready to eat. Žana grabs him. "What have you got for me?"

I'm about to say that he can't have found out anything yet when Dino surprises me. "I didn't ask him anything yet, but when I was playing near him, I heard him ask one of his friends who the tall girl with Amra was."

"He said that?"

"The tall *pretty* girl is what he actually said."

She grabs him in a quick hug. "Oh Dino, you've earned an ice cream for sure!"

"And Maše too?"

"And Maše too!"

She promises to give him money for ice cream as soon as we get home, and Dino runs off to tell Maše the good news.

"Can you believe it?" Žana gushes. "He noticed me, he's interested already. I'm so happy!"

"Now can you go talk to him?"

She blushes and lowers her eyes. "Absolutely not."

I have to go help Mama with the food, and when I get back to Žana, I see the most amazing sight. My sister, who was so anxious and trembling about the idea of talking with Haris, is now surrounded by boys! She's laughing and gesturing, telling them some funny story I can't hear from here. And the boys are entranced! This is the Žana I like to see.

"Is that your cousin Žana?" asks a voice beside me.

I startle and turn to find Haris. "Yes, that's her."

He smiles as he watches her, and my heart lurches for Žana. He's interested, this is it!

"I think I'll go check out those two-colored eyes you told me about," he says, and heads over to compete with the other boys for her attention.

But then...

Is she turning into a magician? I see her glance up, spot Haris, and all of a sudden, she's gone. Using the cluster of boys as cover, she's slipped away. I catch a glimpse of her going into the changing room.

I sigh. *Oh, Žana, what am I going to do with you? He's just a boy, even if he's the one you like.*

I don't go after her right away because I don't know what to say. Instead I eat some ćevapi with the boys. Haris looks around for her a bit but then stays and talks to his friends. I hear the buzz of a Vespa, and soon another boy arrives. His friends introduce him as Orač, explaining that his name is really Mirsad but they call him Orač for his last name, Oračević. He has brown hair and large, gentle gray eyes.

All of a sudden, just for a second, I feel a flash of what Žana must feel. Seeing Orač makes me a little queasy, a little breathless. For a moment I feel like I ran too far or like I'm about to give an important speech in front of a huge crowd.

It passes quickly, but now I think I understand. How can looking at a boy change the way I breathe, the way I think?

I don't know if I like it. It is intoxicating, but I don't like not being in control.

Whatever I'm struck with, it doesn't hit me as hard as it did Žana. In a moment I recover, and I can chat with the boys and eat my ćevapi as usual. Sejla comes, and Belma and Ćućana, and later we go find Žana where she's sulking in the changing room under the poster of Samantha Fox.

"I'm so foolish," she moans, half laughing, half crying. "But when I saw him coming I panicked."

"Silly little cousin," the sophisticated Sejla says, ruffling Žana's hair. "Welcome to love."

19

THAT NIGHT WE have a strategy meeting. Belma, Sejla, Vedrana, and I all sprawl on the floor mattresses and give Žana advice. Some of it is silly—Vedrana thinks Žana should pretend to be hurt or even drown so that Haris can save her. Some of it is clueless—my advice is simply that she should talk to him and they can see if they like each other. Belma thinks she should pretend to be interested in one of Haris's friends to make him jealous. Sejla's advice is the most practical—she wants to orchestrate seemingly accidental meetings so that Haris can fall in love himself and make the first move.

"Because it's obvious you're never going to be brave enough to do it yourself, Žana," Sejla chides. "You'll have to trick him into pursuing you. In fact, you should ignore him completely. That's what really drives boys wild."

"How can I ignore him when he's all I think about?" Žana moans.

I wonder about all of Žana's worry, all her schemes. When I saw Orač, I had an immediate reaction. Maybe love is instantaneous and all the plans and schemes in the world can't make it happen. If Haris meets Žana and feels it, he feels it. If he doesn't, he doesn't.

Just then we hear a timid knock downstairs. I check my clock. It's after ten. Who could be dropping by this late?

Žana, with the predictable, illogical leaps of love, says, "Maybe it's Haris." We just roll our eyes and go down to investigate.

I open the door to find Hana, a huddled little bundle of tears, staring at her feet. When she looks up, her left eye is a livid bruise of blue and purple and black.

"They left us," she sobs. "M-my father and mother l-left us alone!"

I pull her inside and, between her tears and wails, I get the whole story.

Without telling them until the last second, her parents went to Germany for the whole summer, leaving their kids to take care of themselves. She doesn't know if it is for fun or business deals, but whatever their reason, they don't want their children around. So without making any arrangements, they just abandoned them, trusting that they'll be alive in three months' time.

"I took my little sister to my aunt's house, but she can't take all of us, she doesn't have the money or the room. They left us a little money, but Mahmut says it isn't nearly enough. He's the one who does all the cooking, you know. Oh Amra, can I stay here? Please? I won't be any trouble, really. I'll just eat leftovers, I can sleep in the kitchen, the garage even..."

We cluster around her, petting and reassuring her. "Of course you can stay," I tell her without even having to ask Mama and Tata. I know they'll welcome her, not just for the night but for the whole summer. Some families are dangerous, but ours is a sanctuary of safety.

"Who gave you that shiner?" Sejla asks, turning Hana's head to take a closer look at her eye.

Hana hangs her head, and I know she doesn't want to say.

"We know it was your dad," Žana chimes in. "What happened?"

"I didn't adjust the curtain right," she says miserably. "He told me to close it and I left a little crack by accident. He said the neighbors could all see in. So he … he …" She covers her face. "He said he was giving me something to remind me to behave while they're away. That's the first I heard they were going. Oh, Amra, why can't I do anything right? Why can't I be good enough? I try so hard!"

I look at my cousins in shock. She thinks it's *her* fault?

Hana sleeps on the floor with us where we sprawl out like a litter of puppies. She falls asleep before I do. The last thing I see before I close my own eyes is the look of peace on Hana's face. She'll stay with us for a few days, then go to an aunt's house. But we'll have a sanctuary for her whenever she wants to come and stay. For the summer, at least, she is safe.

WE SETTLE INTO a happy routine: rising mid-morning, heading to the river when the sun is properly high enough to sunbathe. Most of the time Mama shows up later with lunch, and Tata comes, too. He tells me that he's been given a vacation of several weeks, and at first this feels wonderful. I have my Tata with me every day. But after a while I start to grow concerned. He has a high-level job. How can he be away from it for so long? But he tells me not to worry, and with so much going on it is easiest just to trust him.

The older teens at Brvice call us the gang, the inseparables, the

sisterhood, because where you find one of us you find all of us ...
except sometimes Vedrana, who alternates between rowdy play
with Dino, and pretending to be much more grown up with us.

After leaving Brvice, we almost always go downtown to
dance and sing in the evenings. Every night, sunburned and
weary, we slather our red skin with cooling yogurt and talk late
into the night, falling asleep at last to the tart-sweet smell on
our skin, resting to be ready for another wonderful day.

And every day, my worries and sorrows and troubles fade farther and farther behind me. Gradually, I begin to think that life is
nothing but sun and fun and friendship.

Žana seems to dominate our group with her passion for Haris,
her need for him. Dino and Maše have earned five or six ice
creams so far. Haris isn't dating anyone. He prefers very tall girls.
He asked about Amra's cousin again. He wishes he could meet her.
With each new tidbit Žana's spirits soar, then crash again when
she realizes she's still too afraid to make a move. She is so open
and loud about her love story that she all but drowns out my own
small crush.

I can't stop thinking about Orač's beautiful eyes. I wish I could
stare into them for hours to figure out their intriguing color.
From a distance they look gray, but up close they are a pale
pigeon-blue with a hint of caramel.

My interest was sparked by my first glimpse but is strength-
ened by something that happens midway through the summer.
Žana has by now exchanged a few words with Haris and can be
in his presence without passing out or running away. Sejla is still
secretly seeing Slobodan. Belma has a pretty, casual boy she's

been seeing but says she doesn't love him—that it's just a summer fling. And I think they are too obsessed with love, feeling just a little bit superior because I haven't been bitten by this bug.

And then...

It is late in the afternoon. Most people have left the river already, to get ready for the night life. We're crossing some of the waterfalls to get back to the right side of the river. Omer, a tall handsome basketball player is there, helping Žana and the others cross the slippery rocks. Omer looks like a Muslim version of Žana's father, exceptionally tall with square features, though his nature is much kinder and his demeanor far more gentle. Gorgeous as Omer is, she has no trouble talking to him. She's throwing her head back, laughing. Wait, is she flirting? Maybe she's getting over her Haris obsession.

I'm far behind them—I forgot my bag and went back for it. I'm so busy watching Žana and Omer that I'm not careful with my footing. There are holes and crevices in the porous rock, eroded by centuries of flowing water. It's hard to tell the difference between firm ground and slippery moss and hidden crevices. One moment I'm on solid rock, the next my foot plunges through flimsy moss and I'm tumbling into one of the hidden caves that pocket the stones and falls. I splay out my arms and catch myself before I'm lost, but my legs feel crushed against the rocks.

"Help!" I cry out, but they're too far ahead to hear me over the loud rush of water. Suddenly I feel strong arms scoop me up like I weigh nothing.

"Are you okay?" a tender voice asks, and I look up into eyes as dark and deep as the Una at night. Orač is crouching protectively

over me, stretching out my legs, checking the damage. In a panic
I have to check the damage, too—did my bikini slip out of place?
No, thank goodness.

"I'm...ow!" I can't be brave—it hurts too much. Right before my
eyes I see dark, blue-purple bruises swelling on my legs like mushroom caps. Those legs that my friends have been telling me are so
pretty, that enemies like Azra have been looking at with envy all
summer, are now hideous.

"Let me see if anything is broken." I watch him as he holds my
feet, rotating each ankle in turn, then moves up to my knees. It
is like paradise and hell, the pain of my legs and the thrill of his
attention. "Is that okay? Can you move them?" He moves higher
to the next joint, my hips, and suddenly we both freeze. He gives
an embarrassed laugh. If anyone wants to check the mobility of
joints above my thighs, they'll have to have a medical degree.

"I don't think anything is broken. But it hurts...a lot!" I have to
bite my lip to keep from crying out.

"Your legs are starting to bruise already. Here. And here. And
here." He touches each place lightly, like the feather of a dove.

"I thought I was going to drown," I gasp. I feel like I'm choking
just thinking about getting caught in the rocks under the water,
and my throat tightens. I'm going to pass out.

"Should I get your friends?"

"No! Stay with me."

"You'll be okay," he says. "Just rest a bit. Can't you swim, then?
I'm sure I've watched you swim."

I'm startled out of my fear. Watched, not seen? He's watched me?

"I...I almost drowned once." I don't want to admit it was my own cousin Azra who tried to drown me. I'm a good swimmer, but ever since then I have nightmares about drowning, about being stuck in the rocks or held down under water. "Ouch!" I try to shift my legs, but a pain stabs through me.

"You need to get to the bank. Can you walk?"

I don't know if it is the pain or the fact that he's so close to me, but my legs don't want to work.

"Here, this will be easier," he says as he scoops me up. I try to protest that I'm too big, but before I know it I'm snuggled against his chest being carried to the river's edge. He sets me down on a bed of moss and, to my confusion, takes off his shirt. What is happening? Am I dreaming this?

"Nothing's broken, but you're badly bruised. The cold will help keep the swelling and bruising down. I'd say put your legs in the Una, but under the circumstances I don't think you'd like that." He kneels at the water's edge and dips his shirt in, soaking it. Then he lays the cold cloth on my injured legs. When the breeze picks up and hits them, my legs go almost numb.

Orač stays with me for nearly an hour, telling me jokes to distract me. Neither of us says anything that we wouldn't say in front of our grandmothers, and yet I've never felt so close to a boy before. I want this to last forever, and when Žana finally comes looking for me, I'm almost disappointed.

Orač leaves me in her care, parting with a long backward look. I'm left breathless. Žana, catching my excitement, makes me tell her everything. Before I know it, I'm in the changing room with all of my cousins and Hana, too, analyzing every detail of this encounter, every word he spoke, until they have me practically convinced that we'll be married by the end of summer! Which is silly because I'm not even twelve yet.

All that day, I think about him. All that night, my sleep is filled with strange movies featuring Orač in the lead role, sometimes as hero, sometimes as villain, so I wake up confused. Today I get to see him! Today I get to talk to him! I find excuses to bring up his name.

But when I see him the next morning he says hello, asks how my legs are, and ... nothing more.

The next time I see him, he waves from across the river but doesn't seek me out.

The third day I find him, corner him, and talk about the carefully curated subjects of conversations I spent all last night planning, things he'll find interesting, clever, and alluring.

And Orač is the most terrible thing: polite.

He listens to me patiently. He answers me in more than monosyllables but doesn't ask me questions or come up with new topics. There are long silences until I think of something else to say. He smiles, and his eyes are kind ... but they are missing the spark I was hoping for.

He's a nice boy. He likes me. He's friendly. But he doesn't feel anything more for me than he would feel for any other pleasant girl.

I never before felt that awful gulf between politeness and true interest, and it is crushing.

It is only weeks later that Žana whispers the truth. He *was* interested, but his best friend Asmir—my cousin—doesn't want him to have anything to do with me. They are in high school, I am younger, and he doesn't think it is appropriate.

"You could talk to him, tell him you know he likes you and that he shouldn't be controlled by anybody," Žana tells me. But I don't have the courage to do that, and do I even want someone who isn't brave enough to want me?

That night, I weep in Žana's arms while she strokes my hair and promises me I'll find true love someday.

VLADIMIR HAS BEEN in love with me since fourth grade. He's a nerd, too, but the boring kind who likes to spout off about things he thinks are interesting without bothering to notice if his audience cares. It's fine for people to be so excited about their passions, but they should still notice when their friends are zoning out. And then there are people who can make anything interesting. Vladimir isn't particularly funny or entertaining, so no matter how smart he is, his conversation comes off as an endless drone.

Once, in the fourth grade, he'd come up to me and told me that I was his girlfriend now. What arrogance, to tell and not ask! No matter how much I'd told him I wasn't, he insisted. Did he think he could wear me down? He'd told everyone I was his girlfriend, and no matter how much I'd denied it, it was something people would ask me about for the rest of the year. He made me feel trapped. It didn't seem fair that someone could claim ownership of me like that.

Eventually he gave up. But this summer it starts all over again. He's good friends with Mahmut, Hana's brother. Now that Hana is staying with me and we're together a lot, Vladimir feels like he has some automatic connection to me. Now that he's older, it's even worse.

He's arrogant and swaggering. His grandfather is a Serb priest, and his father has some position in the Yugoslav People's Army. Vladimir likes to strut around telling people what to do and think. He's good-looking, too, and he knows it. Now that he has Hana as an excuse to approach me, he's relentless. Every day he comes to sit with me on the rocks. I'm polite, but he doesn't get the message like I did with Orač. Or he'll swim over to me and grab my feet, threatening to pull me in. It's something a lot of the boys do to tease the girls, and most of the time we don't mind, we just giggle and splash one another. But the way Vladimir does it is creepy. He doesn't even really try to pull me in, he just holds on to me like a leash.

At first, none of the others notice how much I hate it. All the girls squeal when it happens to them. I usually do, too, if another boy is doing it. Most of the time it is fun and innocent, so they don't see that this is something different, and no one intervenes when I shriek and kick. They don't see how he holds me like I belong to him. Like his privileged position entitles him to touch me. If he tried to hug me or kiss me against my will my cousins would yell at him, the other boys would punch him. But they don't think him grabbing my feet is a threat. And I don't know how to make him stop.

He thinks he's flirting, winning me over. But even though I

sometimes cry after, I wonder if it is serious enough to tell any-one about. It's just my feet, right?

Finally one day, when he's holding my ankles, I find the cour-age to say loudly and calmly, "Vladimir, I don't want you touching me anymore. I don't like it. I'm not interested in you that way. Please leave me alone."

He stares at me like he can't believe his ears. Finally, with everyone watching, he drops my feet. "She's just playing hard to get," he snickers to save face. But he never grabs my feet again.

I think it's over. Later that weekend I'm having a sleepover with all the cousins. It's hot and the balcony is open, the curtain blowing gently in the night breeze. When we hear a song out-side, we think it must be a neighbor's radio. It's a famous song by Bijelo Dugme called "I've Agreed to Be Everything She Wants."

> *I've agreed to be everything she wants,*
> *here I am selling my soul to my devil*
>
> . . .

But it's not a recording. "What on earth?" I say, and fling the curtain all the way open to find Vladimir, Mahmut, and a couple of other boys beneath my window.

"It's just like *Romeo and Juliet!*" Belma sighs. "Being serenaded at your balcony!"

But Žana sees my annoyance. "Who is it, Amra?" she asks.

"Vladimir," I say with dismay.

With more enthusiasm than talent, he's belting out the lyrics of the despairing love song while his friends sing backup and play guitar and tambourine. Vladimir is gesturing passionately, throwing his arms wide and then clutching his heart in pantomime agony.

"Go away!" I hiss at him.

He ignores me and keeps singing.

"Oh my goodness, he's drunk!" Žana realizes. There's no legal age for alcohol in Bosnia. Most teens try it once or twice, but it is discouraged, and no one I know ever drinks. Most would get in major trouble. Vladimir thinks he's immune to trouble, though, and keeps on singing.

"Stop it right now!" I command as loud as I dare. My parents will hear at any moment, and they'll think I want this! What boy would come and serenade a girl if she didn't give him some kind of encouragement? He's trying to trap me again.

"Amra, I'm not going to leave until you agree to go out with me!" he slurs loudly from below.

"How romantic!" Belma swoons.

"No, it's not! Vladimir, hear me now! I will never go out with you! I never liked you that way, and now I don't like you at all! Get that through your thick head!" It's hard for me to be so blunt, but I'm learning you can't be gentle with some people.

Then, to my horror, I hear a knock at my bedroom door. My parents.

"Amra," Mama calls. "Turn down your TV, it's way too loud. I like Bijelo Dugme, too, but you'll wake the neighborhood."

I'm saved! She thinks it's just the TV! How she thinks that is beyond me. My TV is a tiny yellow bubble from the 1960s with a giant antenna, a fuzzy black-and-white picture, and a scratchy sound you can just barely hear. She must be half-asleep. But I thank my lucky stars I'm not in trouble with her ... yet. If only I can stop that silly, selfish, arrogant Vladimir!

It is Žana who saves me. When Mama is gone, Žana slips down the hall to the bathroom and comes back a moment later with the big bucket of chocolate spread. The spread is all gone—it was soaking clean in the tub—but the bucket's not empty.

"Cool off, boys!" she shouts, and flings the entire bucket of frigid water right on Vladimir's head.

Well, no boy can be romantic looking like a half-drowned rat. He slinks home, and peace is restored to the neighborhood.

I'm really upset at first—how dare he? But under the giggles of my cousins and friends, I start to see the humor of it. Before long, I'm laughing along with them. People might think they can tell me what to do, but with a little help, I'm learning to assert myself. Žana especially gives me the confidence to say what I want, to be who I am. No silly boy can force me to do anything.

As I drift off to sleep around 2:00 A.M., I think about the two contrasting experiences: the boy I want who doesn't want me and the boy who wants me who I don't want. Both make me a little melancholy, but it's a different kind of sadness than any I've experienced before. There's a spice to it. It is almost a pleasure to feel these pangs, because they are new, and because they show me that I can feel so much more than I could a year ago.

20

ŽANA AND VEDRANA'S parents travel back and forth from Belgrade to Bihać all summer. In Bihać, they are staying with Feza, another of Žana's aunts, but today they join us at Brvice. Her father, Đorđe, acts like he's making a big concession by going with us, like he's Sultan Suleiman mingling with the peasants. He sits at the long table on the island, choosing for himself the place of honor and the best bits of food, and argues with anyone who tries to talk with him. What makes him so arrogant? It can't be education. My parents are both well-educated and they respect everyone. We Bosnians love a good argument—with the emphasis on *good*. Arguing can be fun if it is a friendly debate and about something minor like whether cheese or beef is tastier in a pie. But Žana's dad has a way of talking that implies anyone with a different opinion is a fool and not worth listening to. Her mom frequently points out that he has a PhD, as if this makes him the supreme authority on everything.

Tata steers the conversation away from some dangerous topics, and diplomatic Mama smooths everything over whenever tensions threaten to get too high.

"How is work going?" she asks when Đorđe gets red in the face over some question about inflation that I don't really understand.

Đorđe loves to talk about himself, but he never gives many

details about his work. All l know is that it's something at the military airport.

"Just fine," he says shortly, and seems about to launch into a tirade about the economy when my little brother Dino comes to the rescue. He worships Đorđe solely because he knows all about planes. Besides that first toy plane he gave Dino, he's also presented him with big posters of military planes—a Galeb (seagull), an Orao (eagle), and a Russian Mig. He brought them after hearing that Dino won a top prize for building and flying his own model glider. Dino has the posters taped to his walls and stares at them for hours, memorizing every detail and dreaming of flying one someday. As far as Dino's concerned, if a man knows about planes, he has to be good, just like his Tetak Ale who started the Aero Klub. Since we were little we'd help him organize glider competitions for the local kids. We would build bigger and better planes out of paper or light wood and compete to see whose could go the farthest or fly the longest time. We have an air current over the city, the Bihać wave, that lets gliders stay aloft without a motor. People from all over the world come here to fly their gliders—real ones, not the toys the kids make.

Aero Klub is one of the reasons l know Haris so well—and another reason Dino likes following him around. Maše, Haris, and his younger brother all competed. l remember long summer days running through big open meadows with them, chasing down our gliders and later lying in the flowers and grass. We'd stare at the clouds, at the gliders soaring through the blue, so quiet and peaceful, and wonder what our lives would be like. Haris, a little older, was in charge of selling ice cream at these events. At the end of the day we'd beg him for leftovers and then sit together watching the sun set, eating mushy melting ice cream cones. I should tell Žana—she might develop a sudden passion for airplanes!

Once Tetak Ale took Dino up in a real plane and he's been hooked ever since. To Dino, planes are about joy and freedom and fun. But when Žana's father talks about planes, they seem to be about work and war.

Đorđe indulgently answers all of Dino's aviation questions. Neither of his children care at all about what he does, so I think he's glad that one young relative is interested. He brought another toy plane for Dino this summer. Last time it was a model commercial jet. This time it is a military plane, complete with detachable missiles.

Now Dino sees his opening and squeezes in beside Đorđe. "What's the biggest plane you've ever seen?" Đorđe tells him all about a huge Russian cargo plane that he says can hold an entire herd of elephants. This sounds a little far-fetched to me, but Dino's eyes light up, and Đorđe, who is a sucker for attention, talks more about his job than ever before. No one else is really listening—they're just glad Đorđe is distracted so they can talk about more peaceful things—but Dino is rapt and I listen, too.

"So you study the airports so you can blow them up?" Dino asks. "I don't get it."

"Well, if there is a war, we can't let our enemies use our airports, right?"

"I guess not. Who are our enemies?" Dino asks. I was wondering the same thing.

"Anyone who wants to end our way of life. We have a long,

proud history, you know. Many times before, invaders have come to our lands, imposing their will on us. Empires have stolen our land. Like the Ottomans. And look at them now!" He gives a self-satisfied chuckle, as if he had been personally responsible for the collapse of the Ottoman Empire.

Other countries have invaded our land through the centuries—Romans, Austrians, Hungarians, Germans, and Croatians. Why does he single out the Ottomans? The Ottomans won't be invading us any time soon. Their empire hasn't existed for generations. I feel like I'm seeing puzzle pieces scattered across a table, slowly arranging themselves but not quite forming a complete picture yet.

We don't learn very much about that period of our history in school. Most of what I know comes from Mama, who would sit with us in front of the ceramic fireplace on long winter evenings when the electricity would go out, telling us stories. My brother and I would eat oranges, and I'd suck at my sticky fingers while the tart juice stung the cracks in the corners of my mouth. As the fire danced, her stories seemed to come to life, much more vital and interesting than anything they told us in class.

In school we learn, in a vague sort of way, that the Muslim Turks, the Ottoman Empire, conquered parts of Europe and then were eventually driven out. They don't teach us much about what happened when the Ottomans were in the Balkans. One story they do tell is that the Ottomans took many young people as slaves, stealing them away from their families. I remember coming home one day as a little girl, upset at the mere idea of anyone being torn from their families. Mama, who knows much more about history than she is allowed to teach in her classroom, had taken me on her lap and explained that though some children were taken from their parents, unlike slaves at that time in other parts of the world, they were sent to be educated and could even reach the highest positions in the government of the Ottoman Empire.

"They picked the best and brightest to go and study in Istanbul," Mama had told me. "It must have been hard for them to leave their families, but it is always hard, and children always leave eventually—for college, for jobs, for marriage. The Ottomans had slaves, and of course that was a terrible thing, but these children weren't slaves after they were educated. They got jobs in the army or the palace or as scholars, and so the people at the heart of the empire got to know and appreciate the worth of the Bosnian people."

That made me feel a lot better.

"No oppressor is ever truly kind to the oppressed," she'd continued. "If they are, it is out of their self-interest. But, at least the Ottomans believed in just laws for everyone, not just for Muslims. When they were here in Bosnia, every religion was protected. Some people became Muslim, but if they wanted to stay Christian, no one stopped them. The same couldn't be said for Christian rulers in other countries. Every Christian country persecuted other religions. Spain expelled the Jews and Muslims. English Protestants killed Catholics. French Catholics killed Huguenots. Here in Bosnia everyone was free to believe whatever they chose. Bosnia welcomed both Muslims and Jews who were expelled from Spain. In fact, Bosniaks preserved one of the

Jewish historic treasures, the Sarajevo Haggadah, for centuries including when Nazis wanted to destroy it during World War ll. A Bosniak hid it from Nazis in a mosque. Even when Nazis occupied our town, my grandfather and uncles did all they could to undermine and resist their rule. This is why one of my uncles ended up in a German camp and another became a leader and later a general in the resistance movement. We are proud that through history, we in particular, as a family, have always tried to do what is right, not what is easy."

l carried Mama's words throughout my childhood, but lately l've come to realize that she was talking about the Bosnia of long ago. Now, things are different. And it's not the Muslims making decisions about everyone else's rights. Her uncle who survived a German camp is now working in the family mill. l wonder why no one talks about him as a hero and why he never got a job after the war?

Dino is still asking Đorđe questions about the airport. He's entranced by planes and flight, but war sounds exciting to him, too. "What will happen if someone attacks us?" he asks.

"Just what happened to the Turks," he says, and makes a slicing gesture across his throat.

Dino's eyes open wide, terrified and delighted, but to him it is just a story. He doesn't realize that by "Turks," Đorđe doesn't just mean Ottomans from centuries ago but Muslims who are Bosniaks.

Muslims like us.

It makes me wonder what my cousin's father sees when he looks at me.

"You see, if there's ever a war, it is my duty to…" He breaks off suddenly, and for the first time I see his look of absolute confidence falter. He looks around at the crowd, his family by marriage. Then he shrugs and smiles to himself. Only Dino and I are listening. Everyone else is sick of the sound of his voice, happy to tune him out. We're just kids, what does it matter what we hear?

And so he goes on, telling Dino about how the airport will be blown up, how many tons of explosives it will take, happy that this kid is interested, maybe wishing he had a son he could train to be like him. He likes Dino, I know it. Who could not like Dino, so happy and open? So why does Đorđe talk about slicing the throats of Muslims, even hundreds of years ago? He loves his Muslim wife, his half-Muslim children.

I think of all of Mama's private history lessons and want to tell him that the Muslims in Bosnia aren't invaders. We aren't Ottomans who decided to stay. We are the native Bosnians of the area who simply decided to change their religion long ago. The Christian church was never strong in Bosnia back then. The Ottomans were sophisticated, educated, the elite of Bosnia when they came, and the elites in Bosnia accepted Islam. *We aren't aliens, Đorđe,* I could tell him. We are your neighbors and cousins and friends, then as now.

"But don't worry, little man," he says, ruffling Dino's blond hair. "Our army is too powerful to be beaten. If we decide to fight anyone, it will be over, just like that!" He snaps his fingers, and Dino grins, so happy to have such an interesting, strong relative to talk to.

I go join Žana and Hana and Sejla at the other end of the table.

They're sitting peculiarly, hunched over, with Žana in the middle. Are they whispering some secret? What could it be?

"Oh, Amra, perfect!" Žana says when she sees me. "Come here and take Hana's place. You're taller. Hana, you can be the lookout."

I'm completely confused. But I do as I'm told.

"There," Žana says. "Now there's no way he can possibly see me."

"Who?" Though I should have known. Haris, of course. "I thought you got over hiding from him." They've been hanging out in a casual way that has Žana simultaneously elated and devastated. She's happy because every moment she gets to spend with Haris is like liquid gold dripping into a cauldron for her to stir for the rest of the day when he's not with her. And she's sad because he's never there for long, and he never treats her as anything more than a friend. She has no idea how to take it to the next level. With us, she talks a big game of grabbing him and kissing him someday. But whenever they're sitting on the rocks or swimming together she just waits for him to give her even the tiniest hint that he's falling for her.

"Usually I want to see him, but not today."

"Why?" I ask, still not getting it.

"Oh, Amra, can't you see? I look hideous!"

I stare at her. I see her suntanned skin, her glorious sun-kissed hair, her arresting eyes, her lips glossy with cherry balm . . . and a swollen red lump right in the middle of her forehead. "You mean *that*?"

"Waaaaa!" she cries, and puts her head down on the table, burying it under her arms.

"She found it while we were in the mill," Hana explained. "When she popped it, it looked like a crime scene."

"A horror movie," Sejla adds. "White pus everywhere. Like an alien exploded."

A whimper comes from Žana's pile of misery.

"And now it's worse than ever," Hana concludes. "All splotchy and red over half her forehead. And I think it is filling up again."

"Noooo!" Žana wails.

"Can't you cover it up or something?" I ask. Žana always brings her makeup to the river, and Hana probably has hers, too. Between them they have enough for a whole beauty salon.

"I tried," Žana says, lifting her head at last. "It just makes a putty-colored mountain, and then it starts leaking through. What am I going to do? Yesterday I asked him to meet me here for lunch!"

"It's really not that bad," I try to tell her, but even as I look at it, it seems to grow right before my eyes, like one of those volcanoes that erupt out of the ocean to make a new island. But I can't tell her that.

Sejla, though, has no problem saying, "I think there's another one starting next to it."

"It's having a baby!" Hana laughs, clapping her hands.

"Oh, you're all so mean!" Žana says, but she can't help laughing, too. "I have a whole pimple ecosystem!"

"What's the big deal?" Sejla asks. "We all get pimples. It's part of life."

"But I want to be perfect for him. How will he ever ask me out when I look like this?"

"I have to tell you a secret about pimples," I say, and lean in close to whisper, so they all have to dip their heads in, too. I wait a while, looking serious, making them think I must have a secret acne cure, some old village granny's potion. Looking around as if I don't want anyone to overhear this momentous news, I say, "*Even Haris gets pimples.* Yes! I've seen it with my own eyes. Just this spring he had a big one on the side of his nose. There was no hiding it. Žana, my sister, if he likes you at all he won't suddenly think less of you because you have a pimple." Even one that looks like a lava-filled archipelago.

"Really?" she asks hopefully.

"Truly," I answer, and I hope it is true. I've known Haris for a long time, and I don't think he's shallow. He might look like a movie star with his classic cheekbones, strong jaw, and wavy caramel-colored hair with summer-blond streaks, but I think he's an easygoing guy. In fact, I think he's so easygoing that he wouldn't bother disturbing the status quo with anyone. If he's enjoying being friends with Žana, it probably wouldn't occur to him to do anything more than that. I think it will be up to Žana to make the first move—a theory I've shared with her before. She's still working up her courage. Today definitely won't be the day!

"Maybe if we just give it a little squeeze," Žana suggests.

"That's how this all started," Sejla says. "You could hardly see it before you started messing with it."

While they talk about what to do, I hear Žana's father raise his voice again at the other end of the long table. Žana doesn't even look up. She's so used to him being occasionally loud and rude that she tunes it out, like the drone from a beehive.

"Agrokomerc was corrupt from day one!" he bellows, and I sigh. People around town have been talking about nothing but Agrokomerc for days now.

Agrokomerc is one of the biggest, most profitable businesses in Yugoslavia. It started as a little chicken farm just over the border in Croatia right after World War II, but since then it has expanded to be a huge industry in our part of Bosnia. It employs thousands and thousands of people who raise and sell chickens, turkeys, and rabbits. It makes chocolate and condiments and salami and every food you can imagine, selling them not just in Yugoslavia but all around Europe. It has become central to Bosnia's economy. The company constructs roads, gives scholarships to the poor for higher education, and builds chicken farms that are helping our region grow out of poverty.

At first, when people started talking about the big fire that broke out at Agrokomerc earlier this year, I didn't pay much attention, except to worry what might happen to all those poor chickens. Now, I hear people say that the fire was set on purpose, so the government would have an excuse to investigate the company.

"Those Pozderac brothers have been lining their own pockets and helping that Abdić gain power, too," Žana's father continues in his authoritative voice. "You'll see. They'll all end up in jail—or worse." I half expect him to do that throat-slicing gesture again.

I don't really know what to think about the Agrokomerc affair. Some people say they weren't doing anything that every other company wasn't doing. Others, like Žana's dad, say they are criminals. I've heard different stories about Abdić, and I don't know what to think about him. Some people say he is playing all sides for his own gain. One day when I ask Tata about it, he doesn't talk about money or investments or promissory notes. In fact, he won't talk with me about it at all. But later that night he talks with Mama about my questions, and I overhear.

"I could have told her, Amra, we aren't a very rich region, are we?" Tata says, imagining our conversation. "We have one big business, that's all. Do you know what we *do* have here? Intellectuals. Thinkers. Diplomats. Teachers. Negotiators. People with ideas who can get other people to agree with those ideas. Do you know what else we have a lot of here in this part of Yugoslavia? Muslims. I don't have all the answers, but think: Who would it benefit to take away the money and the thinkers, eh? Who would want to strip the Bosnian Muslims of what little they have?"

"I'm glad you didn't talk with her about it," Mama says that night. "She doesn't need more worries." Now, I hear Žana's father saying that he's glad Agrokomerc is failing and the people in power are being removed. He doesn't say Muslims outright, but everybody knows Agrokomerc is run by Muslims and has lifted more Muslims out of poverty than any other.

"Don't worry," Žana's father concludes with a smug air. "Slobodan Milošević will see to it that any counter-revolutionaries get what's coming to them."

I've been hearing that name more and more often, hearing his voice on the radio and seeing his puffy face on TV. Most of our news comes from Belgrade. At first, I didn't pay much attention. His name made me think of Sejla's Slobodan. Then later he started saying things that made Mama and Tata exchange worried looks, and I listened harder to what he was saying. He said things that almost—*almost*—sounded like what every politician says. *There has to be room for everyone in Yugoslavia. This is our homeland.* But subtly, and getting more obvious with each speech, he makes it clear that what he really means is that there has to be room for Serbs in Yugoslavia. That this is the Serb homeland.

"Counter-revolutionary" is the worst thing you can accuse someone of being here. The revolution—communism—was supposed to bring about a better life for everyone, the brotherhood and unity that Yugoslavia officially stands for. Anyone who is against that is an enemy of the state. It is a charge that no one ever returns from. But what does it mean to be an enemy of the state? That could be anything the state decides it is on any given day, right? It depends who is in charge of the state. The opinions of Belgrade seem to matter more than those of Bihać.

I think of my father's fear, of his long "vacation" from work, and though the day is warm, I shiver.

"Žana, stop picking at your face!" Žana's mother suddenly shouts out across the table. Everyone falls silent, then from here and there I hear giggles that people try to stifle.

"Mom!" Žana shrieks, and runs off in mortification. Of course, we go after her.

21

WE RUN TO the place where we know we'll find safety and comfort and acceptance.

"Come in," Dika calls without hesitation when we rap on the door, not even asking who is there. "Ćućana went out to look for her dad. Oh, you girls know you never have to knock. Come in any time, day or night. The door is always unlocked." This is typical of the Bosnian attitude, but even more necessary for Dika this summer because it has become harder and harder for her to walk, even around the house. She might not be able to unlock the door to a visitor... and if she falls, someone might have to break the door down to help her. So she leaves it unlocked. It's perfectly safe. Whatever other problems we might have, burglary isn't usually one of them.

"Oh, Dika, I'm doomed!" Žana says melodramatically and throws herself down on the couch beside Dika's little nest. She has everything within arm's reach: blankets, coffee, snacks, pills, and books.

"What is it this time?" Dika asks with an indulgent smile. "The end of the world, right? That's how it is at your age, I remember. Everything is the end of the world."

Žana blurts out her problem.

"Can't see your true love because you're not perfect, eh?" she asks. "Let me tell you, if he can't handle you when you have a few problems, he's not worth having. No matter how much you love him, it isn't real unless he's worthy of you." Dika knows this better than anybody.

"It feels real," Žana murmurs, already distracted by a tin of mixed cookies. She's digging through them for her favorite kind.

"Why don't you join me in a cigarette, and we can figure out your troubles together? Do you want one, Amra?"

My mouth gapes at her. Is she really giving us permission to smoke right in front of her? "No, thank you," I say as politely as if she offered me coffee.

"It's terrible for me, I know. But how much worse could I get?" She gestures to her wasting body and laughs. I guess when most of your life is pain, you embrace the small pleasures even if they are bad for you. I think of Amar's love of sweets. When I look a little shocked at this too she winks at me and adds, "Don't give anyone else a chance to laugh at you—always laugh at yourself first. It shuts them right up."

With a defiant look, Žana accepts a light from Dika and takes a puff. Dika leans comfortably back and blows a perfect smoke ring like the most elegant dragon.

"What do I do about this pimple?" Žana asks.

"First of all, don't worry about not meeting Haris for lunch. When he shows up and you're not there waiting for him, it will only make him want you more. If boys think you care too much they sometimes lose interest. But if you appear indifferent or even run away, they're more likely to chase you. They're like dogs, really. The only problem is figuring out whether they're lap dogs or guard dogs or good, honest, working dogs."

"But once he sees me like this he'll never want to look at me again," Žana wails. "Should I try to squeeze it again? It keeps filling up, a never-ending supply of pus. My mom says I should never pop them, it only makes it worse. She says that's why I have bad skin. I guess she was right."

"That's the last thing a girl needs—for her mother to be right!" Dika chortles. "So many people will tell you what not to do. The strange thing is, they mostly tell you not to do the things that feel the best. Now, some of those things are truly bad for you. But other things, well…Let me tell you, there are few pleasures as great as popping a really ripe zit."

We gasp and giggle. Only Dika says exactly what she thinks and feels.

"I remember I had a huge one on my chin," Dika continues. "Not when I was a teen, either—just a couple of years ago. It's awful to be at the age where you get both pimples *and* wrinkles! Now, your mom is right about one thing. You shouldn't mess with a pimple when it is just starting out. The secret is all in the timing. You have to watch that pimple like a cat watches a mouse hole, waiting for the perfect moment. Let it grow…and grow… and grow…until you just can't bear it any more and you're sure it will explode and take out half the neighborhood!"

We shiver in disgust but laugh at the same time.

We are all human, we all have bodies that can be incredibly gross. Maybe it feels so good because the gross things are what binds every human together. Rich and poor, Serb and Bosniak, we all get huge pimples that we just have to pop.

"That makes me feel better, but it doesn't help with Haris," Žana says when we all stop laughing.

"Oh, that's easy to fix. Go in the bathroom and pop whatever is left. Your tiny little minnow of a zit will never compare to the mighty whale that was on my chin. It only feels huge to you because it's yours. Yes, I know it will get all red afterward. All you have to do is jump into the Una and swim for half an hour. The cold will make it shrink right down to nothing. Don't you know that models plunge their face in ice water every morning? The Una is almost as cold. Whatever redness is left will just look like you're flushed from the cold water or the sun. Believe me, if Haris doesn't think you look perfect after that he's a fool!"

Just then the door opens. We think it must be Ćućana. But to my horror, it is Žana's mom. Like a flash, Žana throws her still-smoldering cigarette into the ashtray. Dika looks like butter wouldn't melt in her mouth.

"Dika, you shouldn't smoke in front of the girls. It sets a bad example. What is this, two cigarettes? Žana, if you were smoking I'll take you back to Belgrade and never let you leave the house again!"

Žana looks panicked at being caught, but Dika doesn't bat an eyelash. "Of course they're not smoking. What do you take me for? They're mine."

"Both of them?" Žana's mom asks skeptically.

Dika shrugs. "You know me. My mind is getting worse and worse. I light one, set it down, and then forget I already have one and light another."

"Well, Žana, I just came to tell you that your father and I are leaving. If you want to stay, go back and look after your sister."

"Mom, we're at the river every day. Vedrana is just fine without me."

"Do as you're told," her mom says, and stomps away.

I think Žana only breathes again once she's gone. "You saved my life, Dika!"

"I knew she'd be silly enough to believe me. Too many people think the mind follows the body, that anyone with a disability has to be cognitively challenged, too. It's a shame … but if it helps my girls, why not use it to my advantage?"

We go back to the river, and as we leave Dika asks us to make sure Ćućana heads home if we see her. "She gets distracted so easily when she's out. At home she has her routines, but out in the world she forgets where she's going, distracted by some friend or a band playing or the beauty of the Una."

We don't see Ćućana, so we head to the rocks and slowly lower ourselves into the frigid water. Žana plunges her head under, holding her breath as long as possible to heal her angry blemish. And Dika was right! You can still see it, but now instead of looking like a huge red barnacle, it is no more than a subtle flesh-colored bump.

But it doesn't matter, because she sees Haris on the riverbank walking with a blonde girl named Ela, who is looking up adoringly with sparkling eyes, showing every last one of her teeth as she laughs at some joke he just told her. Žana ducks her head under the water again and lets out a scream from her soul. Only silent bubbles rise to the top.

"THEY'RE JUST FRIENDS," I tell her the next day for what must be the thousandth time. Žana is too devastated to sleep, to eat, to do anything.

"Not if she has anything to say about it. Did you see her? She was looking at him like a wolf looks at a lamb. She was practically licking her lips."

"That's just how Ela is," I tell her. "She flirts with everybody."

"Oh, what do you know?" Žana snaps at me, but immediately sees the surprise and hurt on my face. "Oh, I'm sorry, Amra! I don't mean to be such a beast. But you've never dated anyone. I need to talk to someone who knows about these things."

"Sejla?"

"She's only ever loved Slobodan, so she thinks every romance will be like hers. Besides, she's given all the advice she has. Oh, I know! What about Emir?" Emir is the son of her aunt Feza, who her mom and dad are staying with until the whole family leaves in a few days. The summer is almost over. Žana doesn't have much time to make her move.

"Emir might have good advice. I know he dated several people before he met his current girlfriend, and now they're in a relationship. He's older than us so he knows a lot. Yes, let's go talk to him, and maybe to his girlfriend, too. I'm sure they can help." I'm really not sure at all, but Žana is so desperate we'll try anything. Dino is already on the case, and if there is anything to discover about Ela, he'll earn more ice cream.

Žana's parents, aunt, and uncle are out, so we go there that evening. Žana is pouring her heart out to Emir.

"How do I tell him I love him? He's like no other boy in the world. When I talk to him the emotions well up so much that I lose my mind. It's like my heart overflows my brain, and I'm all feelings and no words. You don't understand how much I love him, Emir. I have to be with him. I'd do anything, absolutely anything to be with Haris." Her voice has risen to such a hysterical pitch that we don't hear Dida come home unexpectedly.

She storms into the kitchen where we're talking and shouts, "You are a Serb!" For a moment she huffs indignantly, as if that sentence says it all. After she catches her breath, she goes on. "You can't be falling in love with some Muslim boy from Bihać." I don't know which she says with more contempt, the word *Muslim*, or the name of our hometown. "You are worth more than that, Žana. I didn't leave this place behind me so that you could come back here to be trapped in the very net I escaped from. You might come here for the pretty river, but your life is in Belgrade. And always remember that you're a Serb—first, last, and always."

I can't believe I'm hearing her right. I'm in the corner, and its clear that Dida hasn't noticed me. I don't think she'd say these things if she knew I was in the room . . . but the fact remains that she's saying them.

I wait for Žana to storm and rage at her mom. *I'm half-Muslim,* she could say. *You're Muslim yourself,* she could remind her mom. This is the girl who defies her parents in everything, from sneaking out with friends to smoking cigarettes. Surely she'll defend her heritage, her history, the town her family came from.

Surely Žana will defend me. Everything her mom is ranting against, that's me.

But Žana says nothing, only grabs my hand and drags me out of the house like it's on fire. That's enough, right? I know Žana's heart. She might not have talked back to her mom right now, but I know she couldn't possibly feel the same way.

Still, she doesn't talk about it, not in that moment, not later that night. And somehow I can't find a way to bring it up.

IT RAINS FOR the next two days straight, so we don't go back to the river before she leaves.

At the train station, Žana squeezes me like she'll never let me go, like she'll grow roots and stay in Bihać forever. "You'll write to me every day, just like last year, won't you? I don't know what I'll do without my sister by my side. And you promise to tell me every single detail about Haris, don't you? Even if he winds up dating that Ela girl. I need to know everything. I need to plan for next summer!"

Žana's mother, overhearing, says, "Don't plan on anything, Žana. We might be going to Germany next summer."

"*You* can go to Germany," she says with a pout. "But *I'll* be here in Bihać with my sister."

My heart, which had broken a little the day Žana's mother condemned us, heals a little bit with these words. Right before she steps on the train Žana whispers, "Remember, think of me every day at 5:55 P.M."

Then she's off to Belgrade, waving out the train window, and I'm already counting the days until next summer.

"Don't worry, Amra," Mama tells me as she hugs me in consolation. "No matter how long it seems to take, summer always comes again."

But this time, I'm not so sure.

22

I STILL WRITE to Žana almost every day, but it is harder now. There is so much I don't say. Not, as before, because I don't know enough or understand the subtle dangerous currents that run through Bosnia...but because I'm starting to understand them all too well.

I don't tell her about the Bosniak politicians and business leaders who are speaking out for more equality and respect for Muslims. I don't tell her about the counter-rhetoric from Serb leaders. She can listen to the radio and watch reports on TV as well as I can. Unless maybe the news in Belgrade is different from the news in Bihać. Most of the news comes out of Belgrade anyway; they say what they want. But we do have a small local newspaper and radio. And just recently local politicians and community leaders have been trying to start a local television station.

I don't ask her why the Belgrade news is always talking negatively about Albanians in Kosovo. Some Albanians are Muslim, some are not. For some reason the news always calls Albanians "rapists" and says they're a danger to Serb girls.

The best cake shop in Bihać is, of course, my cousin Zuhra's, but the second best is Kod Trove, a shop run by an Albanian family. I don't know what the shop was originally called, but there are old cruel tendencies to put down Albanians, to call them unclean.

The owner got the cruel nickname Trovo, or "Poisoner" after someone who wanted to devalue Albanian businesses spread a rumor that he was poisoning people, so in defiance he changed the shop's name to Kod Trove—"At the Poisoner's"—and won the town over with the deliciousness of their delicacies. Their pistachio ice cream is really to die for, and their cakes are amazing enough to overpower racism. Their shop is near the apartment where we used to live, and whenever I had money I'd go get their "hairy cake"—a confection of fluffy dough dipped in chocolate and rolled in coconut. I'd eat until I either ran out of money or got a terrible stomachache. Even Zuhra would take me there before we went to the hairdresser's next door. They might be the competition, but they were too good for her to resist. Trovo and his wife are so nice and friendly, and I liked hearing them speak Albanian to each other in their shop. The Belgrade news said they shouldn't speak Albanian, though. I could ask Žana how this nice family could be a danger to any girl, except maybe to her digestion. No Albanian had ever done anything bad that I'd ever heard of.

I also don't write to her about the rumors I overhear, the whispered conversations adults have in the next room when they think I'm not listening. Muslim officers are being removed from the military. Muslim-led businesses are being investigated, fined, shut down. Popular local Muslim journalists are suddenly taking long vacations, their voices mysteriously silenced.

No, instead I talk about my schoolwork, about weekend trips to the Una, about food and family and fashion. I tell her about the new lipstick Tetka Fatma gave me, a bold strong color I've been too afraid to wear outside of my own house so far. And as much as I can, I tell her about Haris. I study him so much, think about him so much, it is almost as if I'm in love with him myself. I can't imagine dissecting any boy this much if he was my own crush.

"Is he still single?" Žana asks with every letter.

I've seen him with several different girls. In the last days of summer, he had his arm around the waist of a black-haired girl as they strolled along the bank of the Una. Once he was holding hands with a cute girl with glasses. But as far as I can tell, he isn't attached to any one particular girl, so I only tell Žana that yes, he's still single. I think hearing about the other girls would make her angry.

So my letters are light and funny. Sometimes my pencil runs away from me, and I scrawl out my worries and fears. But I hardly even know what I'm afraid of. There isn't anything overt. No one is saying outright that Muslims can't have jobs, that they aren't wanted. I don't hear taunts or see violence in the streets. Most of it is so easy to ignore. There are only whispers and a feeling that something is coming. So I have to scribble out those parts, cover them up with drawings of hearts or flowers, or glue on celebrity photos from magazines. I'm so afraid that Žana would just dismissively say, "Oh, Amra, you worry too much!" and quote to me that Yugoslavia is the land of brotherhood and unity. I believe she'd take my fears more seriously, but what if she didn't? And she'd reassure me that no matter what is happening in the world, nothing will affect our bond. And that would probably make me feel a little better, for a little while ... the same way Žana feels better when I tell her that Haris is still single.

Above all, I don't tell Žana what happens just a little while after she leaves Bihać. There are still a couple of weeks left in the summer, and since Tata hasn't yet been called back to work we decide to take a short family trip to Slovenia.

I think Mama and Tata really want to do it to take our mind off our troubles, but the main excuse is that Dino needs a treat. I've had my treat with Žana coming to visit, with the glorious sunny days and giddy nights with my cousins. Sure, Dino had Vedrana, who is his own age, and they enjoy playing together, but it isn't the same as for Žana and me. I think he's felt a little left out, a little like the baby of the family that he is, not allowed to do any of the exciting grown-up things his big sister can do.

First, they get him a pair of Hugo Boss swim trunks. This is an astonishing gift, and I have no idea where they might have gotten them. Probably Tetka Fatma had something to do with it, as usual. We've all heard of this fabulous designer, but we've never seen something by him in person. Designer clothes are almost mythological. They live in magazines and in our dreams, not in real life. Later, when Mama and Tata ask him what else he'd like most of all, he says without hesitation, "A BMX bicycle!"

Dino and I know about the movie *E.T.*, even though none of the people in my family have ever seen it. Only one person my age in the neighborhood has a VCR to play movies on. Alma's grandmother in Chicago got it for her, and she has a small collection of bootleg video tapes she watches over and over. She's told us all about *E.T.*, reenacting scenes and lines of dialogue, telling us about the kid and the alien riding his BMX bike magically through the sky until Dino almost believes BMX bikes can actually fly. I keep waiting for her to invite me over to see it. I'll drop by her house with some homework, any excuse, hoping she'll bring me in to watch *E.T.*... but she never has.

Even as he asks, Dino knows it's an impossible dream. BMX bikes are from the Western world, far too rare and expensive for us to afford. Everyone longs for one after the movie *BMX Bandits* came out, starring a beautiful new actress named Nicole Kidman. We can barely even dream of a bike like that.

Luckily he has a next-best choice. "How about a Pony bicycle?" he asks, with almost as much enthusiasm.

Made by the Rog company in Slovenia, Pony bikes are almost a national symbol in Yugoslavia. We tend to value things made in the West, and Slovenia is as far west as you can get in Yugoslavia. The fact that it shares a border with a real Western European country makes its products seem somehow more elite.

In our communist land, bicycles are the transportation of the people. Even though there are plenty of cars, almost every family has a bike. The most popular model is the Pony, an old-fashioned-looking bike that comes in a variety of cheerful colors. Dino has his heart set on a light-blue one with a white seat and whitewall tires.

Mama and Tata exchange a look that Dino misses completely but I'm old enough to recognize. How much meat and chicken will we have to give up, how much bread and *ajvar* will we have to eat to afford a new bike? Mama's pay is several months late— she is still owed from teaching before the summer. *We can finish fixing the house next year,* Mama's eyes say. *I can get my suits mended instead of replaced,* Tata's eyes say. The unspoken conversation happens quickly. Then they smile and say yes and make plans to get Dino his Pony.

There aren't any available locally, so the plan expands to take a long weekend trip through Croatia to Slovenia, where the bikes are made. And if we're doing that, why not stay with Tata's brother and their family in Vrhnika? Once his family finds out we'll be there, everyone wants to come, and the last word when we board the bus for the six-hour ride is that twenty people will be there!

The trip starts out with a festive feel. I almost forget how much I miss Žana. I almost forget the suspicions that cloud my mind. Packed so tight we're almost sitting in one another's laps, we chat and laugh and wait desperately to stretch our legs at the brief midway stop at Metlika. There's a little ice cream shop by the station, and of course Dino and I clamor for a cone. Mama looks like she wants to say no, but in the end Tata buys a cone for each of us.

There are so many more flavors here than we have at home! I get a scoop of hazelnut ice cream, while Dino sticks to a combination of chocolate and vanilla. Mama and Tata usually save money and just take a taste of ours, but today they splurge. Mama selects strawberry. Tata takes his time picking out whatever flavor is the most unusual. Finally he decides on a double scoop of tropical coconut and mango, suggesting an exotic tropical island on the other side of the world.

I've only just taken my first lick when the bus driver rings a bell announcing that it's time to reboard. "No food allowed on the bus!" he tells us sternly when we try to walk on with our cones.

I want to argue that plenty of passengers were sneaking sandwiches and snacks in their seats, but he looks too intimidating for me to speak. In the end we have to either throw our cones away or miss our ride. Watching those four cones melt on top of the garbage can is one of the saddest things I've ever seen.

Finally we arrive, and we're enveloped in the whirlwind of family. I haven't seen most of them for years, since the last time we went to my dad's village of Šumatac in the wild mountains. The uncle we're staying with is nicknamed Brko—Mustache—because he's the only one of Tata's brothers who has facial hair. There are so many aunts and uncles and cousins, some of whom I adore, like Aunt Rahima and her family, who run a farm and sell the things they grow and the animals they raise for Agrokomerc. Other family members I'm not so sure about. Uncle Mustache's son Duško is a strange, silent young man who looks at me oddly. Maybe he looks at everyone that way—I don't know, but I find it very disturbing. He's an artist, and the house is filled with melancholy canvases of people suffering. I avoid him as much as possible.

On the first day we pick up Dino's bike, then sightsee around the city of Ljubljana. I stare into the shop windows like a kid in a candy store. Everything here is so fancy and expensive! The houses all have beautiful landscaping and neat lawns. And all the houses are finished! I never realized how many houses in Bihać are under construction like ours, with bare facades or boards over the windows, with people living in one room while the rest of the house is completed. This town looks like a movie set, everything designed to be perfect.

"You can go inside," Mama tells us, "but don't touch anything. If you break something in these stores we'll be bankrupt!"

She's half joking, half serious, and I'm upset enough by it that

I'm afraid to even go into the stores. Later Tata notices my serious face and asks me what's wrong. "I don't really like just walking around," I say, noncommittal. He thinks it's just a teenage thing, that I'm too grown up to enjoy walking with my parents anymore, and he falls silent. It hurts that he might think this, but explaining how I really feel would be too complicated ... and might hurt him worse.

Slovenia, this western region, seems to be moving on miles ahead of Bosnia. I remember seeing nature shows about wolves hunting for deer. They don't bother with the strong, fast ones. Instead they look for the weak ones, the ones trailing behind. Is my homeland like the weakened deer, easy prey? Why is Slovenia so prosperous compared to us?

There's one thing I do like about this city, though. The houses are very charming and neat, and each one has flower boxes in all the windows facing the street with rainbow masses of flowers tumbling out. I come upon a table with a flowery tablecloth on it, and pots of flowers surrounding printed brochures. Sturdy women with red-dyed hair stand around it, engaging in heated discussion. But I get the impression they're not angry at one another, but angry at the same thing. They all wear big badges that say SLOVENIJA, MOJA DEŽELA.

"What does that mean?" I ask one politely.

"Slovenia, my country," one says shortly, then says more in Slovenian that I can only catch bits and pieces of, something about their own language, their own country. Another woman jumps in saying, "We should be our own country. Who cares about Yugoslavia? We don't need Yugoslavia, only Slovenia."

My mouth gapes open and I start to back away even before Tata takes me by the arm and pulls me away.

"Don't listen to them," he says. "Don't let anyone see you listening to them."

I'm shocked that they say things like this... and that they're allowed to, so loudly, right there on the street. No one at home would ever dare. What would happen to someone in Bihać who loudly said that Bosnia should be its own country? The idea of breaking up unified Yugoslavia is practically criminal.

And then I wonder, why don't they want to be part of Yugoslavia?

As we're driving back in my uncle's car Mama notices that I'm lost in thought.

"Look out the window, Amra. See those horses training in the field?" She points to a trio of gray horses lifting their legs in such perfect unison that they could be dancing. "Those are Lipizzaner horses, the smartest, most perfect horses in the world. They were bred in this area centuries ago. Do you know why they are such brilliant horses? Because they have a little bit of everything in them—Spanish and Arab, and the horses of Slovenia." She pats my hand. "They are like us, the Bosnians. A little bit of everything."

ON THE SECOND night, we gather for dinner. A big, traditional Bosnian meal that, like everything with us, turns into a happy party. We've been roasting a whole lamb the entire day, and the house is filled with heavenly smells. The house is so neat, even with all this chaos. Uncle Mustache's wife has polished the floor to such a high shine that I'm practically skating on it as I help bring platters from the kitchen to the terrace where we are eating.

Ivanka, my uncle's wife, is bringing out a special delicacy, the lamb's head. Some people love to eat the mushy brain, but my favorite is the tongue, sliced thin with a rough texture on one side from the taste buds. I'm looking forward to this delicacy when Ivanka, hurrying to serve it on a big platter surrounded with roasted potatoes, slips and tangles up with Aunt Rahima. The lamb head goes flying! Its burned-out eyes seem to stare at me in slow motion as it soars over our heads and out to the grass just beyond the terrace.

I want so much to laugh. To see my aunts in a tangled mess of dimije and legs and arms, to see that lamb head out on the grass like it was trying to run in the meadow once again! I look at Mama for silent permission, and only when I see the corners of her mouth start to curl do I let loose with laughter. Soon we're all hysterical, especially once we realize the aunts aren't hurt. They have more cushioning to protect them!

The TV is on in the next room, visible from the terrace, set to one of the two channels we get in Yugoslavia. There are cartoons from 7:15 to 7:30 P.M., and even some of the adults are laughing at the animated show. News comes on at 7:30, and I start to lose interest, but suddenly in the middle of a predictable news report the anchors interrupt the broadcast for breaking news. In a dramatic voice, the announcer says that there will be an immediate political cleansing in the Bosanska Krajina region—the area that contains Bihać, Cazin, and Velika Kladuša—the land where Agrokomerc has been expanding. The anchor says that counter-revolutionaries are trying to undermine all of Yugoslavia through their actions in Bosnia, but the government will make sure that anyone who stands against Yugoslavia will be punished.

We stop eating, stop mid-bite. That word, *counter-revolutionary*, rings in my ear. That label is a death sentence.

Ivanka, a Slovenian, suddenly remembers something she has to do in the kitchen.

I hear my family's voices all around me, but I scarcely know which one is talking at any time.

"They want to bring down Hamdija Pozderac," someone says. "He lifted us out of poverty."

"He was going to be the next president. A Muslim president. They couldn't allow that."

"They want to bring down any respected Muslim."

"They won't even let us call ourselves Bosniaks, let alone *be* Bosniaks."

"Are they using him to go after the company, or are they investigating the company to take him down?"

"Does it matter?" someone asks. "The end result is the same. Muslims lose."

I look to my father, who is white with speechlessness. Dino, moved by a fear he cannot understand, presses against my side.

Aunt Rahima's voice breaks through like a dirge. "We were just getting ahead. When I was younger, it felt like the state was robbing every bit of profit we managed to make. To each according to his needs, from each according to his abilities, I know, but why farm if the state can just take it all away, make you sell at a loss? But thanks to Hamdija and leaders like him..." She looks to Tata. "We were finally doing well. All of the farmers, all of the canners and bottlers and packagers and distributors. And now..." Her voice trails off, and she sniffs, then goes on as if talking to herself. "When I was younger, not on our farm, but on other farms we knew, all around Bosanska Krajina, farmers rebelled because they couldn't make the state quotas. How can you make a cow have more calves? How can you make the rain fall? We were all doing our best. Farming is uncertain. They were called counter-revolutionaries because they asked for a reasonable break. The government said, if you can't make quotas here, you can move to another place where you can grow enough. The military came in and forcibly relocated them. Relocated! What was their location? No one ever saw them again. We know what really happened to them. Whole families, women and children gone, the land left empty rather than let Muslims have it. We kept our heads down, stayed silent, and were spared. But what will happen this time?"

Drops of sweat glisten like ice on Tata's forehead.

The phone rings, making everyone jump. Uncle Mustache excuses himself to answer it. He comes back with a look of confused fear and says, "Mehmed, it's for you."

"For me?" Tata asks, swallowing hard. "Who even knows I'm here?"

Everyone falls silent trying to listen to the conversation in the other room. But all Tata does is stand with the phone to his ear. After a long silence he says into the receiver, "Yes, I under-stand," then gently hangs it up in its cradle.

"The State Security Service. A car will be here for me in twenty minutes," he says like he's speaking his own death sentence. The State Security Service is the secret police. "They think I'm going to cross the border, flee the country. They want me back in Bihać." He looks at Mama helplessly. "Why would I go? What do I have to flee from? I've done nothing wrong."

Mama looks at the front door, the back door, the windows. Twenty minutes. He could borrow Uncle Mustache's car and be miles away by the time they come. He could hide in the base-ment, we could say he drove back to Bihać on his own.

Tata reads our thoughts. "If they say twenty minutes, they're already there outside the door. Already watching. I better brush my teeth and get ready." He forces a painful smile on his hand-some face.

When he leaves, he's wearing his best suit, looking as sharp as an old-fashioned movie star. His thick silvered hair is swept back in a wave, and his cheeks are shaved smooth. Whatever happens, he won't look guilty.

It is so civilized. No one has to drag him. When the car pulls up—it must have been just down the street—he walks calmly out. He's said his goodbyes inside. No one goes out with him. No one dares to show their faces to whoever is inside that dark-tinted black Opel Senator, an elite executive car. It's not the police, not an official car from Tata's bank. Whoever is in there is a name-less, faceless agent of the powers in charge. The State Security Service works in darkness, anonymous and deadly.

We gaze from a darkened side room, the one my cousin uses as his studio. Surrounded by those tortured souls we watch my father being driven away into the night.

Death is certain, at least. When my heart broke from Amar, at least I knew what to feel, who to mourn. But I have no idea what will happen to my father, and somehow that is worse. I want to run after him. I want to go home. But there's nothing to do tonight. Maybe nothing to do at all. Begging won't get him released. It might only get Mama arrested, too. All we can do is wait.

The household moves slowly, speaks quietly now. All the festivity is gone. In a trance, I help my aunts clean up, numbly drying the same dish for five minutes. That night we sleep downstairs, surrounded by the harsh chemical smells of oil paints and mineral spirits, with the faces of the damned grimacing down on us from our cousin's canvases. There's one of a woman, her skin so fair and ghostly that it floats in the darkness of a graveyard. She's beautiful, but her face is frozen in a moment of pain. Knives surround her, coming at her from all angles.

We want to leave, to at least wait for news in our own home. But we depend on the bus schedule and have to wait long hours until the afternoon to depart. At the stop at Metlika, we don't even get off. Out the window, as we pull away again, I see ice cream cones in the garbage. They couldn't be ours, could they? Maybe the past days were just a dream. If only we could go back to that time, before Tata was taken away.

But no, the ice cream shop is a trap. The owner never tells kids they can't take ice cream on the bus. Every single one buys a cone. Every single one has to throw it away unfinished. They are set up for disappointment.

AFTER WE ARRIVE home in Bihać, life seems to exist in a time warp. It is nothing but waiting. Mama makes phone calls and contacts friends, but no one can tell her anything. Tata has vanished, made to disappear by the magicians called the State Security Service. It is dangerous to even ask questions about those who are taken, or they might join the prisoner on a trip with no return. The State Security Service is everywhere, and no one knows who they are. They are among us, the tools that control the system. They keep us in fear.

Finally, days later, the secret police come back. They are nocturnal creatures to me, skulking during the day and only coming out at night. We are almost in bed, despairing that one more sun has set without him, when the door opens and Tata comes in.

He doesn't look like my father—he looks like my grandfather. He's lost so much weight. His wrists stick out like bird bones from the grimy cuffs of his once spruce-white shirt. His jacket, folded over his arm, looks like it has been pounded on rocks. I can't see any injuries, but the dark sleepless circles under his eyes look like bruises.

He almost collapses into Mama's arms. Dino and I run to him. And then, just for a moment, the strongest man I know breaks down and begins to weep.

My father cries easily, for he is a man of big emotions. But they are gentle tears. He cries when a baby is born, overwhelmed at the marvel of life. Or he will cry just to look at Dino or me, happy that we exist. Only when Amar died did I see him break down completely in agonizing grief. He does the same now. The world he believed in is gone. Tonight he cannot speak.

We're sent to bed, but late in the night Dino comes to my room and wakes me up. I wasn't really asleep anyway. "Amra, there's a man downstairs with Tata." Thinking he's going to be arrested again I run down quietly with Dino. But what can I do? Can I fight this man if he tries to take Tata?

The door is cracked, and I see a man in his forties with steel gray hair sitting on our best chair. "Mehmed," he says to my father, "my order in Belgrade was to find something dirty on you and put you behind bars, cleanse you as a counter-revolutionary with the other Muslims. They're coming for you. I looked, I never looked as hard as I did in this case. I pushed your employees, I threatened them to give me one thing, anything that would condemn you. Nothing. Not a single employee was willing to tarnish you even after my threats. That has never happened before. There's always someone afraid, someone with a grudge. But they love you and they respect you, more than they fear me. You're clean, and I'm honored to meet you."

Through the crack I see the man hold out his hand, and Tata, after the slightest hesitation, grasps it as if the man were an old friend. "If you ever tell anyone about this, my head is gone," the man says. "So is yours. Let's drink together."

Tata never drinks, but he did that night. The man didn't say much after that, and neither did Tata, but I heard a few things mumbled. *It's coming. I can't stop it.* When the man finally left, we crept away out of sight and heard Tata in the bathroom, vomiting over and over.

This man may be gone, but the people in power are coming for Tata. There will be political investigations, court cases . . . maybe deaths. This is not over, it has only been paused for a moment.

He talks about what he was accused of the next day. Tata didn't have anything to do with the promissory notes for Agrokomerc, but the fact that some of the money flowed through his bank was excuse enough for them to subject him to days of psychological torture. They said it was part of a conspiracy to make money for the business at the state's expense. They claimed Agrokomerc was working with my father's bank to commit fraud.

"Whatever happens, Dilka, I need you to know that I have done nothing wrong. If this proceeding of theirs is based on facts, we will have nothing to worry about. But I don't think they are basing their investigation on facts. They have a deeper agenda. A darker one."

I still don't understand why this is happening. Improbably my mind goes back to that tape Tetak Ale played. Did someone report that to the secret police? That's the only time I know of that Tata was associated with something forbidden.

"No, this is about bringing down powerful Muslims, and when the big fish are in the net, even small fry like me can get caught. But I will never change my principles. My goal will always be to be good to others. I believe if a man keeps to that first and foremost, he has nothing to fear."

I am so proud of my Tata for saying this, but somehow angry, too. It sounds so naive. I want to tell him to fight, to yell at his accusers, to run away if he has to. Anything but this passivity and hopefulness and trust in the goodness of human nature. It seems to make him shrink every day. I want to fight for him myself, but I don't know how. I think of all the things Đorđe said about Bosniaks. I think of self-hating Dida who despises Muslims even though she is one. If people like them detest Bosniaks, there is no point in waiting and hoping, no trust in living an honest and good life.

Deep inside, I know that if the state decides to take him away forever, there is no fact or counter argument that will convince them otherwise. So why fight in a battle that was lost before it even began?

From Mama, from my aunts and uncles, I hear more. While they were interrogating Tata, they also interviewed every single employee. I've known many of them all my life. Šico—Mr. Sharp—was the man in charge of pencils. When I was a little girl, I thought he was the most powerful man in the company, because he had an endless supply of perfectly sharpened pencils, and it was up to him who got one. He always pretended to think a long time before deciding if I was worthy of a brand-new pencil. In the end, he always gave me one. Another favorite of mine was the old lady in a pink coat and pink stockings who pushed a tray of coffee all around the office. Tata said she made the best coffee and always said it loudly enough for her to over-hear. He said many people will compliment you to your face and talk about you behind your back. The best compliments are the ones overheard.

The secret police interviewed them and everyone else,

looking for one bad thing about Tata. His employees had only praise for him.

"Come on," the secret police would say. "Every man has done something bad, and it is always the underlings like you who know about it. Crooks don't bother to hide from the guy who sharpens pencils. Don't be afraid, tell us what he was hiding."

But neither Šico nor any of them had a bad word to say about him. Even people who had been passed over for promotion had nothing negative to say. Even his enemies had grudging respect. If anything, they hated him because he was honest and incorruptible.

Days of interrogation, a 350-page report, and the secret police couldn't come up with a single thing to tarnish his reputation.

But he is tarnished all the same. The world found him guilty just because he had been questioned. His reputation is now gone forever. He has no job, and most people are afraid to even think of hiring him.

As the year drags on, Tata doesn't recover his upright posture, his look of vibrant health. He never sings anymore. His eyes are always haunted. Sudden sounds startle him. Family learns not to knock on the door because that sound makes him panic now. He spends long sleepless nights pacing the kitchen, drinking glass after glass of water. We soon learn that his unnatural thirst isn't from stress, but from a medical cause. He has diabetes.

They broke the most honest man in Yugoslavia.

23

NEWS TRAVELS FAST, and without telling anyone, all my friends in Bihać know what happened. Former friends, I should say, because they've all abandoned me. It is survival of the fittest, and our family is the injured gazelle left for the lions to devour.

It wasn't even as bad as this after Amar died. Then, I think people shunned me because they didn't know what to say, or maybe had a superstition that death hung around me because my brother had died. People were uncomfortable then, but gradually it ended. Now, I learn what it means to be completely ostracized. Even my Muslim friends don't want to hang out with me. None of Dino's friends will play basketball with him. It is as if my family has a deadly, infectious disease no one wants to catch. I want to defend my dad, but if anyone heard me, he'd only be in more trouble. And could I be labeled disobedient, a radical? Could they take me away, too?

In class, my fellow students drag their chairs as far from me as possible. No one speaks to me, no one will sit near me at lunch. Teachers ignore me, pretending I'm not even there, refusing to call on me if I raise my hand. I'm worse than invisible. It is as if I have a stench no one can endure. In a way I guess I do. The label of counter-revolutionary is so awful that it might as well be catching. The stink might rub off on them.

Even Hana doesn't want to hang out with me anymore. Lonely,

abused Hana, who only survived the summer because my family took her in without question, has turned her back on me.

Everyone stays away from us now. Everyone except those who truly love us. There are many who stay loyal. Family and a few friends will come over boldly in daylight just as before. Other friends, more timid, come by after dark or call up for quick chats. Some people look away when we pass them in the street or at the store. Others give no more than a cautious nod, afraid to commit themselves to more.

Which will Žana be?

In between her funny stories about classmates, her fantasies about Haris, pasted-in photos of movie stars from magazines, and lip-print kisses where she shows off her newest shade of lipstick, Žana says in almost every letter that her parents don't want her to come here next summer.

"They have all kinds of excuses," she writes to me. "Last time Mama said we're going to Germany for the summer. Then they say they want me to take extra classes. As if! Just today my dad said something about me going to Tovrljane for the summer to work in the orchards and learn to make plum jam. Can you imagine? That's in the middle of nowhere with a lot of old farmers and girls who have never worn a high heel in their entire life! The summer is for fun, not work. Don't worry, Amra—there's no way I won't be there this summer. I mean it. I'll do whatever it takes. I have to see Haris again and be with my sister for another glorious summer!"

The only ray of hope I feel is that she never says anything about Tata. There's not a hint that her parents won't let her come because he's being investigated. So maybe there's still hope. I haven't written to her about what happened in Slovenia. We don't even talk about it at home. What if the wrong people hear?

In her next letter she tells me she has a new idea. "My dad used the old line, if I don't get my grades up I can't go. Well, I'm going to beat him at his own game! I told him I'll just flunk out of school completely if he doesn't let me go. We'll see who can hold out the longest! I'll fail every test and get held back a year, and our family will be the laughingstock of the whole school! I'll tell the teachers I have a bad home life and that's why I'm failing. Dad will have to give in!"

I can't tell if she's serious, and of course I have to advise her to keep working hard to get good grades and find another way to come here. But I'm still happy that she's so determined, even if more and more often the last line of her letters isn't, "I have to see my sister next summer!" but rather, "I have to see Haris next summer."

But how will we even feed Žana and Vedrana if they come? Right now we're living entirely off Mama's salary—a teacher's salary so small it can barely feed one person. And even that small pay is always a month or two late. The refrigerator is always empty.

One day Tetka Fatma comes to visit, dressed up as usual in the stylish clothes she gets from Italy. She always looks so chic, maybe not like a model, exactly, but like a model's mother who taught her daughter everything she knows. Today she's wearing a pleated silk dress that swishes in a calming way as she walks, like a dervish going into a trance. She never seems to be under stress no matter what happens.

My parents and Dino are off visiting someone, so I'm having an early dinner alone before going upstairs to start my homework. She finds me at the table greedily eating ajvar pepper spread along with a cold potato and bread. I'm happy to have that much. My stomach has been rumbling all day, filled with nothing but the school's lunch of a thin slice of chicken salami on bread.

"It's nice to see a young person with such a good appetite," Tetka Fatma says. "But where's your meat?" There are no vegetarians in Bosnia, or at least not many. Tetka Fatma would call someone a vegetarian if they just ate chicken and fish, but not red meat! No lunch or dinner is considered complete without some form of meat. But meat is so expensive, we only see it once a week, if that.

"Oh, I ate it already," I say, covering for my family's poverty.

Tetka Fatma gives me a suspicious look, then heads to the fridge.

"No, Tetka, don't—" I begin, but she already has the door open, staring at its meager contents. A jar of mayonnaise. A jar of ajvar. A heel of bread that has seen better days.

"Amra," she says in the gentlest voice, "why didn't you tell me? Or more importantly, why didn't Dilka tell me? I could have been helping all this time."

"You do help, Tetka," I tell her, and it's true. She never comes empty-handed.

"Oh, that's just hospitality. This is a matter of need. No, darling, don't hang your head. There's nothing to be ashamed of. Each step forward requires some kind of sacrifice, and every family is challenged and tested in some way. You are just going through your challenge now. Just remember it won't last forever, and it's not your fault, or your mom's, and certainly not your dad's. It's the fault of ..." But here she trails off, afraid or unwilling to speak of such serious things with me.

From then on if we have a good meal it is all because of Tetka Fatma and Tetak Ale. She is as diplomatic as possible. "I accidentally doubled the recipe, can you take this off my hands before it goes bad?" Or, "A friend with a farm gave us this chicken as a present, but I'm sick to death of chicken, so will you take it?" Once she asks Dino to go for a walk with her downtown and he comes home wearing a new pair of much-needed shoes. "They were practically giving them away, it would be a shame not to buy them." Another day it is, "Try this toothpaste, Amra. It makes my mouth too tingly, but maybe you'll like it."

And to whatever else she brings, she almost always adds a jar of the honey they collect on their bee farm out in the countryside. Our cupboards are so full of it that I don't think we could eat all this honey in four years. But Tetka Fatma reminds us that it keeps forever. "If the world ended and aliens found a jar of honey a million years from now, they could still lick it up," she declares.

Even with their help, we'll be in dire trouble unless Tata can find a job.

Unemployment is rare under communism. And for a man with a college education—one of the first and few of his generation in our region to be so well educated—it is unheard of. But now no one will touch him. It doesn't matter that he didn't do anything wrong. If he had the slightest fault he'd be in prison ... or worse. But Tata never even brushed his hair the wrong way.

Finally, his old economics professor Ejub Alagić gets in touch with him. He's the president of the main board of Unatrans, a large transportation company in our region. He said Tata can come and work as the head of one of the working units. Tata is a banker and economist, and knows nothing about transportation, but he desperately needs a job so he accepts.

Despite having a friend on the board, there are problems right away. There is corruption and theft among the workers. Employees are stealing car and bus parts and selling them for personal profit. My Tata isn't in a position to stop it, and it goes against his nature to look the other way. He can't work at a place like this, even for the money we so desperately need. So eventually he goes to look for a job out in Mostar, where the stigma against him isn't as fresh as in our hometown.

Just before he goes, we all visit Mama's elderly Aunt Nevista, who is Žana's grandmother. I always chuckle at her name—a nickname that means "bride." She was called that when she married into the Četić family, and even though she is more than seventy years old now, she is still called the bride. She has a way of fortune-telling where she throws beans to see a person's future. Just for fun, she casts Tata's fortune. "You'll soon have a very big job and make a company more money than they can count," she tells him. "Yes, you will definitely get something very big. Your bellies will all be full from this job!"

I think of the old fortune teller whose predictions about Amar came true in an unexpected way and wonder how Nevista's words will manifest in the world.

In Mostar, my dad meets Hasan Poljskić, a Muslim, who is the director of the Hepok conglomerate and runs their subsidiary, APRO Plastika. The company has produced a ton of bags that they haven't been able to sell. Right now they're sitting in a warehouse, making no money for the company. They've even had to fire people because they couldn't unload these bags. Hasan says it would be cheaper to burn or bury them than to store them much longer. They're ready to cut their losses, but they're willing to give a desperate man one last chance to sell them. He won't get a salary, though, only a commission. His only hope of being paid is to do the impossible and sell these unwanted bags.

If anyone can do the impossible, it is my Tata. At least, if the impossible involves getting people to like him and want to help him. Even if none of his old friends would stick their neck out enough to actually give him a good job, that doesn't mean they won't help him in little ways. And since I think my Tata knows more people than anyone else in Yugoslavia, those little ways can all add up! They have to. Under communism there are no jobs in private companies. We are told that everything is owned collectively by the people, but in reality, all jobs are controlled by the state. So if the state shuns you, you are a dead man walking.

When he was at the University of Sarajevo, Tata helped pay his tuition by working on the accounts for the school's national youth organization. He was even the one who organized the summer trips and camps to Croatia for the students. So he got to know everyone in the college, from freshmen to seniors and all the professors and staff. For as long as I can remember, wherever we go, people stop and greet my dad. All across Bosnia, in

Slovenia, at the Croatian seaside, people run up to him, full of fond memories.

Now, bags in hand, he goes to those people. He doesn't ask for help, just tells them what he's trying to do. Everyone knows what happened to him, and they sympathize even if they're too afraid to shout their sympathy. But they do what they can. Most of the people who know him are influential now. That first generation of college educated people after World War II have all gone on to successful careers. Some of them run department stores, working as buyers or in the marketing departments. Dad approaches each one as if to catch up, and by the end of the conversation they offer to display the bags in their stores. It costs them nothing to do this little favor. If the bags don't sell, they aren't out any money.

"It doesn't hurt that you're so handsome, and so many of the salespeople are women," Mama teases him. Invigorated by the work, and by hope, Tata is looking better lately. Not like his old self, but I can see a glimpse of the man he was.

NEAR THE END of spring, I get two pieces of good news.

"They said I can go to Bihać!" Žana writes to me. "They say I have to stay at Asmir's house with Aunt Zumra. I'll go there at first to get them off my back, but you know Zumra doesn't want me there, so she won't make a fuss about Vedrana and me staying with you. And my dad won't even notice. He's gone for weeks at a time lately. Sometimes months. Mama says he's underground, whatever that means. First he works with military airports, then he's underground? Planes aren't underground. It makes no sense. What could he possibly be doing? I don't care, as long as I get my way! See, Amra, I told you that nothing could keep us apart. Oh, and make sure you find Haris and tell him I'll be back. I want him to be excited to see me!"

Then, soon after, Tata manages to get the bags placed in Robna Kuća Beograd, a chain of department stores with a branch in almost every city in Yugoslavia. Slowly, one by one, they are starting to sell. Tata gets his first payment—smaller than he expected, but he says that now that the bags are in Robna Kuća Beograd, they can really take off.

With cash in his hand for the first time in almost a year, he tells my mom, "Dilka, I'm going to buy a cow. And not just any cow—a young cow." A young cow is more flavorful and tender, and therefore more expensive.

The butcher kills the cow according to the halal way—though of course no one talks about that—and turns it into roasts and fillets and ribs and stew meat, transforms its intestines into juicy spicy sausages, and after months of nothing but bread and ajvar, now our refrigerator and freezer are stuffed full of meat! And Tetka Fatma's is even more full! She's storing most of the cow for us because our little freezer can only hold a fraction of it. That night we have delicious steaks, and my body gets some of the nutrients it has been missing. For the first time in ages, we all feel hopeful. If Tata gets paid like this all the time, we'll have nothing to worry about.

Aunt Nevista was right. Tata did get something big—as big as a cow! And thanks to his success, our bellies are very full indeed.

My last worry is gone. When Žana and Vedrana come next week, we'll have plenty to feed them. They won't see the fear, the poverty that darkened our year. When Žana is here, all should be sunshine.

But there is always a cloud on the horizon threatening to block out the sun. I don't know what my life will bring, but I know enough about the world to fear that it will be something dire. I'm not so naive as to think that life will be good again just because I have another summer with Žana. But maybe under her influence I can at least pretend to have another summer of innocence.

THE THIRD SUMMER

24

TWO SUMMERS AGO, we'd get up before dawn, no matter how late we went to bed, to throw on our bathing suits and run to the Una. But this morning we lie unconscious under the covers until the sun is high in the sky.

Žana and Vedrana got in to the station at 1:00 A.M. last night. Since Zumra didn't want to bother staying up so late to meet them, it was decided that they would stay at our house the first two nights, and then go to their aunt's for the rest of their stay— something nobody was happy about. Žana swears she won't stay there but told me not to worry about it last night. "Nothing is going to spoil our reunion!" she said as she hugged me. In that moment—if only for that moment—I forget the horror of the past year. That's all I ask for, just a few moments like that.

We didn't walk home—we danced home. "Even though we're far apart all year we listen to the same music," Žana said. "By the time we're together again we can sing the same songs. See, it's like we never left!" We shook and shimmied down the streets to songs like "Walk Like an Egyptian" and "Don't Dream It's Over."

None of us speak English, but we sound out the words and understand a few of them. I wish I could study English in school. A privileged few do, but I have to study Russian instead. My knowledge of English is so limited that for the longest time, when I saw the words *The End* after a dubbed American movie I pronounced *the* as "tuh-huh-eh." I thought each letter was pronounced individually. It was only recently that Žana, who has a little more exposure to the language, set me straight.

Anyway, it's the feel of the songs, not the words, that strike us. Even without knowing what the Bangles are saying or why, exactly, we should walk like Egyptians, every teen around the world can appreciate its happy bounce. And Crowded House sings with a universal language of love and longing and melancholy that every person my age understands.

I hear Žana murmur and turn over, cuddling her pillow, still half-asleep. I'm shocked when I look at the clock—it's almost noon! I don't think I've ever slept this late unless I was sick. *Am I sick?* I feel fine, but for some reason my body doesn't want me to leave this snug comfortable nest. It's like my bones and muscles are overruling my brain, demanding rest.

Žana yawns, turning it into a funny roar. "Can you imagine? We used to be up to watch the sun rise."

"I don't know what's happened to me," I say. "I feel like I could sleep another hour. What about you, Vedrana?" I roll over to ask her, but she's gone.

Žana laughs. "Mama says teen brains need more sleep to calm them down. I don't know if that's true, but I know she needs to throw cold water on me every morning to get me out of bed for school. What about you?"

"I'll ask my Tata to get me up extra early some days. It used to be easy because I'd jump right out of bed. Now when he comes at 5:00 A.M., I beg for ten more minutes, just ten more minutes. And he feels so bad making me get up! But if he lets me have ten more minutes I get cross with him for letting me sleep! So now he will and he won't. When I beg for more time, he'll say, 'Okay Amra, I'll let you sleep, I definitely will, don't mind me being here, you go ahead and sleep, I'll just open the curtain, you close your eyes…' He talks so much that I can't fall asleep again!"

"What time does your school start?"

"Eight."

"Why on earth do you get up at five? You can't need that much time to get ready."

"To study for a big test, or sometimes just to get in more math practice."

"Well, I'm sure you go to bed early…when I'm not here anyway!"

I don't want her to think I'm too much of a goody-goody, so I don't tell her how I have volleyball practice every night, and then sometimes stay up until one studying. No matter how tired I am the next morning, I'd never dare be late. The only thing I can do to redeem myself in the eyes of my schoolmates and neighbors is to be the best I can be. The best at school, the best at volleyball. Maybe then I won't be a target. But it's been getting harder and harder over the last year, and now that I can finally let my guard down, I want to sleep forever.

"But the day's wasting!" I realize. "We should be down at the Una."

Žana gives a long, full-body stretch and closes her eyes. "We're not kids anymore," she reminds me sleepily. "Little kids get up at dawn and go swimming. Teens sleep late all summer and then go to the discotheque."

The discotheque! It even has a magical name: Hollywood. It makes me think of everything foreign and American and exciting. Last summer we talked about going, but by the time we worked up our courage, Mama found us getting ready and decided we were too young. I didn't argue, but Žana told her that plenty of kids our age went there every night during the summer. I remember Mama looked at me, and I think she might have changed her mind if I'd begged her. But I didn't, and she only said, "Next summer. You girls have plenty of time."

I have to admit I was a little bit relieved. We've walked by it lots of times, and I'm always a little intimidated by the people I see there. It doesn't matter that I know a lot of them. By daylight they're the older brothers and sisters of people that I've known all my life. But somehow a transformation happens by night at the discotheque. Some alchemy of eye shadow and glitter and sparkly clothes turns them into much older, much more sophisticated people. We'd see the flashing multicolored lights from inside, and I'd feel like that was an entrance to an entirely different world, one I didn't think I could navigate.

"Don't you want to go to the Una every day this summer?" I ask Žana. Even though we're the same age, sometimes she seems so much older than me in social things. In other ways, though, I feel decades beyond her.

"Sure we will. Just not every day, maybe. And not so early in the morning!"

"But the Una has been a part of every summer!" I say, shocked. "The Una *is* summer for us!"

Žana sits up and pushes her disheveled hair out of her face.

"Just think of the dancing, and the boys, and the fun! Brvice is cool, and we'll definitely still go there. I have to work on my tan, after all, and I don't want to miss out on your mom's amazing lunches. But this will be the summer of the discotheque."

The idea is exciting, scary, and a little melancholy. Mostly, I'm glad I'll have Žana with me for my first trip to the discotheque. I feel like it's a place where anything could happen—and that *anything* could be good or bad.

We tell Mama and Tata our plans when we finally manage to drag ourselves downstairs. Vedrana was up hours ago and already left with Dino for the Una. Mama seems a little disappointed when we say we won't be going there ourselves today.

"We need to wash our hair and try different ways to style it," Žana tells her, ticking off our chores on her fingers. "And then of course decide on our outfits and makeup. And nail polish! We barely have enough time." She turns to me. "Oh, Amra, wait until you see the dress I brought for you! It's like molten silver, and it doesn't have any back at all!" She glances at my parents, who are torn between looks of happiness and concern.

"Where did my little baby go?" Tata wants to know. "It feels like just a few months ago you were running around the house in a diaper, and now you're wearing dresses that are only half there." He shakes his head but he's smiling.

I wonder if Žana can notice the change in him. Does she see how loosely his clothes hang on his tall frame now? Does she see the new wrinkles in his forehead? Tata always had lines on his face, but they were happy lines, smile lines around his mouth and crinkles in the corners of his eyes. These new lines are from worry.

He's been traveling a lot, all around Yugoslavia, meeting buyers everywhere from huge department store chains to elite little boutiques, trying to sell the overstocked bags. Already he's had a great deal of success. With his easy charm, he's managed to talk up these bags until they're a budding new sensation. Through persistence, friendliness, and a little bit of luck, I think he's creating the first major home-grown fashion trend in the country. Always before, we wanted foreign things, styles from western Europe or America. Now there's a uniquely Yugoslavian thing we all crave. It is a rare feeling of unity in a country that feels increasingly divided. Maybe some people don't want Bosniaks here. But surely they must see that we're not so different from one another if we all love the same bag! Maybe the Sebastian bag is the thing that unites us.

"Oh, Žana, I forgot I have a special present for you!" I cry, jumping up. Žana always brings me presents, like the magical dress she mentioned, and I never have anything for her besides little things like a hair clip or a fancy pen, all things that are regifted. I'd never bought her anything. This time, though, I have something rare and wonderful that is impossible to get.

As I unwrap it from its bed of crinkled tissue paper Žana's eyes light up. "Oh, Amra!" she breathes, reaching out a finger to stroke it. "It's a Sebastian bag! Where in the world did you find one?"

She picks it up reverently and strokes its black nylon surface. When she lets her fingernails trail over it they make a pretty little scratching sound.

"Oh, Sebastian, I think I'm in love!" she gushes, hugging the bag to her chest while she whirls ecstatically around. "Isn't he the most beautiful thing you've ever seen?"

I nod, thinking what a strange thing a trend is. The Sebastian bag is really nice, a good-sized nylon bag that's big enough for holding a few schoolbooks. It has a single adjustable strap that goes over the shoulder, wide enough to be comfortable, and a big opening with a flap, held closed by two quick-release buckles. It's basically a messenger bag, durable and perfect for a high school or college student. It's more expensive than anything I could afford, but it's not as pricey as imported designer brands.

Somehow Tata has transformed this basic bag into a Yugoslavian icon.

Its black material is simple but rich-looking with a glossy sheen, and goes with everything. It's embellished by three downward-pointing golden chevrons that make it look a little bit—but not too—military. Like a soldier who decided to go out for a night on the town! But the real glory is the name, *Sebastian*, written in red below the golden chevrons. The first "a" in the word has been turned into a playful trio of that letter, stitched in gold and bursting out of the name in a fanciful swirl. The sophisticated name combined with those whimsical golden letters and the overall utilitarian usefulness of the bag combine to create the perfect product.

All it needed was the right salesman. I wonder how many great works of art languish in studios because the artist doesn't know how to talk about their own work?

"Amra, thank you, I love it," she says, exploring the little side pockets. "I can keep my makeup in this one, and maybe snacks in that one, and it will hold at least one change of clothes. This is perfect! I tell you, they are the hottest thing in Belgrade right now. Everyone wants one. A few people I know are lucky enough to have a Sebastian bag and they say they get offers every day. One boy traded his for a bike, can you believe it? Well, it was an old bike, but still! And now I have one! You're the best sister ever!"

"You should be thanking my dad," I tell her. "He's the one who is in charge of getting them into stores. He's the one who told the world how wonderful Sebastian is."

Žana throws her arms around Tata, and I see him beaming. I know how much he misses his job at the bank, but he takes pride in doing a job well, no matter what it is. He must feel so happy to have taken a failed product and turned it into a success. He hasn't gotten paid since the cow money came in, but surely if so many bags are selling he'll make enough money now. Or soon. Definitely soon. He has a lot more due to him, but something is holding it up. Mama hasn't gotten paid for almost a month either. We're used to waiting for good things to happen. At this point, just having something good to wait for is a treat in itself.

And there's still plenty of beef in the freezer!

"I never thought I'd have one. Are they going to get any more in the shops?" she asks my dad.

"I hope so. I've had the stores make a waiting list."

"Oh, that's brilliant! People always want whatever they can't get. But if you don't give it to them sometimes they just forget about it. A list though—that's genius! Then they're committed. They live in hope and think about it every morning. Is today the day I'm getting my Sebastian bag at last? Do you have any more?"

"I have some of them in my car. The ones I bring around to stores to demonstrate them."

"Do you realize how much money you could make if you walked down any street in Belgrade with a bunch of these bags? You could sell them for ten times what the department stores charge. The price was going up and up and up, and by the time I had enough money scraped together they were gone."

Tata looks a little shocked at the idea. "These aren't my bags, they belong to the company. I have them just so I can demonstrate them." I know that Tata keeps careful records and took the cost of Žana's bag, and the identical one he gave me, off what they will pay him in commission. Eventually.

I know most salesmen would do what Žana suggested, make a little money on the side that no one would ever know about. But not Tata. No matter what happens, he's far too honorable to sell something that doesn't belong to him or do anything even remotely unethical. I wish there were more men like him in this country.

Mama and Tata go to the Una while we take a long time over breakfast, nibbling on bread and honey as we catch up. Even with our constant stream of letters we always discover so much we've forgotten to tell each other.

As for me, there's one thing I haven't forgotten. I just haven't known how to bring it up. It's about Haris. Strangely, she hasn't said a thing about him since she arrived. Has she forgotten him, fallen out of love?

Eventually I'm the one who brings him up.

"Whew! It's about time!" she says, grinning. "I had a revelation over the last year. I realized last summer I did nothing but talk about Haris. It must have been so boring for you."

"I didn't mind."

"Because you're so polite. But I tried that with my friends back in Belgrade, and after a couple of weeks of it they told me straight-out to shut up. You should have said something!"

"That would have been rude."

"See? But sometimes friends need you to be a little rude, to put them in their place. I'm still totally in love with Haris, but I decided I don't want to be the kind of girl who talks about nothing but boys. I mean, is that all I am? A girl in love? I'm so much more than that. I decided not to talk about him nearly as much. In fact, I made a resolution not to mention him at all until you did. You sure took long enough—I was going insane! So, how is he? Is he still single?"

Her big smile starts to falter when I don't answer right away.

"Amra, what is it? Is he dating someone?" Her eyes grow bright. Is she about to cry? "Tell me!" she insists. "Whatever it is, I have to know."

"There is something I have to tell you about Haris. I didn't know how to tell you. It's very sad news…"

25

ŽANA GETS READY for the night in a dream, a faraway look in her eyes. She puts on her makeup with slow precision, like every line, every stroke of a brush is casting a solemn spell. I almost wish I hadn't told her about Haris's mom. But I had to. What if she had seen him and started talking to him like everything was normal? Both of them would have been hurt.

I don't want to wear the slinky silver dress she's brought for me—there's a pall over everything now that makes me feel I should wear something more solemn—but Žana insists. "There might be sadness in the world, but that doesn't mean we shouldn't look good. Here, I brought a frosted gold lipstick. I think the contrast with the silver will look amazing." But her eyes are missing their usual sparkle.

When I first told her, tears sprang to her eyes. Now she says, "I need to be strong. We should go out and have a good time, like everything is completely normal. And in a way it is, for us, I guess. But for him, everything has changed. What will I say to him if I see him?"

She's been asking me the same thing since she first laid eyes on him, but tonight her question has a different tenor. She's not just worried about herself anymore, she's worried about Haris, too.

"I don't think you'll see him tonight," I tell her.

Žana gives a long sigh, then forces a smile. "Let's go out and dance wildly, Amra," she says. "Let's dance until we're sweating, until we're almost passing out. Let's dance until we forget that there's any such thing as sorrow in the world."

Despite Žana's melancholy, the night still feels like one of the biggest adventures of my life. At least, until Vedrana decides she wants to go, too, and my parents let her.

"I wasn't allowed to go at her age," I whisper to them out of her hearing. I don't want her to feel like she isn't welcome. I just think it's strange that we had to wait two years.

"That's because *you* didn't have a responsible older cousin that I trusted completely to accompany you," Mama says and kisses me on the forehead. She does trust me, I know … but she also gives occasional inspections. Sometimes when I got home last summer she'd stop me in the hall and say, "Blow!" I'd have to puff into her face so she could be sure I wasn't smoking. But I know most kids—like Žana—wouldn't hesitate to lie to their parents. Sometimes I resent these random checks. But I always pass, and she always kisses me right after, so that I can feel her soft cheek, smell the Nivea cream she uses, and know that someone loves me enough to keep me on a good path. "I know she'll be safe with you."

Now that younger Vedrana is going, too, the discotheque doesn't seem quite so intimidating. At least I won't be the baby of the group.

"And it is best that a person have all the fun while they can, while they're young," Tata says. "Who knows what may come later? Maybe it is better to regret the things you do rather than regret the things you didn't do." Is he thinking of Amar, how he didn't have much time in this world? Or is he thinking of my future, the future of every Bosniak?

Mama laughs. "That advice might be good for someone like our Amra, but don't let Žana hear it!"

They're only pretending to keep it from Žana. She revels in her slightly bad-girl reputation and grins back at Mama. "Better still, don't regret anything at all!" she says. Thank goodness her spirits seem to be lifting. I was afraid the news about Haris would cloud the whole summer.

It is a typical Bihać summer twilight, warm but with a deliciously cool breeze coming off the Una. I missed this freshness the few days we were in Slovenia. Even when we go to the Adriatic Sea in Croatia or the wild Šumatac mountains to visit Tata's brother, the air isn't as pure as it is here in my hometown. It is like the Una is breathing on us, a cool life-giving breath.

"Shh, can you hear it?" Žana asks suddenly. We stop walking, stop talking, and cock our heads to catch whatever sound she's talking about. I hear the deep thud of a beat first, like distant war drums. No, these are drums of peace, a driving beat that is all about energy and life.

As our ears focus we pick out melodies, a magical distant fairy-song in a language we don't speak but understand nonetheless— the language of emotion. It is so faint I don't even know if I'm imagining it.

"It's right there, on the other side of the Una!" Vedrana says excitedly.

"The wind must be blowing just right if we can hear it," I tell them. Maybe I've heard it before but thought it was only a neighbor's radio. Tonight, there's no doubt it's coming from the discotheque, a siren song beckoning us onward.

"What are we waiting for?" Žana asks, and grabs our hands, tugging us along until we get to the Blue Bridge. The linden trees seem lit by pixie lights as the stars twinkle through the boughs.

"Slow down! I'm not used to walking in heels!" I totter to a halt and rest a moment, rubbing my calves as the river rushes below. I feel like a tiny lone drop in that river sometimes.

I don't get nervous about my dress until we get near the crowd of teens hanging around the terrace and park that are near the discotheque. It had taken me a whole summer to get used to wearing a bikini at Brvice, but suddenly I feel naked again. To be wearing a bathing suit by the water is one thing... to wear this slinky, slippery, almost-not-there dress out at night is somehow another thing! I can feel the material sliding all over my skin, and I'm aware of every inch of myself.

Nobody looks at you in a bikini or Speedo. Every young person at Brvice is almost as naked as a baby. In fact, just two years ago the city put up a bronze statue called *Djevojka sa Une*, "The Girl from Una," a nude sculpture symbolizing the magical beauty of a girl growing up by our emerald river. The river is about freedom, and part of that is the freedom to show as much skin as you like, or to show none at all if that's what you prefer. Freedom isn't just about uncovering but about covering, too. Here, though, the contrast between my small dress and the fully clothed boys makes me seem more undressed by comparison. Why is it the norm for women to wear skimpy things? What if men wore little shimmery spangled loincloths when they went out to dance? Before I know it, I can feel eyes on me.

Žana is used to it. Vedrana doesn't notice it. I'm both shocked and thrilled. Do they like what they see? Do I care? Yes and no.

"Should we wait for Sejla?" I ask.

"I think we should just go in. She said her brother is coming tonight so she can't be with Slobodan. Isn't theirs a beautiful love story?" Her smile is wistful, and I know she's thinking about Haris. Then she shakes her head like a bird fluffing its feathers. "Come on, let's start dancing!"

We pay the entrance fee and get our hands stamped. The stamp feels like a ticket to the adult world! When we walk through the door, we enter another realm.

One winter night Mama told me and Dino the tale of Ali Baba, the poor woodcutter who stumbles on a cave full of treasure. Dino liked to hear about the danger and heroism, but my favorite part was her description of the fabulous treasure. There were trees wrought in gold, Mama had told me, hung with fruits of precious stones—amethyst plums and ruby apples and emerald pears. The floor was strewn with pearls that glowed like lanterns. Diamond birds perched in silver cages. Everything glinted and glittered, lighting up the darkness of the secret cavern.

The discotheque is like that, dark and bright all at once, filled with treasure. Only the treasure isn't gold and jewels, but friends and music and life.

I'm hit by three repeating guitar chords, strong and insistent, commanding my attention. *All you've got is this moment. Twenty-first century's yesterday. You can care all you want.* The man's voice is smooth and compelling, like he's trying to lure me somewhere.

"Who is it?" I shout to Žana over the din.

"INXS, an Australian band," she shouts back. She knows everything about pop music, movie stars, and fashion from places I've barely heard of.

"What's he saying?"

She shrugs, and the movement of her shoulders turns into a dance. Suddenly we're in the thick of a hundred bodies, dancing, jumping, arms in the air and hips swaying. There's a fierce, free gleam in Žana's eyes, and before I know it she's lost in the music and the movement, her body one with the beat.

I've never really danced in front of people before. I love to dance in my bedroom or even outside with my friends on the terrace by the hotel where a band plays covers of Bosnian and foreign music. And I've been to a few concerts at the sports hall where, other nights, I'd watch volleyball games with Tata. My friends and I saw the famous Bosnian groups Crvena Jabuka (Red Apple) and Plavi Orkestar (Blue Orchestra) but we were just there for the music. I've never danced in a place where everyone is dancing.

"Am I doing it right?" I ask Žana, but she can't hear me and only shakes her head in time to the rhythm, her wild hair backlit by a pink light.

I soon realize there's no wrong way to dance. One girl to my right keeps throwing her head from side to side, while another is shaking her hips with her hands. The boy with them is simply swaying to the beat with his eyes closed.

This feels amazing. There's not a single worry or care. There's no yesterday or tomorrow. There is only now, my body, my sweat, my movement.

Then, I don't know how many songs later, Žana stops dead still and grabs my arm hard enough to hurt. "He's here," she breathes, and I can't hear her over the pulse of the music, but I can read her lips.

At first I think it's strange that Haris is out tonight. But then I remember the last few years, how the people who loved me did their best to force me out of isolation, into the world. What are friends for, if not to make you forget obsessive thoughts, at least for a time? He's with Sejla's brother and a few others, and he looks like he'd rather be any place other than here.

For the first time since their eyes met so long ago, Žana shows no timidity. Events have stripped away her anxiety, made it unimportant. The crowd seems to part before her, her long strides look like the prelude to a dance. I follow in her wake as she makes her way directly to him.

"Haris." She just says his name, and the sadness and sympathy seem to well up from her, a bottomless spring of flowing compassion. She takes his hand. "Come outside with me." As if they were a couple, or best friends, or brother and sister, they link hands and seem to merge into one as she leads him out of the noise of the discotheque.

I'm left with Sejla's brother Samir as the other boys in their party move onto the dance floor. We slide into a corridor near the back exit where the walls muffle the music enough for us to speak.

"I haven't had a chance to talk to Haris since his mother died," I tell him. "Is he doing okay? I'm surprised he came out tonight."

"We made him," Samir says. "He's been locked in his room for the last two weeks, ever since her funeral. I didn't know what to do. It's like he's dead, too. When he finally agreed to go out we practically had to drag him. He was like a robot—a broken robot."

"I can't imagine the pain he must be going through. If anything happened to either of my parents..."

"I know what you mean. My parents can be pains in the butt, but if I lost them..."

We both fall silent for a while.

"I'm glad Žana took him outside to talk, though," Samir says. "Once we got him here I started to think it might not have been the best idea after all. He hasn't really talked about it, and I don't know how to bring it up. I mean, I said how sorry I am of course, but what good does that do? I don't know what to say after that. I feel for him, but somehow it can't come out in words. I feel pretty useless."

"Žana is the opposite. Emotions are her language. I think she'll be able to help him."

When I told her about Haris last night, as I was leading up to it, she thought I was going to tell her that he had a girlfriend. She was agitated and almost angry, stalking around my room, already planning five steps ahead to win him back.

Then when I told her the whole truth, she stopped pacing and stood for a moment, utterly still. She'd been so ready to have her heart broken, that the news of his mother's death froze her. In that brief time something transformed in her. She stopped being a girl with a crush on a boy and became a girl who honestly cared about the boy.

She'd been ready to have her heart broken for herself. Instead her heart broke for him.

Samir heads off, and almost immediately Asmir, Zumra's son, comes over. "You're here? Žana, too? My mom says Žana should come over tomorrow morning, not too early."

"Oh. Žana said she'd be able to stay with us this summer," I say.

Asmir shrugs. "I'm just telling you what she said. It makes more sense for her and her sister to stay with you guys. Honestly, I'd prefer it. Žana and my mom are like temperamental cats around each other, always with their tails up and their fur puffed, hissing. But I guess Žana's mom and dad want her to stay with us."

Between this news and talking about Haris's loss, I start to feel a little blue again. It won't be the perfect summer if Žana isn't staying with me. We won't have those late nights eating hazelnut chocolate and gossiping on the mattresses on the floor, or long lazy breakfasts, or giddy makeup and hair styling sessions in the bathroom. It won't feel like she's really my sister if we just meet for a while every day and then go our separate ways. But how do you argue with parents?

No matter how much I long for a return to some golden moment of a past summer, I can't have it just by wishing. Maybe I can't have it at all. Nothing is ever perfect, and nothing is ever the same as it was. I'm starting to realize that. This summer, life has changed. But am I changing along with it?

I cheer up when Sejla and Belma come. Hana is here, too, and tells me that her parents are going to Germany for the summer. Then she waits, looking down at her shoes, to see what I'll say. Another girl might point out that after my father's troubles started, she was just like everyone else, keeping her distance so she wouldn't be associated with a suspected counter-revolutionary. *You let me down,* I could say, *so why should I help you?*

But you don't have to agree with someone's choice to understand it. I know why she did it, even if I wouldn't do the same thing myself. At least, I hope I never would. Anything she does can be forgiven because of what she has to live through at home. What would I be like if I had a father who beat me? Nothing is black and white anymore. With all that has happened, my life is now all shades of gray, and I understand Hana better than I ever could have a year ago. When I see her, nervous and sad, opening her heart to me and hoping I won't reject her—as I'd have every right to do—my own heart melts.

"Are you staying with your aunt again? You can come stay with us, too, whenever you want," I say casually. "We had a lot of fun last summer, didn't we?"

She looks up at me with grateful tears in her eyes. "Yeah, I'd like that."

After that, we lose ourselves in dancing. Usually we're all in a group, mostly girls together, but sometimes a boy we know dances with us. I have no idea what time it is. I'm sweating and my cheeks feel flushed. I know my hair must be a mess by now—I'm tossing it around like a wild woman, and whenever I stop it glues itself to the sweat of my face and neck. Sejla, Belma, Hana, and I link hands and dance. For a moment, Sejla forgets Slobodan, Hana forgets her terrible father. I try to do the same, willing myself to forget what has been done to my family…and in the hypnotic pulse of the music I almost succeed. I want to enjoy this innocence, don't want to let it pass me by. That's what Tata wants for me. Here, life is neon lights and rhythm.

I feel a hand on my shoulder and turn, mid-dance.

"You look like an Amazon," a boy says, very close to my ear. In flashes of strobe lights, I see dark hair, dark, tanned skin, very pronounced dark eyebrows, eyes full of fun and mischief. He's wearing a vivid purple T-shirt. He flashes me a megawatt smile and dances away from me.

"Who was that?" Belma asks.

I shrug, but Sejla shouts back, "That's Emir. He's best friends with Adnan, the son of that imam who people say can do magic."

That adds yet another layer of mystery and excitement to him, having a best friend whose father is a magician. I've heard of his father, the imam who does what he is not supposed to do. Mama took a cousin to this imam once, a girl with mental health issues that no one else could help. Her parents were strict believers who were scared to take her to the imam, but Mama did even though she didn't believe in any of it, because she had empathy for a desperate mother. Fate is fate, Mama realized after Amar died, and no magic will save a child. The imam prayed over the girl, gave weird instructions to sew a feather into the girl's pillow by the light of a crescent moon... but of course it did nothing. She was never cured. Still, it makes Emir somehow more unusual.

I keep on dancing, but those quizzical dark eyebrows, that impish smile stay with me.

When exhaustion finally catches up with us, we order a drink. I'm astonished at the high prices. Coke is the price of a good meal somewhere else, and Schweppes tonic water, which I really like, is almost as bad. Coffee is cheapest, sparkling water the second cheapest. I don't like coffee at all, but I might die of dehydration if I don't have something soon, so I pick budget over taste and buy a small fildžan and cringe my way through it. Then we head outside. I don't know about the others, but I'm ready to go home. My body still seems to pulse with the bass, in the same way you can feel waves rocking long after you've left a boat and are back on dry land.

When I see Žana and Haris I start toward them but then stop. They're sitting on a bench under a linden tree, their knees touching, their heads angled toward each other. There's nothing at all romantic about their postures, but they're talking so intently I don't dare disturb them.

I'm chatting with my friends when a voice says "Hey" from behind me.

"Do you always sneak up on people like that?" I ask him.

The boy with the dark, expressive eyebrows grins at me. "Like a panther," he says. An unlit cigarette dangles from his lips. I don't like smoking—not the smell or how it looks—but somehow I can't look away from that cigarette bobbing as he talks. Or am I actually looking at his lips?

The butterflies in my stomach feel different this time, making me excited and curious instead of frozen. I want to flirt, even if I don't really know how. I want to figure out what it is that I like, what attracts me to a boy. There's a confidence in me I never felt before, and it is surprising, like another person inside of me nudging me to act. Is this from years of watching Žana, or am I simply blossoming into my own self? I'm ready for exploration. Who knows what tomorrow will bring?

"Got a light?" he asks me.

Flustered, I reply, "I don't smoke."

"I know," he says, moving closer. "I know all about you."

For a second I can barely breathe, and I feel a little flutter in my chest. The light scent of his cologne floats from his tanned skin on the breeze off the Una.

"What do you know?" I ask him.

"Everything. I know what you hide behind that good-girl front. I know you're sweet and smart, and I know you can dance."

"How do you know all that?" Has he been asking people about me? I feel warm and wonderful but not yet fully in control.

"I can guess it all just by looking at you. In fact, I know every-thing ... except your name."

"Amra," I whisper. I can feel a drop of sweat trickling slowly down my back. Is that leftover from dancing, or is this boy's pres-ence actually making me sweat?

"I'm Emir. I haven't seen you here before."

"It's my first time."

He leans ever closer so no one else can hear. "Your first time is always special. Can I walk you home?"

"I ... I don't know." Maybe somewhere else it wouldn't be such a big deal, but here in Bosnia, people tend to hang out in groups, even if they're interested in one another. To go off alone with someone is practically like going steady. And I don't even know this boy! I guess it would be safe—we have a connection through cousins and friends, even if we never met before tonight—but the implications frighten me more than any actual danger.

Sejla comes over and puts an arm around my shoulders. "What's this? Has my little nerdy cousin made a conquest?"

I feel my cheeks burning. I know she's teasing, not being mean, but the end result is the same. She sees my embarrassment and looks instantly sorry. "What do you want with my beautiful cousin, eh?" Belma and Hana come over, too, a little army to keep me safe.

Emir laughs and holds up his hands in surrender. "All I want is a nice walk by the Una under the moonlight. Is that too much to ask?"

"You go on, Amra," Sejla says. "We'll make sure Žana and Vedrana get home safely." She hugs me close and whispers in my ear, "Have fun...but not too much fun, little cousin!"

I'm in a daze as we walk back to my house. He's so close his shoulder brushes against mine sometimes, and each time I feel a surge like electricity run over me. Where did this boy come from? Why is he interested in me, and not older Sejla or more glamorous Belma? How is this even happening? Yesterday I was a girl who had never been to a discotheque, and tonight a stranger is walking me home? I can barely follow his conversation, saying nothing more interesting than *yes* and *no* and *huh* to everything he says.

Soon enough, we're almost home! What if Mama and Tata see? Will they be mad that I let a boy walk me home or that I left my cousins behind? I'll have to introduce them, and I know I won't be able to speak. Then Mama will ask him all sorts of questions. What if she does the cigarette breath check on me in front of him? This is exciting, but it also makes me sick with anxiety. I'm not ready for this!

I stop at the house just before my own. "This is it."

"This one?"

"No, that one."

He takes my hand and leads me up to my doorstep. "You know, I never did light my cigarette," he says. "Maybe that's just as well." Still holding my hand, he pulls me a little bit closer. His face is so close it blurs. His breath is warm on my lips. A sweet breath that smells like bubblegum, not cigarette smoke. His lips almost touch mine...

And I jerk away.

"Thank you for walking me home," I say primly. "Good night." Before he even knows what's happening I run inside and slam the door. I lean my back against it as if he might try to break the door down, but a few seconds later I hear his footsteps as he walks away. When I'm brave enough to peek out the window the street is empty.

I feel like I've let someone down, but who? Him? Me? Part of me wanted to kiss him, to see what all the fuss is about. When I watch Sejla and Slobodan kiss it seems so natural, so romantic. When Žana fantasizes about kissing Haris someday, it sounds right.

This didn't feel right. It didn't feel *wrong*, exactly, but definitely not right.

I'm not my cousins, I don't have to be like them, do what they do. Sejla is Sejla, Žana is Žana, and I am me. I'm the author of my own love story, not acting out someone else's script, and I know that when I have my first kiss I want it to be special. I want it to *mean* something, not just be something I do on a whim, or for the experience, out of curiosity.

When I kiss a boy, I want to be in love with him.

But what if I love the wrong boy, like Sejla, or Žana? One boy is Serb, the other Bosniak, but both parents say he's the wrong kind of boy for their daughters. Would my parents ever say that? I don't know. The idea of love, already so complicated and intimidating, seems so much harder in a world of the "right" and "wrong" kinds of love. I don't believe it—love is love. But part of me is starting to understand how complicated things can be, even those things that should be easy, like love and friendship.

My bedroom door eases open, and Žana and Vedrana come in. While Vedrana goes to the bathroom to brush her teeth, Žana curls up with me and tells me about her night.

"We understand each other now, I think," she concludes. I'm glad that Žana sees who Haris is beyond his looks, beyond the appeal of the unattainable.

"Are you a couple now?"

"Of course not! Do you think I'd mention that kind of thing at a time like this? But we talked so much, about his mom, about life and death, all the big things, you know? He said he's never known anyone as sympathetic as I am. I feel so close to him now. It's not the right time to figure out all the rest, but I think...no, I *know* that we're closer than anything now."

"Closer than us?" I ask. I don't know if I'm jealous or just curious.

Žana laughs and hugs me. "No one can be closer than us, Amra."

And I realize that this is the only kind of love I need right now. The perfect, uncomplicated, forever love of Žana.

26

THE PHONE RINGS early in the morning, just as Žana and I are heading downstairs. Mama answers it. "Good morning! How are...Yes, of course. But it's really no trouble having her...I understand, but don't you think the girls would rather...I'll let her know."

Mama hangs up the phone so carefully I think she must be using all her self-control not to slam it down. "Is anything wrong, Mama?"

"That was Zumra. She says she expects Vedrana and Žana to be there this afternoon. I'm sorry, Žana. I know you wanted to stay here, and we love having you. But what can you do if that's what your mom and dad insist on?"

"Oh, you just wait and see what I'll do!" Žana says, and stomps her foot. Mama barely manages to suppress a smile.

"How are you going to change your parents' minds?" I ask her when we're back upstairs. Žana is packing angrily, taking out her feelings on her underthings, Vedrana is sulking, and Dino is complaining loudly about the unfairness of it.

"I have no idea. But there's no way I'll waste the whole summer at Zumra's, away from my Amra." She scrunches her brow, but we can't think of a solution.

To my relief, we decide to go to Brvice today. The discotheque was exciting, but maybe not something I want to do *every* night!

There were so many emotions, some joyous, others confusing, that I was overwhelmed. I can't stop thinking of that almost-kiss. Should I have allowed it to happen? Will I get another chance? I feel a little dizzy teetering on the edge of adulthood, balancing so delicately I worry about falling. Each summer gets harder, it seems. How many summers until things are impossible? Or maybe there comes a time when everything gets easy, when the long dizzy climb is over and I'll be secure, and sure.

Žana stands out on the balcony, looking as romantic as Juliet, while I brush my hair and get dressed. "All ready?" I ask.

"Just about," Žana says, and leans far over the balcony to the apple tree, stretching her fingers toward a tiny green apple.

"Žana!" I shout.

She jerks her hand back. "What?"

"I thought you were going to fall over! You shouldn't lean on the railing like that. And you shouldn't pick green apples! By the time autumn comes we won't have any left to ripen." It takes several months for apples to swell from hard little nubbins to juicy sweet red orbs.

"Oh, come on, don't tell me you never pick green apples?"

"Never!" I tell her honestly.

But almost every kid does, now and then. Not me—not from fear of the consequences but because it's not who I am. I don't know what the appeal is for the other kids—green apples are so sour they make your whole face twist up, and they're hard enough to hurt your teeth. Even worse, if you eat more than a bite or two, they can give you diarrhea. I guess part of it is the idea that you can get away with something, a little theft that most people will ignore. And part of it is a test, the way some people want to eat the hottest pepper. Dino has made himself sick more than once in a challenge to see who can eat the most green apples.

I've never stolen an unripe apple.

WE HAVE A perfect day...for a while. It's early afternoon, and Žana, Vedrana, and I've been swimming and sunbathing, expecting Ćućana to join us at any time. But so far she hasn't shown up. We decide to go look for her.

"Hello? May we come in?" We've knocked a few times at Ćućana's little house but for the first time no cheerful voice comes singing out to welcome us.

"Should we be like the aunts and let ourselves in?" I ask. I know it's the norm here, especially among the older generations, but I don't like to just barge in no matter how welcome I know I'll be.

"I think we should," Žana says. "What if something's wrong?"

"Dika, we're coming in!" I call, and we let ourselves in. "Ćućana, Dika, are you here?"

The house is dark, the curtains drawn. That's strange. Dika always has the windows wide open to let in the breeze and the sounds of passersby, and to gaze on her beautiful pear tree. I hear a little noise from the back of the house.

"Oh no, Žana, help me!" I cry. Dika is on the floor just outside the bathroom, her head bent uncomfortably against the wall, her skirt hiked up showing painfully wasted legs that remind me of

Amar. She's unmoving, and her hand, when l grasp it, is ice cold. Her wooden walking stick is laying nearby, snapped in half. "No, Dika, no! lt can't be!"

Then, like a miracle, her eyes flutter open.

"Amra...Žana...l'm sorry...l don't have any tea ready for you..."

With an almost hysterical laugh l pull her up to a sitting position and hug her, sharing the warmth my skin has soaked up from the sun all day. What a Bosnian thing to do—apologize for a lack of hospitality when you've collapsed on the floor.

"Žana, get her other side." We all but carry her to her usual nest on the sofa. Her legs can barely move on their own. It's strange, as a little child it never occurred to me that an adult could need help with anything. They were the ones who helped us. Now l know that everyone needs help in some way. "Dika, what happened?"

"Oh, it was my own silly fault. Instead of waiting for Meho or Dževad to come home l tried to go in myself. It wasn't to...l have a..." She breaks off, embarrassed, and glances at the empty bedpan tucked discreetly behind the sofa. "It wasn't that. l wanted to fix myself up a little bit. Poor Meho hasn't seen me with my hair done and makeup on in so long. l thought if l went slowly and was careful l could do it myself, surprise him." She laughs. What an amazing soul that she can laugh about this! "See, girls, the price of vanity? But my walking stick apparently wasn't made to support all my weight leaning on it, and when it broke, down l went!"

"Should l call a doctor?"

"What for? I'm just fine. Well, as fine as I ever will be again. Nothing that a doctor can do at any rate."

"Where are Meho and your kids?" I ask. "We can call them."

"Meho is at work, he'll be home soon. And Ćućana is...well, I hoped she might be with you. She went out for a walk earlier this morning. I gave her a sandwich to take to Meho. He's working at a neighbor's house a few blocks away. It's not far, she should have been back by now. Have you seen her?"

"Not today. Is she doing okay?"

"I don't know. She's been more absent-minded lately. She stares into space for a long time, but when I ask her what she's thinking about she just smiles and says *oh nothing*. She's gone for so long, sometimes, and I feel so helpless stuck here, not able to do anything for her."

"I'm sure you do a lot for her," I assure her. "Just having someone as sympathetic as you for a mother must make her feel so loved."

"Who knows what goes on in Ćućana's head? I wish she'd tell me more. I wish I knew what she was thinking, where she goes. What if someday she doesn't come back?"

"She would never do that," I tell her. "She loves you too much." I say it with confidence, even though in the back of my head, the back of my heart, I think of Amar. He left us, and no amount of love could stop him from going on that journey of no return. But I've learned not to lie exactly, but to cover up the harshness of life with half truths when it will comfort someone. And what I told Dika is true, in a way. Ćućana wouldn't leave her on purpose. But life might take her away someday all the same.

We stay with her until Meho comes home. He's so tender and patient with her, helping her adjust her weak legs, bringing her little treats from the kitchen. He may not have the best job, and people say he's not very bright, but there's more to human worth than intelligence and money. He has a kind and loving heart, and that makes him worth ten of that man who abandoned Dika before their wedding.

"I have to go to Zumra's now," Žana groans when we leave. "What am I going to do? I want to be with you, fixing our hair and getting ready for another exciting night at Hollywood. I don't even know if she'll let me go! She'll probably give me a ton of chores and then if I don't finish them or if I do one thing wrong she'll ground me. You know she doesn't like me, so she'll look for any excuse to ruin my fun. Oh, Amra, this could turn into a miserable summer."

As we pass the magnificent pear tree she absently yanks a tiny green unripe fruit from a low-dipping bough. She doesn't even try to eat it, just throws it at a tree trunk for the pleasure of hearing it bounce off. "Žana, how could you?"

"I didn't even notice what I was doing! It's just such a habit to pick them. Zumra gets so furious when I do..."

We both have the idea at the same time.

"No!" I say.

"Yes!" she counters. "Of course, why didn't I think of it right away? I'll attack her prize apple orchard. I'll pick every single one of her silly green apples and leave them in a big pile. She won't have any ripe apples at all this fall."

"Žana, that would be too cruel! You know how she loves those apples. She makes desserts with them and shares them with all the neighbors. They're her pride and joy."

"Exactly! Hit her where it hurts, and she'll be glad to get me away from her."

"So glad she might just send you all the way back to Belgrade. Besides, it's just mean. Think of all the people who will miss out on those sweet, juicy apples. It's not just about Zumra. And she's not really so bad, is she? She might not be the nicest to you, but you do provoke her every chance you get." Žana has taught me greater confidence, and now it backfires when she sees I've become assertive enough to stand up for what I think is right!

Žana pouts. "I guess you're right. But it was a really good idea."

We pass several other apple trees on the way back to Brvice. Every house has one or two, though not as many as Zumra's little orchard. Žana controls her impulse to snatch one from every tree we see.

So many apple trees in Bihać...

"Žana, I have an idea! What if you could do it without actually being mean?"

"How?"

I tell her, and she laughs with delight. "Amra, you're so clever. I think it will work!"

We go home so Žana and Vedrana can collect their bags, and then they leave for Zumra's house.

At home around dinnertime the phone rings again. Mama answers.

"What? Zumra, slow down, I can't understand you. She what? Please, stop yelling in my ear. No, if she did that it was very wrong

271

of her. I don't think calling her mother will do any good. They're at Đorđe's home village, and always working outside in the gardens there, you'll never reach them. They're expecting her to stay in Bihać. I understand, you must be very annoyed. Well, I suppose we could, if you really insist. Yes, why not both? Tonight? But wouldn't you rather ... of course, I'll be expecting her."

Mama sets down the receiver and turns to me with a stern expression that is trying to hide a smile. "Do you know what your cousin did?"

I have a good guess.

"That troublemaker Žana plucked half the green apples in Zumra's orchard and left them in a big basket on her dining room table. Zumra is livid! How could Žana do such a thing?"

I don't mean to confess, but somehow I can't help myself. "We had an idea that if Zumra thought Žana had destroyed her apples she wouldn't let her stay. Then she could come here."

"Oh, Amra, that was very wrong of you. You know what those apples mean to Zumra. They're the thing she's most proud of, other than her sons Asmir and Zlatan. Didn't you think about her feelings at all?"

Her chiding makes me feel terrible, even though I'm innocent! "But Mama, she didn't actually destroy the whole orchard! She just made Zumra *think* she did. We decided if Žana just made her believe that she ruined so many of her apples she'd get mad enough. But Žana didn't want to actually do it." This isn't exactly true, but I know Žana would have thought better of her first idea ... eventually.

I tell Mama how we got all of our friends and cousins together to help. Dino got the most people—what boy doesn't like this kind of mischief, and I know Dino has plenty of experience swiping apples and cherries. I told them that we have to search the entire city of Bihać for apple trees, and from each one pick one—and only one—green apple. "Everyone is fine with kids taking one," Dino said. "It's like a tax they pay, one green apple in exchange for us leaving the ripe apples alone." Once they understood it was to help Žana, a popular favorite, everyone was all for it. It was odd enough to intrigue people, too.

We spread out like a mob of crows, flying all over the city, looking for all the apple trees. We made a game of it, tiptoeing and stifling our giggles even when the homeowner was watching us, making such a pantomime out of it that no one got mad. One old man told us he was glad to see teens having nice clean fun instead of smoking and necking all day. Another woman who used to be one of Amar's teachers when he was little said she would make us a pie of sweet apples when hers were ripe.

"Žana didn't even take any from Zumra's grove, not even one. All our friends brought Žana the apples they collected and she made a big pile to make Zumra think she'd vandalized her orchard."

"Well...I suppose that's not quite so bad," Mama says with her hidden smile. "But you and your friends were still stealing apples."

"I didn't steal any, Mama." It's true, technically, though I did go along on the hunt. "But...it was my idea." I hang my head, ashamed that I instigated a crime, even a minor one that saved my summer. But beneath that childish feeling of shame is another feeling: pride in my audacity, my willingness to take risks I never would have dreamed of a mere two summers ago.

"Well, I suppose most children steal a green apple now and again."

"Did you, Mama?"

"Are you kidding?" she asks, and I think of course, my Mama would never sneak a green apple. But then she goes on. "Didn't you know I was the green apple–eating champion of my school? I once ate three in five minutes without throwing up or . . . having the other thing. In fact, one boy was so mad I won that he pushed me in a big mud puddle. That's what I got in trouble for with my own mama. She had just braided my hair so neatly—you know how big and curly my hair gets when I don't keep it short— and then it was all muddy. Mama didn't mind that I stole green apples, though. She told me that as long as you don't take any more apples than the wind might blow down, it's not a crime. Now, go upstairs and make sure your bedroom is ready for company. Žana and Vedrana should be here in time for dinner."

27

"JUST ASK YOUR mom for it," Žana says. "It's only one egg."
But she doesn't understand, and I don't want to explain. One egg
isn't a big deal to her, but it is to us. Money is so tight that Mama
says she'll have to cut back on the food she brings to Brvice. She'll
only bring a feast once a week, and even that means we'll have
to eat more simply at home. Luckily Hana is spending most of
this summer with an aunt, though she still comes over occasionally. She'll meet us tonight at the disco and then come back for
a sleepover.

I know Mama will do her best to make sure Žana doesn't
notice how we cut our rations. Maybe instead of a chicken Mama
will plan a bean soup we make together and have two days in a
row because she says she wants to pass on the recipe her mother
taught her. There's just honey on the table, not butter or jam.
Mama says it's so Žana can have the special treat of Tetka Fatma's
honey ... but I know the honey is free, and butter and jam are getting more expensive by the day. We still have the meat from the
cow, but most of that is in Tetka Fatma's freezer, and she wants us
to save it as long as possible. Instead we eat sausages that Tetka
Begija smuggles out from the factory kitchen. Fatma brings us
vegetables from her garden even more often than before. We'll
never starve, but we have to be careful.

I'm in on the conspiracy, raving about my favorite ajvar

spread so that Žana and Vedrana also want the pepper relish on day-old bread rather than expensive cheese and pastrma on fresh toast. I don't want them to know how tight money is, for several reasons. Maybe pride is one of them, but also I don't want Žana to feel like her visit is a burden on us, that we have to cut corners elsewhere just to feed her. I've learned what to share and what not to share, even with those closest to me, instead carrying it inside of me. As these things pile up I feel like I'm carrying a sack over my shoulder, adding one rock at a time.

Now, Žana is telling me about a fabulous hair tonic that will give us big beachy waves. The only problem is that it needs sunflower oil and an egg. Maybe we could spare the egg—it's only one egg, after all. Maybe Mama would even give us the egg. But I know already the look that would be on her face. *How frivolous,* she'd think. How wasteful when that egg could be poached atop a nutritious čilbur tomato, onion, and pepper stew, or used to make a tasty cake. At the same time she might remember what it was like to be my age, to want to experiment and experience. She might think one egg was a small price to pay for a night of teenage happiness.

"You just *have* to try it," Žana goes on. "You'd think it would make a goopy mess, but if you wash your hair first and then comb it through with your fingers and scrunch it as it dries, it gives your hair so much volume. We can have the biggest hair in the discotheque! And the oil adds a shine like you wouldn't believe. Come on, Amra, just one egg?"

I can't resist her pleading. "Okay, but you wait here."

I'm on a stealth mission, like a special forces army officer sneaking behind enemy lines. Mama and Tata are in their rooms, but either one could come down at any moment. Tata probably wouldn't even notice, but Mama keeps such a tight inventory of food in the house that she probably knows the first and last name of every egg in our refrigerator! Even if she doesn't catch me in the act, she'll surely notice one is missing.

I'm a girl who won't even take a green apple, and here I am stealing from my own family! I feel bad, but I don't know how to get out of it without revealing my family's embarrassing poverty to Žana. I silently take a bowl, a tablespoon of oil, and one precious egg, along with a fork to whisk it all together. As I creep upstairs, I wonder how I can ever make up for this crime. But I also feel…I don't know, exactly. A sense of danger, a thrill of getting away with something. There's just a tiny part of me that understands why Žana sneaks an occasional cigarette.

But most of me wants to cling to my childhood where things are simple, where it never occurred to me to disobey anything. It was so easy living in a world without moral choices. When I was younger, I also had Amar, who would help me puzzle through every dilemma. Now, every choice I make, even one as tiny as an egg, seems to be a compromise and cost me a little bit of pain.

Back upstairs we beat the egg and oil together, and wet our hair—we don't have time to each take a shower if we want to get out tonight.

"Žana, you must have made a mistake. Maybe this is one of those hair masks you let soak in and then wash off?" My hair feels sticky, and I can't get over the idea that there's food on my head.

"Be patient, Amra. Just keep working it in and then scrunch

it with your fingers. It will take a while. Believe me, this is better than mousse and hair spray combined."

I wouldn't know—I've never tried either. Hair spray reminds me of Azra, who uses gallons of it on her huge, teased hair. Once someone holds your head underwater until you think you're about to drown, you don't want to imitate them in anything! Of course, Mama uses it, too. When she and her sisters get their hair done they spray it until it is helmet-hard, then stay out of the water for days to keep the style intact. I guess my hair was short for so long I never thought about using hair spray. Now that it has grown out a lot, though, I like the idea of using something to give it a special style.

She's right! It takes a while, but somehow the sticky egg doesn't dry to a crust, but instead holds our hair in full shiny waves.

"But is it going to stink later?" I ask her. We might go from being the queens of the discotheque to the girls with food in their hair!

"Maybe if we left it on for two days, but since we have to be home by midnight we should be fine."

"But if any rats or mice start sniffing your way, you better run!" jokes Vedrana.

As we're walking down the stairs, Žana holds me back, letting Vedrana go first. "Amra," she says, low and serious. "This is the night."

"What do you mean?"

"Tonight I tell Haris how I feel. I was worried it might be too soon, but he needs someone to comfort him. I think if he knows how much I care it will help him."

"I think you helped him a lot already... as a friend."

"I want to be more than his friend, you know that. And I think he should know it, too."

A change has come over her after last night. She's no longer that uncertain girl full of self-doubt. I recognize it. Žana is gradually becoming her truest Žana, just as I am becoming my truest Amra.

"I know what I want, and I believe I can get it," she adds.

I follow her downstairs, wondering about the way she phrased it. There's a boutique next door to the discotheque that sells jeans in all colors: not just dark blue and light blue, but gray and green and red. I think I want a pair of red jeans more than anything else in the world! I know I'll never get them—they're Levi's and cost far too much—but if I could afford them, if I had plenty of money to throw around, that's how I might say it: "I know I want those jeans, and I believe I can get them."

Is that the way she wants Haris? I wonder how much of love is the challenge of finding a partner, like a prize?

Is love about winning?

When Emir walked me home and wanted to kiss me, did he really like me, or did he see something that caught his eye, something he wanted to own, if only for a night? I don't want a love like that. But then...I was entranced by Emir's lips, his scent, his smile. I just couldn't "afford" what he was offering—where the currency was emotions.

I know Haris is more than a prize to be won for Žana. Especially after their hours of heart-to-heart talking last night, she cares for the person as well as the handsome boy. Their connection last night was real, so why am I analyzing this so much?

279

We meet up with Sejla and Belma. Ćućana isn't allowed to go to Hollywood, and anyway, I'm sure she's home taking care of Dika by now. It's dark, and she always goes home before nightfall if we're not with her.

When we get to the discotheque Žana squeals, "It's Madonna night!" Unbeknownst to us, Hollywood is having a theme night. They'll be playing a heavy rotation of Madonna songs, and some of the girls here are even dressed like Madonna. Some imitate her most recent, most daring look, with fishnet tights. I see a couple of real bustiers, and even more tight, cropped black shirts under short denim or leather jackets. Others go for her earlier style, bright colors, layered clothes, tons of rubber and plastic bracelets going halfway up both arms, and of course her trademark hair bow. A few even copy her sweet and innocent look with puffy white tulle and lace gloves.

Music pumps through the door as we get our hands stamped. *Something in the way you love me won't let me be. I don't want to be your prisoner so baby won't you set me free.* I know the word *love* because it's in so many American songs I've figured it out. Other than that, I don't know what she's saying, but I admire the defiance in her voice. She's a person who won't stand for any insult. That's someone I would like to be. I've taken tiny steps in that direction, I think, but what kind of journey will I have to take through life to reach that destination?

"I wish we'd dressed up like her," Žana says.

"You look better in your own style," I tell her. "Besides, what if you win him over and then later some other girl dressed as Madonna comes over and he thinks it's you?"

She laughs, and we dance together and with our friends through the rest of "Borderline," then "Lucky Star," and "Holiday." I wonder if Emir will be here tonight. I wonder if this time I'll kiss him. I don't think I will...

But I still like thinking about it.

A boppy voice singing "I think we're alone now" replaces Madonna—they can't play only Madonna songs, I guess—and suddenly, from across the dance floor, I see Emir. Our eyes meet...

And he looks away like he never saw me before in his life.

I stop dancing, still breathing hard.

"What is it?" Žana asks.

"Emir. He...he looked right through me."

"He what?" Žana shouts over the music.

"He must think I'm just a little girl, not grown up enough to..."

She grabs me by the shoulders, and we're the only still ones in a sea of moving bodies. "Amra, forget him. It was interesting for a few minutes, but he's nothing to you, right? Don't even think about him. If you not kissing him is enough to make him lose interest, well, then he's not interesting enough for you. There are so many boys in the world! He's not even that cute."

That last part is just a lie to cheer me up.

I start dancing again, but my heart isn't in it. I know I look older. That's what happens when you're six feet tall! All it takes is a little makeup and less dowdy clothes, and I look almost like an adult. But in my heart, I know I'm still a kid. Now Emir knows it, too. I feel like I just got denied a membership to a club I wasn't sure I wanted to belong to in the first place. The rejection stings...but there's a little relief, too.

Gradually, I start to feel better. How can a person be glum when listening to Madonna? She's so daring, audacious, scandalous—all the things I can't imagine myself being. I feel like I'm living on the edge just by listening to her music. It feels like everything is allowed in America. You can just do whatever you want. What could be better than that?

I think of all the whispers in my family, all the history we can't talk about, all of the present moments we don't let ourselves address. Why can't we—not just my family but my people, the Bosniaks—be ourselves, talk about our past, about what makes us who we are? Madonna is loved for being open and free about everything. But here, that can ruin lives.

I cheer up even more when I see a very tall boy wearing overalls with deep bulging pockets. Everyone calls him Sejo Bajkanov—Sejo, son of Bajkan—because his father's name is Bajkan. He's really nice, a cheerful person, the kind that never asks anything of you, only what he can do for you. As he approaches I catch a whiff of almost overpowering cologne. I wrinkle my nose but try to hide it so I don't offend him.

"Hi Sejo Bajkanov!" I call, and introduce him to Žana and Belma. Sejla apparently already knows him.

"What did you bring us today?" Sejla asks him.

To my amazement, Sejo Bajkanov looks around stealthily and then starts pulling out packages wrapped in paper. "Tonight I have livanjski sir cheese and pastrma on some bread still warm from the oven."

"Warm from being in your pockets, more like," Sejla teases, but she eagerly takes one of the packets.

"Wait until you taste the pastrma. Seasoned with the finest onion and garlic, sliced so thin I could see your face through it." He's talking like a deli owner promoting his favorite product.

"What's all this?" I ask him, smiling.

"Didn't you know, Amra? Oh, that's right, you never used to come here. Well, when I first started coming to Hollywood of course I expected all the girls to want me. Right?" He nudges Sejla playfully. "But for some reason none of them were interested. So I figured since I'm not going to be kissed, I might as well eat all the garlicky pastrma I want. I'd sneak some in, triple-wrapped so the management couldn't smell anything, and have a nice snack when I got tired of dancing."

"Why not buy something here?" Žana asks.

"The food is no good, all cold and stale, and have you seen the prices? Soon I had the bright idea that if I couldn't be the most popular boyfriend, I could be the most popular friend—and who is more popular than the person who gives you food when you've danced yourself into starvation? So I bought overalls with the deepest pockets I could find, and now I bring snacks for everyone."

"You should charge, Sejo Bajkanov," Sejla says, but he looks aghast at the thought.

"I'm not doing this for money! I just like how happy people look when I feed them."

I think Sejo Bajkanov and my mom would get along well.

He leans closer to me and Žana. "Sorry about the cologne," he says. "I know it's horrible, but I need it to mask the smell of the pastrma. If they smell it at the door they'll never let me in. They'll say I'm ruining their profits."

We each take a bite or two from the sandwich Sejla took, and it fortifies us enough to keep dancing. The only problem is that he mixed a salty meat with a salty cheese, and now we're even more thirsty than before. I could run out and drink directly from the Una!

"Maybe he's not coming after all," Žana says, looking anxiously toward the door.

Just then they start playing another Madonna song. *I made it through the wilderness . . . Didn't know how lost I was until I found you.*

"I don't know this song, do you?" I ask Žana.

"You haven't heard it? It's the best. 'Like a Virgin.' Listen!"

Madonna's voice blares through the speakers.

"What does it mean?" I ask.

Žana whispers in my ear. A friend with relatives in America told her.

"Oh my goodness! She can say that?" I giggle, wishing I could understand the rest of the song. What a thing to sing about. Madonna can truly sing about anything! I wish I could do the same, let every thought and feeling out in song, in writing, in speech, without fear. With Madonna I get a glimpse of what I've missed my entire life. What Bosniaks have missed.

"Amra, there he is!" Žana says a few songs later.

On the edge of the dance floor, bathed in romantic pinkish light, is Haris. He's alone tonight and stands near the doorway, away from the crowd, looking around as if searching for someone.

Of course, he must be looking for Žana.

Žana grabs my hand and gives it a squeeze, then starts slowly toward him. Our fingers stay linked until the last second, her arm trailing back behind her. When we part I watch her, moving as if she's in a slow-motion movie scene. As if on cue, the DJ starts to play U2's "With or Without You." Which will it be for Žana? With or without?

I can see her hands clench and open as she wills herself to courage. The moment is perfect. She's halfway across the dance floor, and I can already see the kiss that I know will happen. Haris is still looking around. He hasn't seen Žana yet, and she's almost reached him.

At last he looks right at her. Even though her back is to me I can feel the magic of Žana's smile, the way her eyes sparkle. His lips move, he's saying something to her...

Then, as suddenly as if she were a pouncing wildcat, a blonde girl slips in between them, shutting Žana out like she doesn't exist. I recognize her—it's Ela, a notorious flirt who never had a moment of shyness in her life. She runs her fingers through her golden hair, tossing it provocatively, and gets close enough to Haris to whisper in his ear.

Žana stands stock still. I can see her trembling from here. Slowly she backs up. One step. Two steps.

Ela is laughing. Haris is smiling.

Then the worst thing of all happens.

Ela kisses him.

They're kissing.

Everyone in the discotheque disappears for me. There is only Žana, alone in her heartbreak.

She runs out the door. As she passes I can see silver tear streaks on the face that was so full of confident joy just a few moments ago. "Get the others," I shout above the music to Vedrana as I run after Žana. She needs me.

This is who I am at my heart, more than anything else: the protector. When someone I love is in pain there is no hesitation, no self-doubt. This is when my strength emerges and I am, most completely, Amra.

28

I REMEMBER HOW it was after Amar died—the numbness, the lethargy, the way my brain would alternate between replaying the same scene over and over again and not thinking at all. I could say that losing a crush is nothing like losing a brother… but who can compare grief? What right would I have to say that my pain hurts more than anyone else's? It's not a scale; there is no balance. She is feeling it, that's all that matters.

Žana felt the pain of Haris's grief for his mother as if it were her own, because she loved him. Now I feel Žana's pain as if it is my own. When you give your heart to someone you double your chance of pain. I fear loving because I know what it is to lose love. Now Žana knows, too.

She falls into bed the moment we get her home and stays there, silent except for her sobs, all night and into the morning. Although there's not much I can do for her, I'm glad I'm with her when her heart is broken for the first time in her life. I felt so alone when Amar died, when Tata was taken away. I had my family, but I didn't have a friend, a peer. I'll be here for Žana and help her, no matter what.

"Come down for breakfast," I urge her. She just shakes her head and curls into a tight ball.

"Come to Brvice," Vedrana begs, but Žana just shudders.

"Haris could be at Brvice," she murmurs from under the

covers. "Haris could be anywhere in Bihać, kissing Ela. I'm never going out again. I'm never getting up again."

Nothing will convince her to get out of bed, so we leave her there and go downstairs. Over hot bread Tetka Begija delivered early that morning, smeared with honey from Tetka Fatma's bee farm, Hana and Vedrana and I try to figure out what to do. Sejla and Belma come over before we've made much progress.

"How's the victim?" Sejla asks.

"Still in bed," I say.

"Forever," Vedrana adds.

"She's just being dramatic," Hana says crossly. "She acts like it's the end of the world." Hana knows about suffering, too. She never likes to talk about the abuse she suffers at home but now she makes a rare, if vague, allusion to it. "Some of us have real problems. How lucky that her only problem is not getting one thing that there are literally three billion more of. One boy doesn't like her, so what?"

"Hana, that's not fair. She's in pain. Whether you think it's justified or not, her heart is broken. Now, what are we going to do? Should we make her talk it through, get it all out of her system? Or just let her sulk for as long as she likes?"

"I think she should go out and find another boy," Vedrana says. "Someone like Omer. She should kiss him right in front of Haris to show him what he's missing." She thinks for a moment, then adds for emphasis, "Kiss him with her tongue!" Sometimes she goes so far trying to imitate us and be as grown-up as possible that she shocks us!

It's not a bad idea. "I don't think she'll be ready for that for a while. But luckily it's early in the summer, so maybe she can find someone to distract her later on." Omer certainly is interested in her, but she hasn't given him any encouragement other than friendship.

"We have to find *something* to get her out of bed," Belma says. "Maybe we can take her to Zuhra's sweets shop. Žana always perks up at cakes and ice cream. One taste of Zuhra's pistachio ice cream, and she'll forget all about Haris."

"We'd have to get her out of bed first," Sejla points out.

"Maybe a makeover?" Belma suggests. "We can do her makeup, and she doesn't even have to get out of bed. She can just lie there. And if she cries, well, I have some waterproof mascara!"

I laugh, then feel guilty for laughing at all while Žana is so miserable. I have to think of something, though! I know she would do anything to help me if I was unhappy ... even if, in the last year, I haven't told her about half of my troubles.

On a hunch I bring over my tiny cheap radio. It has a cassette player, but I usually have to fight with it for ten minutes just to get the cassette door open. Today the machine is sympathetic and opens right away and even starts to play the grainy copy of a copy of a copy of an Azra tape. I bring it upstairs. At the first sound of singer Branimir Štulić's voice, Žana stops crying. The slightest smile touches her face.

"Yes, he knows what it is to suffer," she says, and lays her head back, staring at the ceiling, letting the emotion wash over her. I think if she could have listened to the whole tape the melancholy melodies would have purified her heart, given her perspective, buoyed her up in a sorrowful sea. But—like usual—the player eats the tape and the beautiful sad voice garbles and then shuts off.

Back to the drawing board, I think as I carefully untangle and rewind the delicate tape. Music isn't the answer. Neither are makeovers or cakes. She enjoys those things, but ultimately they're shallow, and this cut goes deep. It's more than just losing a boy. Her confidence is shattered. Two years she's invested: daydreams, musings, and fantasies, all with Haris as the leading man. Thoughts of him were her distraction in times of stress. When her parents were fighting she would let her mind stray to Haris, and for a while everything seemed a little better. I know she contrasts this love with her parents' relationship. This is a true love, neither selfish nor mercenary. I wonder how much she actually analyzes why her mom married her dad? Does she realize that her mother is ashamed of who she is and thought she could "better" herself by marrying a Serb? But Žana's heart would never work like that.

I know how it feels when the world you believed in suddenly turns upside down, when your entire mindset is forced to change. What does it matter whether it is because your eyes open to the prejudice around you or you see the boy you love kissing someone else? It is shock, it is pain.

After that you have to find a way to endure. And slowly, you must learn to find joy again. Each time my life was shattered—by Amar's death, by Tata's investigation, by what is happening to Bosnia—it took me a while to rebuild it. My parents helped, of course, but it was always Žana who made me feel alive again. Her love, her sisterhood, saved me.

Now I have to find a way to save her.

"Žana," I whisper, touching her shoulder. She doesn't respond, just stares unblinking into space with her bloodshot eyes. "Žana please, you're scaring me. You look like…" Without warning I start to cry. I don't even realize I'm doing it until tears fall onto her arm. She looks like she's dead. Like there's nothing behind her eyes. How can she be so alive one moment, then like a blown-out candle the next—all that vibrancy extinguished? In her depression she's just lying there, staring, like Amar did as the light faded from his eyes…

If this were a fairy tale, my tears would be enough to save her. They'd touch her skin and she'd magically shake off the sadness, smile at me, and be my cheerful Žana again.

Instead, she doesn't even seem to notice them.

I want to yell at her, shake her until she snaps out of it. *What about me?* I want to ask. What about Vedrana and Sejla and Belma, Mama and Tata and Dino? What about our beautiful Una? Aren't you here because you love us? Or were you just here because you loved him? I hear the phone ringing downstairs. Ten rings, then it stops. Why didn't anyone answer it? Then I remember Mama and Tata went with Dino to visit Tetka Fatma and Tetak Ale earlier. My cousins and Hana must feel like they don't have permission to answer the phone in our house. When it starts to ring again a moment later I reluctantly leave Žana's side and trudge downstairs to answer it.

"Amra?" It's Mama, and she sounds upset. "Oh, thank goodness! Is Dino home with you?"

"No," I say, the hairs on the back of my neck prickling at her tone. "Didn't he go with you and Tata?"

"He did, but he went outside to play in the river." The river where it flows near Tetka Fatma's house is shallow and gentle, just right for a kid to wade and try to catch minnows or frogs with a net. "And now...Oh, Amra! When we went outside to call him one of the neighbors ran by and said a boy had drowned! They were gone before we even realized Dino was missing and...what if..." Her voice breaks in a sob and I feel my body go numb, my stomach turn ice cold. It was always there, the death, the disaster, waiting to strike my family again. I let my guard down.

Somehow I find the strength to say, "Mama, it wasn't Dino. It couldn't have been. He knows better than to go in the deep water, or maybe the person was wrong. Maybe..." But I'm weeping, silently, with a sinking feeling in my heart. "Mama, I'm coming to look for him. Where did they say it happened?"

"They didn't say, they ran off to help, somewhere up the river. What if..."

"Mama, it's okay, I'll be right there."

"Don't stop here, go right upriver. We'll go, too."

I quickly tell the others what happened.

"What about Žana?" Sejla asks. "Do we leave her here alone?"

I think for a second. "No. Žana is coming with us."

I run back upstairs. "Žana, get up!"

"Leave me alone," she mutters from under the covers.

I don't have time for this, and I'm in no mood to be indulgent. "Get up now and help us!" I fling the covers off her and she squeals, then scowls at me.

"What are you doing? Go away."

"This is no time to think about yourself. You can be unhappy later. Right now, we need you. Dino is missing."

"What?"

I hastily explain. In an instant, Haris and Ela might as well not exist. She leaps out of bed and scrambles into her clothes. Most tellingly, she runs out of the house with us without washing her face, fixing her hair, or putting on a drop of makeup. Her golden-brown hair is tangled in the back, and the remains of last night's mascara are smudged around her eyes. She looks feral ... and has never been more beautiful.

We run to the Una, stopping everyone we know and telling them as quickly as we can. A web of searchers expands from us, all heading toward the Una's beautiful, treacherous waters.

We see someone standing on the riverbank, scanning the water as it cascades over rocks. "Who was it?" I grab this stranger by the shoulders, almost shaking him. "Who drowned?"

"I don't know," he says. "They say it was a boy."

"How old?" I demand.

"Not a little child. Maybe a teen? They told us all to look, everywhere, downriver. I don't know much, just what my neighbor said."

We run and stop everybody. People have heard rumors, gotten confused phone calls, half truths and errors. It's a child, no, a teen. He drowned, no, he was saved. Tears are streaming down my cheeks, and I try to keep myself together for Dino, for Mama, for Tata, because I can't be of any help to anyone if I curl up in a ball and cry until all the horror is washed away. The more time passes without finding him, the more I believe that he's gone.

This whole time, Žana never lets go of my hand. Her troubles are forgotten in the wake of this. How small her sorrow seems against this greater one.

It isn't until we reach a set of treacherous waterfalls downstream of Brvice that we learn what really happened. There's a crowd here, some pacing the shore, others standing like statues, tense and watchful. I see two wooden lađa boats in the water, with people paddling as near to the waterfall as they dare. There's another boat, capsized and swamped, and I remember how Dino always begged to be allowed to take out Uncle Ejo's boat by himself.

That moment with Azra comes back to me, the freezing swirl of emerald water coiling around me like a beautiful deadly snake, and my throat closes up thinking of the terror of drowning.

I see Asmir on the bank, soaking wet, a hollow look in his eyes. "Who is it?" I beg him to tell me.

He looks at me and sighs, then shakes his head, and I feel the ground open up under me.

"We know them," he says. "The twins, Senad and Damir, and their brother Adis."

I've known them for years. Dino went to school with the twins when he was younger. Their father is an artist who sets up his easel on the banks of the Una to paint its beauties.

"They were in a lađa, and they got too close to the waterfall. That's what people are saying. I wasn't here. I heard the shouting and came later. When the waterfall hit their boat it flipped over and they all fell in. They're not good swimmers." He scrubs a tear from his eye. "They thought they were safe in the boat. Their father jumped in to save them, but he needed to be saved himself. From what they say, everyone here was so panicked, so afraid, they just watched. The only one who dove in was Naser."

I know him, too. He's a grown man with the mind of a child, someone who the neighborhood bullies mock and tease. Of all of them, he was the one willing to risk his life to save four lives.

He only saved three.

Senad, a beautiful, funny, clever boy who was Dino's age, sank under the water.

Žana puts her arms around me and whispers in my ear, "You can be relieved. It's okay. You can be glad it's not Dino and sad for Senad at the same time. You can feel everything, Amra." She squeezes me tight and I let myself weep into her hair, weeping for the boy who is gone and for the fear that never leaves me, that there will be more loss in my life.

As I absorb comfort from Žana, I realize again how different we are, each shaped by our natures and our experiences. Žana's laughter and love protected me from pain when she was here, but I will never escape the realities of my life. I am Bosniak, and that has brought me hardship. I am a girl who lost a brother and therefore will never be as carefree as Žana. She is a balm on my broken heart, but that is not enough to erase the deep scars.

In my heart, in my soul, I know I will have heartbreak and loss again. Maybe not today, but one day. And I know that my scarred heart is strong. Somehow, I will take whatever life throws at me.

I look at the weeping father, the sodden boys. I see the place where one is missing, where he will be forever missing in their hearts. They will see him every day, as I see Amar, in my thoughts, my memories, in voices I hear in a crowd.

But Dino is still missing, and the undercurrent of panic still lingers. He didn't drown, but where is he?

I don't know what draws my footsteps there. Both of my brothers are lost to me right now, so maybe there is some small comfort in seeking out Amar, even if I can never hug him again. Without any real plan, my feet carry me to the cemetery where Amar is buried.

THERE IS A beauty to cemeteries, a peace, despite the melancholy. Before Ramadan my mom and I would join all the aunts to clean the graves of our family members. We'd run into other friends or relatives and remember those who are gone. The older women, the devout, would wash themselves in the fountain, cleansing themselves before prayer. The whole ritual was cleansing for all of us, giving us time to reflect, to remember.

The past is here, beneath the ground. Centuries of loss and mourning, so many generations of lives lived and remembered. Memory, that's the part we should hold on to. Sorrow is natural, but what is important is that all these people existed. They were real, alive, vital, like Amar. Some died full of years with their families around them. Others died alone on a battlefield calling for their mamas. And now that I think about it, not a single generation of my Bosniak family lived without experiencing violence against them for who they are. Will my generation follow this pattern, or will we learn? How can we be cruel to one another when death comes for us all the same in the end? The bad and the good are buried here, the cruel and the kind. They are all the same now, except for the memories they leave behind.

"There he is," Žana whispers, and we run to him.

He's sitting on the mossy ground, leaning against the stone that marks Amar's grave. This grave is fresh but others here are old, their stones eaten by lichen, slowly crumbling. This is an ancient Muslim cemetery, a centuries-old resting place. Dino is holding a cheerful yellow flower from a little shrub we planted on the grave. People here plant flowers along with leaving cut ones, and our cemeteries are alive with butterflies.

"Dino, what are you doing here? We were so worried! We have the whole city out searching for you."

He lifts his miserable tear-streaked face and wails, "I'm sorry! I'm so sorry!"

But he's not looking at me—he's looking at Žana.

"I didn't know. I thought it was fun at first, and then I did it because it made you happy." He looks up at her with glistening bloodshot eyes. "And for the ice cream," he adds sheepishly. "I wanted to stop, but Maše talked me into keeping it up." He swallows hard and seems to get a year older all of a sudden when he adds stoically, "No, that's not fair. It's my fault. I can make my own decisions, and I chose to do it. It doesn't matter what Maše said. I have free will." It's a phrase that Tata uses when he talks about always doing the right thing no matter how many people around you are doing the wrong thing.

At first I don't even know what he's talking about. My brain is so a-whirl with the image of Dino beneath a swirling Una whirl-pool that I can't think of anything beyond the relief of holding him again.

"I didn't mean to hurt you, Žana. I didn't realize what would happen." He bursts into sobs again and breaks away from me to throw himself into her arms. "When I saw you sad, saw you broken, I realized it was all my fault. I let you think Haris was in love with you. Vedrana told me what happened. You never would have cared about him at all if I hadn't told you those lies, and now your heart is shattered."

He'd told us that he was getting his information from Haris's brother Halid, or from overhearing Haris talking about Žana. He'd gotten so many ice creams over the summer in exchange for his information. Now he tearfully confesses that he made it all up.

"Oh, Dino," she says, holding him tight. "Don't feel sad. My heart isn't shattered. It hurts, a lot. But do you know what? While we were looking for you I forgot all about it. Haris who?" She gives a rueful little laugh.

"I just liked seeing your face light up whenever I told you that he liked you," Dino says. "You've been so nice to me, gave me the skateboard, helped me make friends. I wanted to do something for you, too. I wanted to put that smile on your face. I'm so sorry I lied."

"So it wasn't about the ice cream?" she asks him wryly.

"Well...it was a little bit about the ice cream."

"You poor little man! Don't you worry about me." She shakes her head, her hair flying all around her face, as if she's trying to shake her sadness away. She looks at me over Dino's head, and I can read so much in her eyes.

"Why did you come here, Dino?" I ask gently.

"I was upset, so I went for a walk along the riverbank. Then I came to the place where they said someone had drowned. It was terrible, Amra. Everyone was staring into the Una like they were waiting for the river to speak, to open up and give the person back. I didn't stay to find out who it was. It just made me so sad. Everything made me sad today. I needed Amar. Oh, Amra, sometimes I miss him so much. He could always make things better. You can, too, but you have Žana now. You're always doing something interesting, and I'm never part of it."

My heart twists with guilt. I never meant to make him feel abandoned. I was just so happy to have a sister, someone who I could learn how to be a teenage girl from.

"I'm sorry, too, Dino. I promise I'm always here for you."

"Who was it that drowned?" he asks innocently. "Do you know?"

I can't tell him that it was his friend. Not now. Not yet. So I do what I never used to be able to do when I was younger: I lie to protect him.

"I don't know, Dino. We can find out tomorrow." His face, puffy with tears, relaxes a little bit.

We all sit in silence at Amar's grave. Then I remember that Mama and Tata must be frantic with worry, and we get up to head home.

"Do you want an ice cream on the way home?" Žana asks with a straight face but a sidelong glance at me. "Maybe two scoops of pistachio, or hazelnut?"

Dino looks horrified. "I'll never eat ice cream again!"

As we walk, Žana and I fall a little behind.

"I'm sorry I was so emotional before," she says.

"Never be sorry for the way you feel!"

"It just seemed so important, then. It felt like it was everything! Like all I am was tied up in Haris, and when that dream was over it felt like there was no *me* anymore. It wasn't that I was so sad that Haris wanted someone else. It was because if I didn't have that, what did I have left?"

She throws an arm around my shoulder as we walk through the sunshine toward the Una. "And then I remembered," she goes on. "I have you, my sister, my best friend, my second self. I have Dino, my funny little brother. When I thought we'd lost him, everything else just faded away. And I have them, annoying as they are sometimes." She gestures to the girls walking ahead of us. "And I have all of this!" She spreads her free arm wide, covering Bihać, Bosnia, Yugoslavia, the whole world. "How can I be sad for too long with all this? When Dino was missing, I saw what true loss would be. Losing him for a little while made me remember myself. Oh, Amra, how could I have been so silly? Thank goodness I have you. All of you . . . but especially *you*."

Before we make it home we run into Mama and Tata, who were heading to Brvice, desperate to find Dino. The reunion is full of tears and laughter. Since we are in Hatinac and close to Dika's house, we go there to make phone calls to spread the word that Dino is safe and sound. Soon, in the typical Bosnian style we are celebrating with food. Neighbors and friends bring things over to Dika's tiny house, and since the night is balmy they bring chairs and tables and blankets, too, and before you know it we're having a banquet on the lawn beneath the pear tree. Mama and Dika sit close together as the stars come out, reminiscing about their girlhood spent in this very spot. Tata and Meho and Tetak Ale talk about balsa planes, and Meho comes up with a new design they can't wait to test.

Žana, Vedrana, Ćućana, Sejla, Belma, Hana, Dino, and l sit in a circle on the grass with our legs all crossed over and under one another's in such a tangle that no one can wander away or get lost.

"You're better off without him," Sejla says late in the night. Dino has fallen asleep with his head on my lap. "You'd just go away at the end of the summer and you'd be heartbroken. If it was going to be true love, you'd just be setting yourself up for sadness. And if it wasn't... why bother in the first place?"

The old Žana—the Žana from this morning—would have argued with her, but tonight she nods. "Do you love Slobodan like that?" she asks.

"Yes," Sejla says, and bites her lower lip. "Only..."

"Only?"

"l sometimes wonder whether l'm setting myself up for sadness, too," she muses. Out of all of us, it's me who Sejla looks at. She knows l understand.

Words from the past come back to me.

She didn't just marry any Serb boy. She married into a family of known Muslim-killers. That's what Mama said when she was explaining why Dida's father disowned her.

No daughter of mine will ever date a Serb. That's what Sejla's father told her. Does the hate go both ways? Or is it hate from one direction, fear from the other?

Have pride in yourself, Žana, and always remember that you're a Serb, first, last, and always. That's what Žana's mother told her. And her father, gleefully miming slicing a throat when slaughtering Ottoman Muslims.

I don't know much about romantic love yet. All that is just an idea, part of some distant future. But I know about family love, the deep bonds of sisterhood that Žana and I share. Žana saved me. When I thought my world was bleak forever, she pierced it like a ray of sunshine, and I felt a love I never could have imagined.

Am I setting myself up for sadness, too?

I look at Žana, half-Bosniak, half-Serb. But that's not her identity. She is not half this or that—she is 100 percent Žana, a thing that cannot be divided. Maybe older generations gave in to prejudice and hate, but not us. Our world is different. Those things are behind us.

Žana throws back her head, laughing at some joke I missed, and I smile back at her. She leans close to me and whispers in my ear, "I love you, Amra, my sister."

"I love you, too, Žana, my sister. Always."

Above us the stars twinkle in the velvet of the summer sky. But the cool breeze that blows from the Una touches my skin, and I shiver.

29

THE REST OF the summer is imperfect only in that it is not infinite.

Picture the best day of your life: That is the rest of the summer for me. For a warm golden moment that expands to weeks, the troubles of the world seem to be over. Tata and Mama are hopeful. There is enough food. Those who love, love in the right direction in a suitable amount. Every day is sunny and kind. Perfect.

Still devastated by heartbreak, Žana decides the best cure for an old love is a new love. Omer, the gentle giant who has been following Žana with his puppy-dog eyes since last summer, makes his move after a basketball game one day.

For Bosnians, sports are a passion. When you don't have much else to look forward to, simple things make all the difference. Omer invites us to watch him play basketball at the court that doubles as a concert venue and the place for my volleyball competitions. I've seen the Bosnian pop groups Crvena Jabuka, Plavi Orkestar, Merlin, and Hari Mata Hari there. I've even sung there myself. I have no particular talent, but I'm not so bad that I can't be an extra body in the school chorus competitions, where quantity of voices can make up for quality.

Dino happily narrates the match for us as we watch. The game is intense, all boyishness and sweat, and afterward, when Omer, still glistening, comes up to Žana, there's a twinkle in her eyes.

Not long after that she starts dating him. But she's always a little coy, a little standoffish. She never goes off with him the way I know she would have wanted to with Haris. Instead, Omer joins our group, a kind of mascot to our sisterhood.

He tries so hard to make her happy. There's nothing really wrong with Omer. His main fault is that he's not Haris. He knows he's not her first choice, but he does everything he can to make her love him. I can tell it doesn't work. Maybe he can, too. But he keeps trying.

I think Žana just wants someone to make her feel special now. Someone who can reassure her that she's worthy and desirable. But when he's not looking, her eyes will wander. I don't know if she's bored, or looking for someone better.

Late in the summer, I find that we cling more closely to each other, and at the same time we look outward for new experiences, new sensations. Žana, in particular, feels more reckless.

One night when Omer isn't there, two brothers hang out with us. Ahmed is sweet and good-looking, with wavy blond hair and big blue eyes. He seems interested in me—something that still surprises me to the point that I don't believe it. He's shy and nice. His brother, though, Mido, is a playboy, a young man who knows exactly how attractive women find him. He's superficially like Ahmed—blond wavy hair, full lips, a strong jaw, piercing blue eyes—but on him it is magically gorgeous instead of merely nice-looking. He's supremely confident in his looks and charm. He'll have one eye on the girl he's flirting with, and the other scanning the horizon for the next one. He flirts like he breathes, naturally and without thought.

So while Ahmed talks to me, Mido works his magic on my

cousins. Even with all his experience, I think he's caught off guard when, instead of merely giggling and flirting back, Žana impulsively kisses him. Mido's look of shock turns to one of surprise, and before I know it they're making out right in front of all of us, and anyone else who might walk by.

I'm terrified that Omer will see or that at any moment Žana will be overcome with guilt. So of course I try to stop her. She wants this to be a balm to her pain, to ease the sadness of not winning Haris, but I know she won't feel good about herself tomorrow. Right now, though, tomorrow doesn't exist for her.

"Leave me alone," she whispers desperately when I pull her away. "Let me at least kiss a boy who looks a little like Haris."

And so I leave her to pretend, wondering how far she'll go in her search for love.

She never kisses Mido again, and through the summer she continues seeing Omer. But there's a constant restlessness in her now. She is on a journey, but I feel like I'm just starting to pack for it. I learned pain and disappointment earlier than Žana, and my path will be different than hers.

I like the way Ahmed makes me feel when he says he's interested in me . . . but I don't act on it. Emir still flirts with me sometimes, and that makes me feel warm and confused. But I don't feel a truly strong connection until I discover from my friend Asmira that Emir's a math nerd like me.

Soon after that, Emir finds me one day sunning myself alone on the warm planks of Brvice. He flops down beside me, and we watch Hadžara with her gourds, safeguarding the children as they learn how to swim while she bobs in her old-lady bikini.

I turn my head and find Emir watching me, his cheek on the sun-warmed wood, his face mere inches from mine. He starts to talk about math, the engineering he wants to study. I share some of my own plans and dreams with him. And I realize that the gentle, contented, vaguely romantic thing I feel when I look at him is enough. I'm so happy to be feeling it, but I don't need more. It's like having a taste of something when you're not hungry yet. This summer has taught me more about love and loss, and I know that love, true love, demands more than what I feel in this moment. Love doesn't come from desperate desire for it. It can't be forced. Not realizing that was what caused Žana so much pain.

One night, to our surprise, Sejla invites us all to a sleepover for the first time. She might hang out with us, but she never fails to remind us how much more mature she is. Like she's only with us because we're her cousins, not because we're interesting enough to bother with. Like she's doing us a favor. So the sleepover plan is strange and out of the blue.

Her house is older, but has beautiful, lush red rose bushes under the windows at the front of the house. When night falls we learn what Sejla's true plan is. Her parents have been cracking down on her, absolutely forbidding her to see Slobodan. But she's decided that with all of us there, her parents won't check on her. As soon as it gets dark there's a tap on the window and she climbs out right into the thorny bushes, and before we know it she's kissing Slobodan passionately. I try to call her in, but she ignores me. I'm terrified when I see this kind of impulsive, reckless behavior in other people. It makes me feel guilty just watching it—guilt by association, as if I'm doing something a thousand times worse by being complicit.

Just a few minutes later, sure enough, they're caught by her brother Samir as he comes home.

"Who's there?" he calls. "Come out or you're in trouble!" He evidently thinks they're burglars.

"Shush, Samir! Don't let Mom and Dad hear you. I'm just... gathering roses."

"With your face all flushed and your lipstick smeared? A likely story. Come out, Slobodan. I know it must be you."

Slobodan creeps out sheepishly as we watch from the window.

"What are you going to do?" Sejla asks nervously, sure he'll tell their parents.

"I should tell them," Samir says, undecided.

"Please, brother! Don't tell them. Or at least, don't tell Dad!" Gentle Tetka Ica would forgive her, but she couldn't bear her father's disapproval. "It's not fair that they're keeping us apart. Have mercy on me!"

"Slobodan, you better go home," Samir says. "No, I won't tell our parents. But I want to talk to you, Sejla."

Sejla defiantly kisses Slobodan goodbye and we help pull her back in through the window. Samir takes the more conventional route through the door and soon meets us in his sister's bedroom.

I think he's going to be angry, berate his sister. Instead he looks at us all soberly, then sits down on the floor with a heavy sigh. "I want you to be happy, but the world is changing," he says to Sejla, to all of us. "You're younger, maybe you don't pay attention to the news. Maybe it doesn't seem as important as the other things going on in your lives. But it will be, I think. Soon we will all be forced to pay attention."

It feels like the air has been sucked out of the room. As he speaks, all of my worries flood back into me. Every fear I've had for our country, everything I've tried to avoid and deny and forget, returns in a rush.

"I know your Slobodan is a nice guy, Sejla. But there's another Slobodan. He's saying that Serbs better be prepared to take up arms and defend Serbs from people like us. Bosnian Muslims are not doing anything to Serbs or anyone, but I am afraid that he sees our very existence as a threat. It's a dangerous time, and I don't want to see you get hurt. This is not the right time to be with a Serb."

"But he loves me, and I love him!" Sejla protests.

"I know," Samir says gently. "But I fear for the future. The way things are going, I don't know if love will be enough anymore." He gets up, shaking his head sadly, suddenly seeming so much older as he walks out of the room.

For a long time we sit in silence. Then at last Vedrana, her face in a puzzled frown, asks us, "What am I? Am I Serb? Am I Muslim? Am I something else? If Serbs hate Muslims, what happens to people like Žana and me? Do we hate one another? Ourselves? Half of ourselves? Which half?"

"I'll hate whatever part of me ever hates," Žana swears, hitting her thigh with her fist. "These troubles, they're for adults. Stupid adults. Not for us. We know what's truly important in life. We're not like them."

"My mom and dad are talking about putting their money in a bank in Germany," Hana says in a tiny voice. "My dad is drinking more. He keeps saying it's coming, it's happening. But he won't tell me what. And if I ask, he…" She bows her head. We all know what she isn't saying.

"Our parents don't tell us anything," Žana says. "My mom just criticizes me. My dad's always away on his 'military exercises.'" I know her dad was just promoted to colonel in the Yugoslav People's Army, a position so important he now has an unlisted number so he can't be bothered by petty requests from the public…or maybe even family and friends. Žana says I'm one of the few people to have the family phone number now.

They talk, on and on, about the things they've heard on the radio, the things they've heard their parents say when they thought no one was listening. For a long time I listen…and then I can't keep silent any longer.

"We can't do anything about the world. All we can control is ourselves. They want to divide people. But we can't let the world keep us apart. Politics, conflict, hate…that's not us. We're better than that. We have to stay strong. We have to make a promise to one another." I feel tears welling in my eyes. "Right now, a real, true promise that no matter what happens, we will love one another, help one another. Even if the whole world falls apart we—family and friends—won't crumble with it." Then I burst into tears and they're comforting me, promising me, and I know they mean it.

THE NEXT MORNING the cold cleansing waters of the Una wash away what remains of our worries from the night before, and by the next afternoon we're sunning ourselves, flirting with boys, talking about our futures. Small troubles—pimples and crushes—consume us. The bigger problems belong to the world, not to us. Our lives will flow as smoothly, as eternally as the Una herself.

We don't let ourselves think that this golden hour cannot last. But there is no flower that doesn't fade and fall and become the seeds of something new.

The day Žana and Vedrana leave is as glorious as any other. No clouds roil overhead to give us any premonition. Žana holds me in a long hug and whispers the promise we made long ago.

"Every day at 5:55 P.M., I'll think of you, my dear sister."

"I'll think of you, too," I tell her. "I'll say a prayer for you. And next summer..."

"Next summer we'll do it all over again. Next summer and every summer. I will always have summers with my sister in Bihać on the banks of the Una."

AFTER

BUT SHE NEVER returns.

During the school year we call and write to each other almost as often. But when summer approaches, she tells me that her parents want her to go to Tovrljane, a little village in Serbia near the border with Kosovo. She says she doesn't want to ... but this time she doesn't say she *won't*. There are no passionate declarations of rebellion. She doesn't swear she'll hitchhike here if she has to, just to see her sister and her beloved city. She grumbles, but she accepts it.

I spend my first summer without Žana.

After that, school becomes a top priority. I settle on a challenging math-focused high school so I can study medicine later. Maybe someday I can help someone like Amar.

Volleyball takes a lot of my time, too. We have an amazing team, but it seems like the better I get, the less my coach likes me. Even though I'm one of the best players, he sometimes keeps me on the bench and puts in a Serb girl who's not as good. When I miss one practice—the first I've missed in a year—because of back-to-back tests, he makes me do nonstop sit-ups and push-ups all through the next session while my teammates practice. My coach seems angry at me all the time, and I can't figure out why.

The girls on my team talk about how their parents might send them away for a while "if anything happens." What is this "anything" they're referring to?

One day I read the headline "CIA-Leaked Documents Predict Breakup of Yugoslavia." Who are these CIA people who think such a preposterous thing? How could anything be broken up? How could any of us be separated? My country is a place of brotherhood and unity. Haven't I been hearing that since the day I was born? I know that Muslims are treated poorly here, but a country can't just disintegrate, can it? Sure, Bosnia had been its own country for nearly a thousand years, but for all my lifetime it has been part of Yugoslavia, part of a bigger, stronger whole. Bosnia is so deeply *everyone's* that it cannot be *anyone's* alone.

And yet people keep talking about war.

War against who? I want to ask. And how do you go to war without a military? Bosnia doesn't have an army. There is only the Yugoslav People's Army. The military of Žana's dad, who is always on his mysterious exercises. I don't know of any Muslims in the army, only Serbs. But they are still *our* army. They will defend us.

I call Žana, hoping to talk about this with her. She can ask her father if it is true. But tonight, like so many other nights lately, when her father answers, he tells me Žana isn't home. From the fall onward I call her every week, but he will never connect us.

So I write to her, tonight and for several more years. In our letters we live and relive our three magical summers by the banks of the Una. *Do you remember . . . do you remember . . . ?*

And we plan for next summer, and the next. We will meet again, spend another glorious summer together, all of us.

Each summer our plans evaporate like wet footprints left on warm rocks.

We continue to live in our fantasy summer world instead of the reality that is becoming irresistibly obvious. It gives me hope for humanity and the future because I know that Žana doesn't feel hate for me, will never feel hate for me. If we can understand this, won't everyone else figure it out eventually? How could adults not figure out what is so crystal clear to us, that hate produces no winners?

In time, it becomes clear that Slobodan Milošević, the president of Serbia, sees Yugoslavia as nothing more than a Greater Serbia, a place for *them* and not for *us*. I don't see how there can be a war in Yugoslavia unless it is fought by the Yugoslav People's Army. And they can't fight me, can't kill me! The army exists to protect me—me, and everyone in Yugoslavia.

But things get worse—the newspapers announce that the Yugoslav People's Army attacked Slovenia, then Croatia after they each proclaim their independence on June 25, 1991. Bosnia and Herzegovina follows in an attempt to escape Serbia's cruel dominion and proclaims independence on March 1, 1992. The Yugoslav People's Army—which it turns out is the army of the Serbs—becomes Milošević's executioner. It arms the Serb paramilitaries throughout Bosnia and Herzegovina, seeding a second army of hate within our own land.

By April 5, 1992, I sit with my family and watch on our bubble TV the largest peace protests Bosnia and Herzegovina has ever witnessed—100,000 out of 300,000 people in the country's capital of Sarajevo march into the streets to protest against the war. But Milošević and the Serb military—the former Yugoslav People's Army (Jugoslovenska Narodna Armija or JNA) and the newly armed paramilitaries won't let us go, won't allow peace. Serb snipers kill six people in the crowd and injure others. And so yet another occupation in Bosnia's thousand years of existence begins.

And so too ends life as I once knew it.

It's harder and harder to get Žana on the phone. One day Dida calls and says I should come stay with them in Belgrade. Belma is going, and I should, too.

But I don't.

Bihać is my home. And besides, I'm not a good liar. If I as a Bosniak pretended to be a Serb, someone would see through me. A parent of a Serb friend working at the airport would discover me before I could even leave the city. What would happen then? And then, to have to live a lie, not just every day but every hour, with every breath I take? I am no Dida, ashamed of who I am or where I come from. I'll do what's right, not what's easy or safe. I am who I am, no matter the cost. I keep hoping that people will come to their senses. I almost believe it can never happen here, to me ... Until one night almost every Serb in Bihać packs up and leaves.

Tata calls Žana's father. "Đorđe, tell me it isn't true. You won't do it ... You can't be a part of it. We were one people, one country. Đorđe, do something, make them listen to reason! You can't bomb our airport, Đorđe. You can't bomb *us!*" The line goes dead, and there are tears in Tata's eyes.

But I still have hope ...

Until Đorđe's army blows up the Željava Air Base so that we can't escape.

Until Serb tanks roll in.

Until my city is under siege by Serbs.

Until my family, my friends, are killed by Serb artillery.

Until I begin to starve in the summer of 1992.

And then I realize this was never truly my country. I am not part of this people; the Yugoslav People's Army never saw me as someone to protect but rather as someone to crush. When reality erupts like a volcano I realize how deeply in denial I was.

WE ARE BOSNIANS. Our door is always unlocked, our kitchen is always ready to feed anyone. Before the siege, in the spring of 1992, Tata came upon a lost French tourist in the hotel downtown. Bernard asked for directions, which sparked a conversation, and before he knew it, the Frenchman was swept up into Bosnian hospitality, taken home and fed like he was part of our family. We didn't have much food by then, or money to buy it. After the first payment that bought us the cow, Tata was barely paid anything for his work selling Sebastian bags. Finally they agreed to pay him in salt, truckloads of it. But the trucks were confiscated by armed Serbs, and he never got anything. Nonetheless, we shared what we had with Bernard, and when he left we had a new friend. He gave us his address, so that if we ever found ourselves in France he could return our hospitality.

The phone lines out of Bihać are cut before the siege. The mail routes have long been stopped. Nothing is going out or coming in. Seeing how desperate I am for contact with Žana, Tata finds a battalion of UN soldiers and convinces two French soldiers to smuggle a packet of letters to Bernard to forward to Žana. When they come to our terrace to collect them, Mama has made tulumbe, golden sugary fried dough treats, crispy on the outside and soft on the inside. We watch them eat but never taste a bit ourselves. These are a thank-you to the soldiers for their small act of kindness. By now, food is far too scarce for us to eat anything for pleasure ourselves. Eating is only for survival.

I pack many letters together, weeks worth of my thoughts and prayers and fears, and Bernard repacks them so they can be sent from France to Belgrade without being censored or destroyed.

It doesn't matter if she doesn't answer me. In a way, maybe it doesn't matter if she never reads them. Writing them keeps me sane. It gives me something to hold on to, something pure and true and eternal in a world that is fractured.

I always felt that my life would be different than Žana's. I never imagined how different, and now I'm not even sure how much of my life is left to me. Now, more than ever, I am grateful for my three summers.

From 1992 to 1995, my faith in humanity hangs by the most fragile thread. That thread is belief in the unbreakable sisterhood we forged during those summers. Because of that belief, I survived the war. I survived the genocide.

Thousands did not.

AUTHOR'S NOTE

I BEGIN WRITING this note on a plane as I sit somewhere in between the two worlds that make me whole—my country of birth, Bosnia and Herzegovina ("B&H" or "Bosnia" as it is referred to in my memoir)—and my new homeland, the United States of America. I survived the Bosnian Genocide that lasted from 1992 to 1995. This experience defines who I am today as a person, a professor, and an author. I was lucky. I lost family members, but the closest ones, the ones you've read about in this memoir, lived until the war ended. My mother lost her hearing after a missile hit our house and exploded. My father's health was so damaged by starvation and diabetes and sorrow that he died a few years after the war ended, a delayed casualty. But I lost uncles and cousins, and many, many friends. I lost a country, and I lost my innocence. But I never lost hope, not entirely.

After the war, in 2001, Biljana Plavšić, a Bosnian Serb politician and leader who served as one of the presidents of the war-time self-proclaimed Republika Srpska—a territory Serb forces occupied in Bosnia and Herzegovina—was indicted by the International War Crimes Tribunal for the former Yugoslavia in The Hague on the multiple charges of genocide and crimes against humanity. She requested a plea bargain and admitted her guilt. After serving less than ten years in prison, she was released and gave interviews stating she admitted her guilt only to avoid being found guilty of genocide. Prior to the war, Plavšić was a university professor in Bosnia and Herzegovina who even spent time in the United States on a Fulbright scholarship. She argued that Bosniaks had inferior genetics. Some of her public statements capture the extent of the Serb nationalists' dehumanization and hate toward Bosniaks. She describes my people as follows:

"It was genetically deformed material that embraced Islam. And now of course with each successive generation it simply becomes concentrated. It gets worse and worse. It simply expresses itself and dictates their style of thinking, which is rooted in their genes. And through the centuries the genes degraded further."[*]

This is a quintessential example of how hate-fueled narratives normalize and justify acts of direct violence. Truth matters. Words matter. Stories matter. They inspire people to take action. It is our choice how and what stories we tell and, in that choice, we decide whether to empower peaceful or violent futures. When a group is dehumanized and depicted as "a deformed material," the most extreme forms of violence such as genocide and extermination of that group are likely to follow. Though telling our stories can be painful for those of us who have survived targeted and identity-based violence as it puts us at the risk of renewed attacks by those who perpetrate hate, truth-telling is necessary and worth the risk I take to tell my story. Truth-telling helps us understand

---

[*] Sells, Michael. "The Construction of Islam in Serbian Religious Mythology and Its Consequences." In Shatzmiller, M. *Islam and Bosnia: Conflict Resolution and Foreign Policy in Multi-Ethnic States.* Quebec, Canada: McGill-Queen's Press, 2002.

and connect with one another and therefore protects us and our societies from future violence, which is why it is important that stories like *Three Summers* and my young adult memoir, *The Cat I Never Named*, are written and read. This emotionally complex story of sisterhood is a warning to us all that if we fail to learn about hate, we are allowing for vulnerability and susceptibility in our society for the most senseless and extreme acts of violence to occur. I know because it happened to me.

In 2016, the International War Crimes Tribunal for the former Yugoslavia found Radovan Karadžić, a psychiatrist and the first president of Republika Srpska, guilty of genocide, war crimes, and crimes against humanity including persecution on religious, racial, and political grounds, and extermination. He is serving forty years in prison for his crimes.

In 2017, the Army of Republika Srpska's commander, Ratko Mladić, was also found guilty of genocide and crimes against humanity. He is serving a life sentence in prison. Slobodan Milo-šević died before his trial in the International War Crimes Tribunal for the former Yugoslavia concluded. These are only some of the people who created the hell in Bosnia and Herzegovina. Others still walk freely, even after participating in genocidal killings, mass rapes, persecution, and extermination of people who bear names like mine. Today, some continue to glorify and deny geno-cide. I respond to those attempts to erase my history by telling my story.

To me, as a survivor, the denial of my lived experience and those of others who perished during the Bosnian Genocide is always the hardest and most painful moment. Survivors of extreme and targeted violence seek acknowledgment of their experience and respect of their identity.

According to my own research, that of other scholars, and the United Nations, anti-Muslim hate in particular has reached epidemic proportions globally. This is why I hope that *Three Summers* will become a source of understanding, connection, and empathy in schools and outside of schools not just for those with Muslim identity but also all young people growing up in the United States who have ever felt displaced, targeted, or silenced for who they are.

Unfortunately, there are many parallels between what we are living through in the United States and what I had survived in Bosnia and Herzegovina prior to and during the war. A convicted war criminal, Radovan Karadžić, has become an inspiration for the far-right movement in the United States and around the world. Many extremists look at the crimes he, along with Biljana Plavšić and others, committed against Bosniaks in Bosnia and Herzegovina and are inspired by their anti-Muslim racism and hate as they seek to perpetrate similar violence in the United States targeting specific racial, ethnic, and religious groups.

None of the indictments or convictions will ever bring back my friends and family nor will they take away the permanent damage inflicted on each person in my family who was subjected to this kind of hate. Some days, I find myself walking through the streets of New York, only to be jolted by a scent of a passerby that reminds me of a Serb soldier who attacked me during the war in Bosnia. In a moment, all the pain and trauma return. But I have learned to live with the consequences and experiences I never chose for myself. I also learned during these three magical summers that we are born into our ethnicity, family, and geography, but we all have a potential to transform and empower the best and most humane version of ourselves. There are certainly days when I wish my life wasn't interrupted by other people's hate for who I am. I cannot change my past nor the consequences of what was done to me and my people. But I can tell my story in *Three Summers* to inspire humanity, resilience, and connectedness. Hate continues to reverberate in the minds and hearts of some who seek a reason to inflict direct violence on an ethnically, religiously, or racially different group from that of their own, but you and I can prevent it together by humanizing the dehumanized.

I wish for *Three Summers* to help prevent hate from ever happening to you or someone else. The most effective response to hate is to dismantle it, to challenge it, and to build resilience to it by learning about others as much as we know of ourselves. It is those connections across ethnic, racial, and religious lines that build connective tissue we call humanity. It is those connections that save us from the next genocide. I ask you to help me build them.

TIMELINE OF ETHNIC TENSIONS LEADING TO WAR AND GENOCIDE

May 4, 1980—Josip Broz Tito, Yugoslavia's dictator, dies.

May 28, 1986—Slobodan Milošević becomes president of the League of Communists of Serbia and intensifies his efforts to promote Serb nationalism and expand Serbia's territory into Bosnia and Herzegovina, Croatia, and Kosovo. He promotes hate and fear of other ethnic groups, including Bosniaks, through the state media he controls out of Belgrade.

May 8, 1989—Slobodan Milošević becomes president of Serbia.

November 9, 1989—The Berlin Wall falls, initiating the end of communism in Eastern Europe.

Throughout 1990—Slobodan Milošević, his government in Serbia, the top leadership of the Yugoslav People's Army (Jugoslovenska Narodna Armija or JNA), and the JNA's Psychological Operations Department articulate and adopt the RAM Plan. This secret plan envisions partitioning Croatia and Bosnia and Herzegovina to annex those territories to Serbia and form a state for Serbs only. This concept becomes known as Greater Serbia. By this time, the JNA was the de facto army of Serbs as the majority of officers in the JNA were Serbs. The plan details how the JNA will distribute weapons to Serbs both in Croatia and Bosnia and Herzegovina that would then support the JNA's efforts to occupy and hold territories beyond Serbia. The plan also instructs the secret police to help train Serbs to form additional Serb paramilitary units in Bosnia and Herzegovina and Croatia, including the region of Krajina where Bihać and the Željava Air Base are located. Over a period of several years, on my way to daily volleyball practices or school, I pass by Dom JNA, a building owned by the army. The building has an outdoor space where I watch young, fit men wearing special uniforms and red berets. They train other soldiers how to fight and pretend-slaughter with knives and weapons they carry all over their bodies. I notice that they are different, even scarier than regular JNA soldiers. Years later, as I follow the proceedings against those accused of war crimes, genocide, and crimes against humanity like extermination of primarily Bosniaks at the International War Crimes Tribunal in The Hague, I learn that soldiers who wore red berets and made me tremble every time I passed by were likely the special operations unit of the Serbian state security called "Red Berets." If that was them, then they were preparing to kill people like me. I just didn't know it then.

December 23, 1990—Slovenia holds a plebiscite and the people of Slovenia vote in favor of Slovenia's independence from Yugoslavia.

August 1990—Ethnic tensions rise in Croatia, particularly in the Krajina region bordering Bosnia and only miles from my hometown of Bihać. Trained, equipped, and armed by the JNA, paramilitary Serb units in Croatia establish several autonomous regions.

March 25, 1991—Slobodan Milošević (president of Serbia) and Franjo Tuđman (then president of Croatia) meet in Karađorđevo (Serbia) and discuss partition of Bosnia and Herzegovina between Serbia and Croatia. Bosniaks are in the way of that partition.

June 25, 1991—Slovenia and Croatia declare independence. The JNA, which by then is openly controlled by Serb nationalists, attacks Slovenia. The war lasts only ten days. There were no local Serbs the

JNA could arm to hold Slovenian territory. The JNA attempts its next conquest. By the summer of 1991, the JNA invades cities and villages in Croatia to take control over regions with a Serb population. Several Serb autonomous regions are proclaimed over the next several years. The war in Croatia continues until November 1995. The part of Croatia bordering my hometown is under full control of the Serb forces, whether the JNA or the Serb paramilitaries.

September 1991—Yugoslav Prime Minister Ante Marković leaks information relating to the RAM plan, which prompts Bosnia and Herzegovina to hold a referendum for independence.

September 1991—the United Nations Security Council (UNSC) establishes an arms embargo on the states once or still in Yugoslavia, but this UNSC Resolution 713 adversely impacts primarily Bosnia and Herzegovina. Croatia has access to weapons. Serbia already controls a well-equipped JNA, which has been arming and training Serbs in Bosnia and Herzegovina. Bosnia and Herzegovina is unable to defend itself, and Bosniaks are left at a risk of genocide during the later aggression of Serbia against my homeland.

October 1991—Bosnian Serb leader Radovan Karadžić openly threatens that "Muslims will be annihilated in Bosnia and Herzegovina."

January 1992—The Bosnian Serbs Assembly proclaims Republika Srpska, a secessionist Serb republic within Bosnia and Herzegovina.

February 29 and March 1, 1992—Bosnia and Herzegovina holds a referendum for independence. The majority of Bosnians and Herzegovinians—primarily Bosniaks, but also substantive numbers of Croats, Serbs, and other ethnic groups—vote in favor of independence from Yugoslavia.

March 3, 1992—Chairman of the Presidency of Bosnia and Herzegovina Alija Izetbegović formally declares the country's independence.

March 1992—Serb leaders order the blocking of roads. (This is why Tata's delivery of salt never makes it to us.) JNA and Serb paramilitaries (which I collectively and simply refer to as the Serb forces) start attacking parts of Bosnia and Herzegovina.

April 5, 1992—100,000 people from all ethnic backgrounds protest against war in Sarajevo. Serb snipers kill six people and injure several more.

April 6, 1992—Bosnia and Herzegovina is internationally recognized as an independent country. April 6, 1992, is also considered the official start of Serbia's aggression against Bosnia and Herzegovina. Initially, the conflict was between the JNA and the newly formed and self-organized Army of the Republic of Bosnia and Herzegovina. The JNA then gradually transforms into the Army of Republika Srpska, which continues to be funded, armed, and supported by Serbia. While labels changed, the Serb military force, as I call it, had one aim—to eradicate primarily Bosniaks (along with other non-Serbs) and form Greater Serbia.

April 15, 1992—the Army of the Republic of Bosnia and Herzegovina is formed in response to the aggression against Bosnia and Herzegovina and is recognized by foreign governments as the only legal army in the country. This army was composed of my friends, family members, teachers, and other people who might have never seen let alone held a gun prior to the war. They are mostly Bosniak, but many are Bosnian Croats and Serbs. Not all Serbs sided with the Serb nationalists. However, the Army of the Republic of Bosnia and Herzegovina struggles against the well-trained and equipped Serb forces that occupy around 70 percent of Bosnia and Herzegovina's territory very quickly while displacing, persecuting, killing, torturing, raping, and eradicating primarily Bosniak populations. I survive

327

because, by some miracle of our will to survive, my hometown, along with a few other towns, successfully resists occupation by the Serb forces.

June 1992—Bihać is besieged by the Serb military occupying both Bosnia and Herzegovina and parts of Croatia bordering my hometown. The life as I once knew it ends, and I spend the next several years living under constant bombing coming both from the parts of Croatia that the Serb forces occupy and from the parts of my own country they took over. Because of the UN arms embargo and much better equipped Serb military, we—Bosnians and Herzegovinians—struggle to defend ourselves. In Bihać, we live under the Serb forces' military siege with the constant threats of concentration and rape camps for nearly 1,200 days. My family and I starve, but we also learn to keep hope alive, to retain humanity, and love one another in the face of the unimaginable. This all happens to us for one reason only—because we are Bosniaks. I tell the story of my survival and the cat that saves my life in *The Cat I Never Named: A True Story of Love, War, and Survival* (Bloomsbury, 2020).

May 31, 2023—The United Nations International Residual Mechanism for Criminal Tribunals in The Hague finds Slobodan Milošević's top allies, Serbia's senior state security officials Jovica Stanišić and Franko Simatović, guilty of a "joint criminal enterprise" between Serbia and Serbia-funded and armed Serb paramilitaries which "had a common criminal purpose to forcibly and permanently remove the majority of non-Serbs from large areas of Croatia and Bosnia and Herzegovina, through the commission of murder, deportation, inhumane acts (forcible transfer), and persecution."[*] (Milošević himself

---

[*] The United Nations International Residual Mechanism for Criminal Tribunals, Hague, 2023.

died suddenly on March 11, 2006, only weeks before his trial's conclusion, thus evading a verdict.)

While justice takes a long time, and in some cases never comes, survivors of humanity's darkest hours understand the power of storytelling to help us grow, transform, and make this world the peaceful place it was meant to be.

WHERE THEY ARE NOW

I have tried to summarize what happened to the people in this memoir after the turn of the last page to the best of my knowledge below.

ŽANA

After the war I went to college in the United States, and I didn't see Žana until my wedding in 2002. I decided to have a celebration in Bihać as well as in our current home in New York. For so long, the only time my family had gathered in a large group was for funerals. I wanted us to gather for a happy occasion. *We may never get this chance to be together again*, I thought.

We never did.

Žana and I never talked about her father, about his possible role in the Bosnian War. We don't mention the war. I don't want my dream to be damaged, our friendship shattered if I learn anything I can't live with.

At this time Žana was married to a Serb man and struggling financially, living in a tiny Belgrade apartment. It didn't help with her in-laws that she is a half-Bosniak. She has two children, a boy named Marko and an older daughter named Una.

The day of my wedding, we were sitting on the terrace of my family house that had been hit by a bomb during the war. It was repaired by then. I was doing well in the United States, so I gave her money to finish her college exams—not as much as it would have cost in the States, but it was a lot for Bosnia, or Serbia. She tried to refuse but eventually took it. We both wept, overcome with so much unspoken emotion between us.

Through the years we talked. I didn't talk too much about my own happiness or success. She told me about her marital problems. Slowly, we drifted, always with so much unspoken about the war.

When I was writing a memoir about my war years as a teenager, I was haunted by the thought of her father's role in the war. Finally, I sent him a long message on social media, confronting him about it. I worried what Žana's reaction would be, but I had to get this off my chest. Did he feel guilty? Proud? Indifferent? Sorry? Did he ever think of his daughter's best friend huddled in a cellar, hearing bombs shake the world overhead?

I wrote him a long note, detailing all that happened to my family, all that I believe he is responsible for given his role as a colonel in the army that invaded my country. I told him I loved Žana regardless and that will never change, but that I needed to transfer the burden of all that pain to him. It was his doing, not mine. I needed to feel that I was not staying quiet but that I was speaking up and telling the truth to those who inflicted the pain on us. I didn't want him to think that his role in my suffering was hidden—he needed to know that I know. I don't need a court decision to adjudicate what happened. I know what I survived. He was one of them, one of our murderers.

And I needed to have a voice, and to be the voice of the people who could not speak from beyond the grave. My silence would be a betrayal of those whose voices were stolen from them. I couldn't tell all their stories, but I could tell mine. It was my choice to tell my truth. It would be up to him to listen.

He never answered me...but Žana did. She wrote that she was angry with me, disappointed in me. She defended her father.

We wrote back and forth a bit after that. She felt that in blaming her father I was also blaming her. She said I needed to get over it. Get over genocide?

A few months after that, Žana posted photos on her social media of her kids holding up the Serb three-fingered salute. Once, maybe, it was just a symbol of national pride. During and after the war it became a symbol of hate, the sigil under which the Serb forces committed genocide against my people.

In that moment I knew that I had lost Žana forever. Later she unfriended me on social media, as did Vedrana and Dida, but the real irrevocable break came the moment I saw those three fingers.

Still, even today, when I happen to see that it is 5:55 p.m., I think of her. I always will.

Losing Žana left an open wound in me, one that will never heal. It also showed the strength of propaganda and narrative, and that none—not even those we love the most—are immune to it. We can all succumb to hate if we're subjected to an environment where hate is normalized. A lie repeated often enough becomes the truth.

DINO

Dino survived the unimaginable with me during the war, and he remains the most supportive brother anyone could ask for. We talk almost every day. If I'm busy, he makes sure to call me until we connect, and he confirms that my family and I are well. If I cannot get hold of him, I do the same until I reach him. We still fear that if we don't hear from each other, it might mean something terrible has happened. Our lived experiences of surviving the genocide against the Bosniaks have scarred us for life.

Dino never had a real childhood except for these three summers. His later and formative memories are of the Bosnian war, starvation, volunteering to remove dead bodies and debris from the streets during the constant bombings of our hometown, and the bombing of our own home in the 1990s. Mama lost her hearing when our house was hit, and Tata, too, suffered multiple health setbacks.

As I left to study in the United States, in 1996, Dino stayed with Mama and Tata. Life was difficult for Dino. We lost Tata while I was a student at Brown University. He never saw Dino or me graduate from college, one of his dreams. After Tata's death, Dino would use one single light bulb as he studied to save on electric bills until I was able to get my first job and help support them. Dino graduated with a degree in economics from the University of Bihać, and now he works for a telecommunication company in Bosnia and Herzegovina. He is married to Arijana and has one child, an incredibly cute and smart boy named Haris.

Dino volunteers and runs a local basketball team with several of his friends in Bihać. For years, Dino took care of Tetak Ale, who recently died. Dino remains the best brother in the world. We only wish that Amar and Tata were with us. Mama lives with me in New York, and she spends her summers in Bihać.

VEDRANA

Vedrana had a very difficult time during and after the war. I can't help but think her actions were reactions to what her father was, and did, during the war. I heard she attempted to jump off a bridge once. She became a heroin addict. Her parents sold most of the property they owned to pay for her treatments. All the money her father made as an officer, any profit he made from the war, went to treat his daughter's reaction to the war. She ended up marrying an Albanian man named Ramadan, maybe to spite her father. To the Serbs who share her father's views, only the Albanians are lower than Bosniaks. She named her daughter Dina, seemingly in honor of my brother Dino, who had been her playmate during those magical summers.

BELMA

Belma went to live with Žana when the war started. For a time she had a Serb boyfriend she loved, but after the war she moved to Sarajevo. She got a degree in psychology and became a school psychologist. It was a job that fit with her nature: quiet, more an observer than a participant. She and Žana remained friends. Žana still travels to Sarajevo to visit her.

ĆUĆANA

Ćućana was getting more difficult as the war approached. She married early, but everyone thought it might be better for her to be established with a family. For a while she seemed fine. She came to see us with her two-year-old son. But eventually her mental health deteriorated. She abandoned her husband and child and became homeless. One summer when I returned to Bihać after the war ended, when I was shopping in downtown Bihać I saw her begging for money. I approached her and asked if she recognized me. She said, "Yes, of course, you're Dilka's daughter, Amra." I bought her food and gave her money and told her to go home. Later I heard that she'd disappeared. She was suspected to be a victim of human trafficking.

SEJLA

Sejla continued to go out with Slobodan. She wanted to study medicine in Banja Luka, where Slobodan was studying engineering. She couldn't get into medical school but got into law school. I remember telling her that college wasn't about just being with your boyfriend but that it had a purpose of improving oneself. She didn't care. She focused on Slobodan, leaving her whole family to be with him. She went to Banja Luka just as the war was starting. Then her big love dissolved, and Slobodan left her. He escaped to Montenegro to avoid being drafted into the war, and Sejla was trapped in a hostile city. Sejla was hidden by a kind old lady, and then my dad, with the help of a Serb friend, paid a bribe that let her escape as a refugee rather than be sent to a concentration camp. She was smuggled out and put on a boat with some other refugees, heading for Sweden. There she lived in a refugee camp before she met her current husband, an Albanian. They have two children, a boy and girl. Sejla and I don't keep in close touch now. We saw each other a few times after the war. She has a strong sense of guilt. I think she realizes she left her entire family behind in order to be with a man who left her alone. She could have been killed, or worse. I think it's easier for her now not to be in touch with me or other people from that time because she's afraid of what that reminds her of. She did finish college and runs a daycare.

SLOBODAN

Slobodan married a Muslim woman and lives abroad.

EMIR

Emir had a Serb girlfriend who left Bihać when all other Serbs left, just before the war. By then, I had met a boy named Davor, who became my first real boyfriend. Emir became an anchor on the local TV station that was started during the war. I was glad he was not on the front line. One day I saw him and his best friend by the Una...soon after, that friend was killed in fighting. Emir then met a Scandinavian woman working for the Red Cross. He told me he was going to marry her and leave. I don't know if he was marrying her for love or to escape or both. Today he is a math teacher and has three daughters.

ORAČ

Orač was injured by a bomb in the war, his body horrifically burned. As soon as I heard he was injured, I visited him in the hospital. A friend snuck me in through the back door. Orač was completely bandaged in white gauze, with only his eyes and his fingers visible. I remember I touched his hands gently, told him how handsome I always thought he was, talked about the butterflies I felt in my stomach that day on the Una when he tended to my injured legs with those strong, gentle hands. He couldn't talk, but he squeezed my fingers. "You're going to be fine," I told him. "You were my first major crush, and I can't wait to see you again so we can reminisce more."

He died the next day.

ASMIR

Asmir was injured during the war. He lost his teeth. He married a very nice and pretty girl named Jasmina. Jasmina and Asmir are happily married. Their daughter visits Žana's children and stays with them, where Dida and Đorđe live now near Serbia's border with Kosovo. I know how hard Asmir fought in the war, but I think he chooses not to speak of it with Žana and her family. I believe he might have even traveled to Belgrade. I never could. I think I would not be able to breathe there. If even Žana changed, what could I expect of other residents of Belgrade? Asmir also turned the family mill and Lučica, the island by Brvice, into a profitable tourist spot.

SAMIR

Samir was supposed to pursue his engineering degree outside Bihać, but the war put an end to that plan. He ended up working on computer networks for the police and for the military that we organized in a desperate attempt to defend ourselves during the conflict. He was so good at it that it became his permanent career. It was very difficult for many who were soldiers during the war to return to "normal" activities like going to college and finishing a degree. Samir still works with law enforcement and has a wife and one daughter, Lamija, who is an excellent student and very talented in art.

HARIS

Haris lost his father to the same kind of cancer that killed his mother. He and his brother, Halid, ended up living with their stepmother. Haris married a Bosnian Croat girl after the war. He became an environmentalist and is in charge of the Una National Park, dedicated to preserving the beauty and health of the Una and surrounding parks and mountains.

SOURCES

Bakšić-Muftić, J. (2014) Bošnjaci i Država Bosna i Hercegovina—
Dešavanja na Periferiji/Bosniaks and State of Bosnia and
Herzegovina—Happenings in the Periphery. *Godišnjak Bošnjačke
Zajednice Culture*, Preporod, (1), Sarajevo, Bosnia and Herzegovina,
76–92.

Becirevic, E. (2014) *Genocide on the Drina River*. Yale University Press.

Bergholz, M. (2010) "The Strange Silence: Explaining the Absence
of Monuments for Muslim Civilians Killed in Bosnia during the
Second World War." *East European Politics and Societies*, 24(3),
408–434.

Biserko, S. (2011) "Perceptions of Serbia's Elite in Relation to the Dayton
Agreement." *Duh Bosne*, 6(4).

Bostedt, F., and Dungel, J. (2008) "The International Criminal Tribunal for
the Former Yugoslavia in 2007: Key Developments in International
Humanitarian and Criminal Law." *Chinese Journal of International Law*,
7(2), 389–415.

Bringa, T. (1995) *Being Muslim the Bosnian Way: Identity and Community in
a Central Bosnian Village* (Vol. 3). Princeton University Press.

Donia, R. J. (2014) *Radovan Karadžić: Architect of the Bosnian Genocide*.
Cambridge University Press.

Hashemipour, S. (2019) "Njegos's The Mountain Wreath: The Text Behind
Serbian Nationalism's Racist Foundation Myth." *Universal Journal of
History and Culture*, 1(2), 203–218.

Malcolm, N. (1996) *Bosnia: A Short History*. NYU Press.

Maslić, S. (2020) "Concentration Camps in the Municipality of Zvornik in 1992 in the Function of Committing the Crimes of Genocide against Bosniaks of the Bosnian Podrinje. *Monumenta Srebrenica*, *9*(9), 177–206.

Holbrooke, R. (2011) *To End a War: The Conflict in Yugoslavia—America's Inside Story—Negotiating with Milosevic*. Modern Library.

Karčić, H. (2022) *Torture, Humiliate, Kill: Inside the Bosnian Serb Camp System*. University of Michigan Press.

Karčić, H. (2021) "Triumphalism: The Final Stage of the Bosnian Genocide." *Denial: The Final Stage of Genocide* (99–112). Routledge.

Karčić, H. (2018) "A War Seen from the Hill: US Helsinki Commission and the War in Bosnia 1992–1995." *Journal of Muslim Minority Affairs*, *38*(4), 493–502.

Khan, M. R. (1994) "From Hegel to Genocide in Bosnia: Some Moral and Philosophical Concerns." *Journal Institute of Muslim Minority Affairs*, *15*(1–2), 1–30.

McNeil, R. (2022) *Grave Faces: A Forensic Technician's Story of Gathering Evidence of Genocide in Bosnia*. Behar Publishing. beharpublishing .com/book/grave-faces-a-forensic-technicians-story-of-gathering -evidence-of-genocide-in-bosnia/

Memorial Center Srebrenica. Genocide transcripts. Potočari, Bosnia and Herzegovina. srebrenicamemorial.org/en/investigations/genocide -transcripts/1

Novic, E. (2016) *The Concept of Cultural Genocide: An International Law Perspective*. Oxford University Press.

Odobašić, J. (2015) *Hiljadu Grobnica u Bosanskoj Krajini: 1992–1995/A Thousand Graves in Bosanska Krajina: 1992–1995*. Preporod.

Joshi, V. (2021) "The Cat I Never Named: A True Story of Love, War, and Survival" (2020), written by Amra Sabic-El-Rayess with Laura L. Sullivan (Bloomsbury). Book review in *Global Journal of Peace Research and Praxis*, *3*(1).

Rogel, C. (1991) "Slovenia's Independence: A Reversal of History." *Probs. Communism*, *40*, 31.

Rutland, P. (2021) *Quo Vadis, Aida?*, directed by Jasmila Žbanić, Deblokada film, 2020. *Nationalities Papers*, *49*(5), 986–988.

Sabic-El-Rayess, A. (2023) "Ending Educational Displacement." *Bosnian Studies: Perspectives from an Emerging Field*, 123.

Sabic-El-Rayess, A. with Sullivan, L. (2020) *The Cat I Never Named: A True Story of Love, War, and Survival*. Bloomsbury.

Sells, M. (2020) IV. "Reflections on the Genocide in Bosnia-Herzegovina and the Bosnians Who Resisted It." *Horizons*, *47*(1), 99–108.

Sells, M. (2009) "Religion and Genocide in Bosnia." Lecture, University of South Florida Libraries.

Sells, M. A. (2002) "The Construction of Islam in Serbian Religious Mythology and Its Consequences." *Islam and Bosnia*, 56–85.

Sells, M. A. (1996) *The Bridge Betrayed: Religion and Genocide in Bosnia* (Vol. 11). University of California Press.

Taras, R. (2019) "Islamophobia Never Rests in the Balkans: Muslim Communities and the Legacy of Exclusionary Nationalisms and Ethnic Expulsions." *Journal of Muslim Minority Affairs*, *39*(3), 282–299. tandfonline.com/doi/full/10.1080/13602004.2019.1652411

Tatum, D. C., and Tatum, D. C. (2010) "Bosnia-Herzegovina: The Kitty Genovese of the Balkans." *Genocide at the Dawn of the Twenty-first Century: Rwanda, Bosnia, Kosovo, and Darfur*, 59–108.

The International Criminal Tribunal for the former Yugoslavia. (2004) "Prosecutor v. Radislav Krstic—Judgment." icty.org/x/cases/krstic/acjug/en/

Turkestani, R. E. (1997) "The Muslim Predicament in the Balkans: Tito's Legacy." *Journal of Muslim Minority Affairs*, *17*(2), 325–334. tandfonline.com/doi/abs/10.1080/13602009708716380

Tyers, C. A. (2009) "Hidden Atrocities: The Forensic Investigation and Prosecution of Genocide." trace.tennessee.edu/cgi/viewcontent.cgi ?article=1097&context=utk_graddiss

United Nations. Resolution adopted by the General Assembly 47/121—The situation in Bosnia and Herzegovina 1992. hrlibrary.umn.edu /resolutions/47/121GA1992.html

U.S. Congress. (2005) "S.Res.134—A resolution expressing the sense of the Senate regarding the massacre at Srebrenica in July 1995. congress .gov/bill/109th-congress/senate-resolution/134/text

Vrkić, N. (2015) "The Unfinished Trial of Slobodan Milošević: Justice Lost, History Told. *UvA-DARE (Digital Academic Repository-University of Amsterdam)*, 189–280.

Yadav, M. (2021) UN Court Confirms Ratko Mladic Convictions and Life Sentence. jurist.org/news/2021/06/un-court-confirms-ratko-mladic -convictions-and-life-sentence/

Zagaris, B. (2011) "The International Criminal Tribunal for the Former Yugoslavia: Prosecutor v. Gotovina, Decision on Gotovina Defence Appeal Against 12 March 2010 Decision on Requests for Permanent Restraining Orders Directed to the Republic of Croatia." *International Legal Materials, 50*(5), 873–893.

Zulic, A. (2018) "Slobodan Milosevic's Propaganda Tour: Mobilization Across Borders, Nationalism and the Creation of the Other," Aalborg University, Copenhagen.

ACKNOWLEDGMENTS

SOME DAYS DURING those magical three summers, I felt like I was caught in a swirling eddy of the River Una, others I was resting in a gentle pool. But most of the time I was hurtling downriver toward some unknown destination, utterly unable to stop myself. Did I even want to stop? There might have been rocks and waterfalls, but the speed was thrilling, too. Isn't that what life as a young person is, a headlong rush into the unknown?

Later, during the genocide in Bosnia that followed the events of this memoir, the unknown defined my life. Every day, I was an infinitesimal moment away from being blown up, executed, or taken to a concentration camp. It is at those junctures that I recognized how the extraordinary is constructed of the seemingly ordinary moments in our lives. The extraordinary is a gift of laughter, a shared family meal, a friend who becomes closer than a cousin, and a cousin who becomes a sister, even if only for a moment, even if only for a summer.

Though I witnessed the worst of humanity, those magical three summers instilled resilience in me. There was permanency to the impact they had on me. I refused then, and I refuse now, to believe that life is anything but beautiful. I am grateful for that boundless sense of hope and resiliency that those summers gave me. Though I no longer speak with Žana, Vedrana, or their parents, I will forever be thankful for those summers of love, exploration, and sisterhood. For me, Žana and Vedrana will always remain my sisters, even if we never speak again. I still love them, even if they don't love me.

I also wish to acknowledge my brother Dino, as well as Belma, Ćućana, and Sejla, who enriched those years of my life. In particular, Dino and I have built a bond that has made every obstacle in life easier for both of us. Our love for each other remains my place of comfort, because I know that I can lean on my brother, and that he can do the same with me.

As I think of the people in this story, I would be remiss if I did not acknowledge those who are no longer with us. Amar, my older brother, was an important influence in my early life. He still is. His brilliance, humility, respect for differences, wittiness, and integral morality have inspired and guided me through life. No one else in our family has Marfan syndrome, but I hope that this story raises awareness of those who are affected by it. Amar was irreplaceable, and he will forever be missed.

Many thanks to the Marfan Foundation for providing research, raising awareness, and supporting individuals and families affected by Marfan syndrome. Amar never had such support. I wish he had. I wish that we as a family had. I also thank one of the organization's board members, who provided thoughtful feedback on this manuscript.

I am grateful to my Tetka Ica and my cousin Nafka for their love and care. They would both hug me so tightly as if it was our final hug. The last time I saw my Tetka Ica, who died recently, was in the summer of 2022, and by then Nafka had already succumbed to Covid-19. My friend Aladin is no longer with us, and years ago, we lost Maše, Dino's best friend.

As I acknowledge Orač for his brief but tender role in my life, I also want to recognize that he, along with Asmir, Samir, Emir, Dževad, Haris, my father, and others in this story, protected us during the Bosnian Genocide. These seemingly ordinary people, many of whom were still very young at the time, took extraordinary risks to protect our city and people from complete annihilation. I would not be here today, writing this story of resilience and sisterhood, without their will to fight for our collective survival.

Now I wish to thank those who have made *Three Summers* possible, and who fill my life today with love, inspiration, and laughter. I thank my two daughters, Jannah and Dinah. They serve as my inspiration and have helped me curate stories for *Three Summers*. My older daughter, Jannah (pronounced Žana in Bosnian), was applying to colleges as I was finishing *Three Summers*, and she surprised me one day as she reflected on some of the stories from my life that have shaped her worldview. Today, she is a resilient young woman, an engineer, and an artist who has influenced my selection of the stories in this book. I am also deeply grateful to my younger daughter, Dinah, a scientist, activist, and mathematician, who too has engaged with me in a true and genuine dialogue, always filled with love, humility, and respect, about the stories she felt modeled resilience. Dinah is the most mature and empathetic sixteen-year-old I have ever known. My husband, Tamer, has shown unparalleled patience, love, and understanding as I have worked many late nights on *Three Summers* (including tonight!), juggling my many different roles, from being a professor at Columbia University to being a mom to our teen daughters.

I am also deeply thankful to Laura L. Sullivan, who has collaborated with me on *Three Summers* and my young-adult memoir, *The Cat I Never Named* (Bloomsbury, 2020). Laura is an extraordinary gift and a rare friend in my life for whom I am deeply grateful. I am excited about the many more stories we will introduce to the world together.

None of this would be possible without Jason Anthony and Rob McQuilkin of Massie and McQuilkin, who have been the most trusted partners representing my work. I thank Grace Kendall, senior editor at Farrar, Straus, and Giroux Books for Young Readers at Macmillan Publishers, for this privilege and opportunity to tell my story. I share my voice with a deep sense of humility and responsibility that comes with entering classrooms and lives of my readers. Ever since I met Grace several years ago, I have wished for a project that we could collaborate on, and I hope that *Three Summers* is only the first of our many co-creations. I am deeply grateful to the entire team at FSG—including Asia Harden, Samira Iravani, Lelia Mander, Allyson Floridia, Celeste Cass, Teresa Ferraiolo, Morgan Rath, and Samantha Sacks, for their contributions to this project. My special thanks to the talented Yogi Fahmi Riandito, who has brought the Una to life with an exceptionally gorgeous, powerful, and communicative cover. I am curious to learn, as I engage with audiences on this book, how many readers will decipher the cover and discover the subtle but meaningful lessons we have incorporated visually.

Last but not least, I thank my students and a team of researchers and educators who work with me at Columbia University on instilling in students and educators internationally the resilience to hate. Without their support on many of our research projects, I would not have had time to write *Three Summers*. In particular, I thank the core members of my research team: Vikramaditya (Vik) Joshi and Tina Keswani. And of course I thank you—each and every one of you—for reading *Three Summers*. Your connections with this story of resilience, sisterhood, love, and hope give meaning and purpose to my lifelong effort to end hate.